WILD ROADS

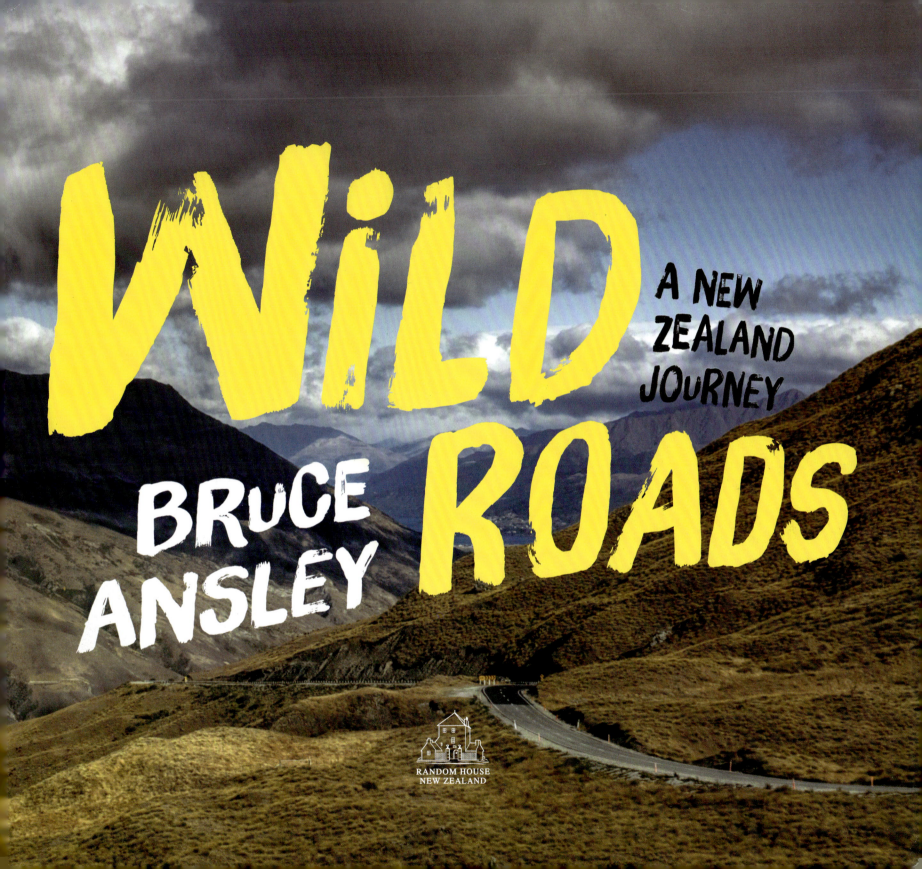

WiLD ROADS

A NEW ZEALAND JOURNEY

BRUCE ANSLEY

RANDOM HOUSE
NEW ZEALAND

RANDOM HOUSE

UK | USA | Canada | Ireland | Australia
India | New Zealand | South Africa | China

Random House is an imprint of the Penguin Random House
group of companies, whose addresses can be found
at global.penguinrandomhouse.com.

 Penguin
Random House
New Zealand

First published by Penguin Random House New Zealand 2015

1 3 5 7 9 10 8 6 4 2

Design by Kate Barraclough © Penguin Random House New Zealand
Cover photograph © Alamy
Typeset in Galaxie Copernicus
Colour separation by ImageCentre Ltd
Printed and bound in China by C & C Offset Printing Co Ltd

A catalogue record for this book is available from the National Library
of New Zealand.

ISBN 978-1-77553-788-5

penguinrandomhouse.co.nz

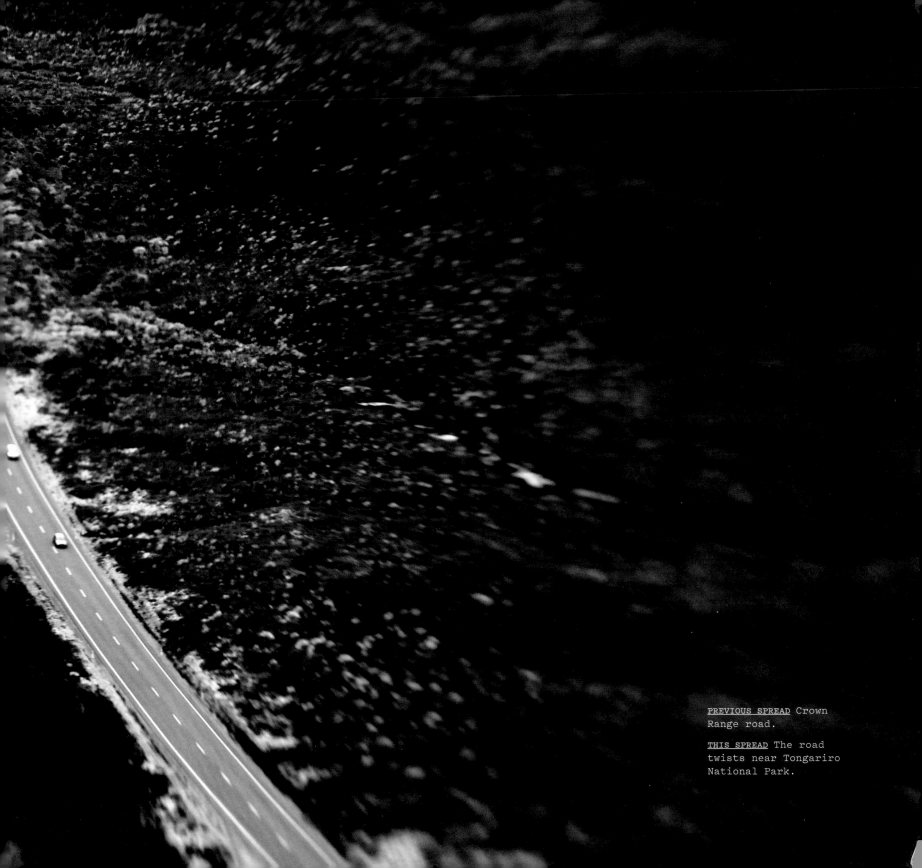

PREVIOUS SPREAD Crown
Range road.

THIS SPREAD The road
twists near Tongariro
National Park.

CONTENTS

INTRODUCTION

A wild road is one which lodges in our imagination, for its past, or difficulty, or beauty, or presence. Roads carry our life force, our DNA. They are our capillaries, our nervous system, our blood and belonging. What we were, what we are and what we do are embedded in them.

Everything anyone wants to know about New Zealand can be found in our roads. They bear our history. Many began as Maori trails. Coastal paths ran the length of both islands: State Highway 1 follows a Maori track along the South Island's east coat. They grew from footpaths to horse tracks to coach roads to carriageways. They tell stories of wars, hardship, intrigue, enterprise, development. They describe where we live and how we live, what is important to us, what we have and what we don't.

If you follow these roads, or even some of them, you'll have a very good idea of what New Zealand is all about, the ways we lived in the past, and the way we live now. You'll have a good time doing it.

New Zealand is a small country by international standards, but I've always believed it to be much bigger than it is. It's long and thin and cut into three by fierce straits which once made us effectively different countries, with several more isolated within. Many of New Zealand's roads are crossings, connecting places so physically different they have stamped that diversity on their people. Better roads and communications have changed us but only to a point: people in Invercargill, Christchurch and Auckland not only sound different, but have their own values.

We can enjoy being tourists in our own land, the magic of strangeness. And, we are curious about New Zealand. Southerners want to visit Hot Water Beach or Tane Mahuta or Waitangi. Northerners want to see Punakaiki or Skippers Canyon or Milford Sound.

For a small country we're a nation of astonishing geographical differences. If you drive over the Haast Pass in the dark, into the complete blackness of South Westland, you're nowhere you recognise. If you take the Rawene ferry across the Hokianga and curl through the dusty roads and tight bends of the little harbours on that coast, you'll have the same feeling of another world.

This is not a guide, or a history. It is a story of New Zealand roads and, through them, other stories which show that we're a nation of contrasts.

The roads have been chosen not just because they are wild, but because they are wildly beautiful, or lonely, or interesting. Almost all of them are accessible by the average car. Only a couple demand something more rugged. I've driven over them all, some of them many times, often in the course of my work as a writer. Driving through New Zealand is my favourite pastime, and is still an enduring romance.

LEFT Wildly beautiful: mountain bends on Skippers Canyon Road, Central Otago.

– CHAPTER ONE –

HIGH ROADS

DRIVING ROUTES

1. THE RIMUTAKAS ROAD
2. ARTHUR'S PASS
3. TAIHAPE TO NAPIER
4. THE LEWIS PASS
5. THE LINDIS
6. THE DESERT ROAD
7. CROWN RANGE
8. DANSEYS PASS
9. TAKAKA HILL
10. SPRINGS JUNCTION TO MURCHISON
11. NAPIER TO TAUPO

LEFT Truck on the Desert Road.

UPPER HUTT   FEATHERSTON

THE HILL

THE RIMUTAKAS ROAD

'NOTHING BUT NUMBER EIGHT WIRE BETWEEN YOU AND ETERNITY.'

Only Wellington has a road like the Rimutaka Hill highway so close to the city, even if Dunedin comes close. It's one of those idiosyncrasies which, like mad winds and politics, make the capital so dramatic. With their steep zigzagging streets, houses cleaving to the angles of their wedged city, you'd expect main roads to be eccentric. The Rimutaka Hill Road certainly is.

Like the capital's winds, and its politics for that matter, Rimutaka road reports are measured on the Beaufort scale. Here's a typical news bulletin:

Motorists trapped in 13 vehicles by snow on Rimutaka Ranges near Wellington have been rescued by police. The vehicles, heading towards Wellington, became trapped after heavy snowfall and ice blocked Rimutaka Hill Road.

Roading contractors and ploughs were unable to clear the road forcing the vehicles to turn back. Police say three trucks are still trapped on the road.

On a fine day it's a nice cruise up a road still difficult enough to be exciting. On a bad one, well, let's just say it's difficult enough to be *very* exciting.

It's not long, only 30 kilometres from Upper Hutt to Featherston, but you get your money's worth of road. The Rimutakas are the range running from Palliser Bay to Upper Hutt. They fill the view from Wellington, and from the earliest days of settlement they were a barrier. Maori used trails and waka to get around them, and early European settlers did more or less the same: they either walked around the coast or went by boat, both wild and difficult, for all Wairarapa harbours were dangerously exposed.

Not surprisingly, a road joining Wellington and the Wairarapa was a priority. The Rimutaka Hill Road, a cart track then, was finished in 1856. It squeezed through the pass between the end of the Rimutakas and the beginning of the Tararuas and was even curlier than the present road. Early photographs show towering escarpments cut with pick and shovel amid a landscape of felled trees and blasted hillsides. What a bleak job it must have been labouring through the rain, gales, ice and snow that you can't miss even today, with your air conditioning pumping.

For a century and a half the road ran true to its

origins. Then it began to change. Today you leave Upper Hutt and drive through the beguiling Te Marua. You're lucky. The section between here and Kaitoke was unwound, or realigned, between 2002 and 2006. Before then it was a rehearsal for the big event, Muldoon's Corner, the sharpest and tightest in the whole road. On this route that was quite a distinction. It was once famously described by the then Masterton Mayor, Gary Daniel, as 'one of the few places where there's nothing but number eight wire between you and eternity'.

True. Sometimes cars simply disappeared into the gullies.

Conventionally, Muldoon's Corner got its name from the former Prime Minister's financial stance, tight and to the right. The *Wairarapa Times-Age* produced a different story, quoting a retired Masterton carpenter who drove the road every working day for 30 years and knew its history. He said the corner was named for the knobbly bit on the cliff face overhanging the road: 'It looked just like Muldoon's grin.'

The grin has been wiped off now. The New Zealand Transport Agency spent $16.5 million widening and easing the corner and a kilometre-

long stretch of the adjoining road, cutting cliffs as high as 55 metres above the road, filling deep gullies, using abseilers to replant near-vertical hillsides, even building fish passes into culverts. They smoothed the bend so trucks could round it without crossing the centre line and pass in opposite directions. Both had been difficult before.

After two and a half years of work the road's 5300 daily users could drive happily through one of the country's most perilous stretches. The frontier-like atmosphere of the old road was bulldozed out of the way. You can sweep to the summit from Upper Hutt without a touch of nostalgia, even when you discover that the old café no longer exists. And bush cover, beaten up as it may be, is recovering steadily.

There is still the Wairarapa side of the hill to come, of course. It writhes downhill through hairpins, crimps, kinks and curls. Featherston arrives with a sense of ceremony, like the tapes and cheers at the end of a marathon.

Is there an alternative? A railway line over the

PREVIOUS SPREAD Heavy traffic over the Hill.

TOP LEFT Tractor pulling a car out of snow on the Rimutaka Hill Road, 1976.

TOP RIGHT Rimutaka Road and Hill, 1948.

RIGHT Lone cyclist takes the bend.

Rimutakas opened in 1878, a few years after the road did. The only major accident on the line was a result not of its precipitous character, but of wind: in 1880 three carriages were blown off the line into a deep, dark gully called Siberia, killing four children. Locomotives laboured up the notorious Rimutaka Incline until 1955, when it was replaced by a tunnel which shortened the journey from Upper Hutt to Featherston from three hours to 45 minutes and opened up the Wairarapa to commuters. But nothing is that simple on the Rimutakas. A cave-in killed a construction worker and trapped 33 others for two days. The builders suggested to the then Ministry of Works that a road tunnel be combined with the rail. Evidently the plan was rejected as too expensive.

According to legend the Americans volunteered to dig a road tunnel during World War I, presumably to service the Featherston army camp. Up to 8000 troops lived there during the war and after eight weeks' basic training, they marched over the Rimutakas to Wellington arriving in worn condition.

But something is always happening on the Hill. The old railway line became a popular walking and cycle track. The Rimutaka Incline Railway Heritage Trust plans to reinstate the old Incline. A car tunnel was suggested again in 2008. Transit New Zealand commissioned a study on the Rimutaka Hill Road and it came back with two tunnel options: one short, near the summit, and the other long. So will we one day be able to drive under, rather than over, the Rimutakas? If so, might we feel we've lost something?

Early workmen would consider the drive a doddle now. Yet for all the work that has been done on this hill road, it was still ranked third most dangerous in the country. Nor has the vicious weather contributed to the toll a whit less than it always did. For all the planning, all the work and money, the Rimutaka Hill retains its basic component: drama.

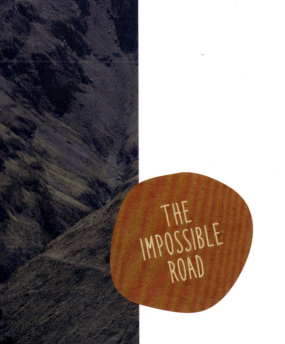

OTIRA

SPRINGFIELD

ARTHUR'S PASS

'BETWEEN THE DEVIL AND THE DEEP BLUE SEA.'

This road is legendary in the truest sense. Fables swirl throughout its length.

It is pure Canterbury. Plains, mountains, rivers, history, people, romance: all concentrate here where the road passes from plains to foothills, lakes and forest into mountains and crosses the Main Divide itself through a miraculous saddle deep in the crags, Arthur's Pass. It is the best-known road in the country.

The road was always critical to the economies of both sides of the South Island. Maori knew the pass well, as one of the pathways for pounamu, or greenstone. They told early European settlers of this route and of others too, for their preferred passage was over the Hurunui Saddle and Harper Pass to the north.

The first European to see the pass itself was Samuel Butler, who was scouting the high country for a sheep station and spotted it from a distance. He later settled on Mesopotamia in the Upper Rangitata Valley, and later still used that station as the setting for his novel *Erewhon*.

The credit for discovering the pass, however, went to Arthur Dudley Dobson, then a young surveyor working in Canterbury. He was told of a pass at the head of the Otira River by a Ngai Tahu chief, Tarapuhi. In 1864 Dobson walked up the Waimakariri River, over the mountains and into the Otira Valley. He did not name the pass he crossed, merely sketched it and gave the drawing to his boss, the chief surveyor Thomas Cass, with a report noting that the western side of the route was very steep. He didn't think a road was possible.

Then the matter became urgent. Gold was discovered on the West Coast. Businessmen could smell money all the way from Christchurch but Dunedin was getting the lion's share of it. They needed a route through the mountains. Prizes were offered. Arthur's brother George was sent off in 1864 to check every possible route, while Christchurch's citizenry danced with impatience.

George came back from the mountains. He had checked all passes, and Arthur's was the best. The name stuck.

The Canterbury Provincial Government wasted no time debating the issue. After all, there was gold in them thar hills. With a third Dobson brother, Edward, in charge, the road was forced through the mountains.

The winter of 1865 was especially hard. Workers lived in tents and primitive shelters. Many were killed or died of cold. Yet a 251-kilometre road to Hokitika was opened to coach traffic in just two years, in 1866. Even now that would be breathtaking speed. These men, a thousand of them, had picks, shovels and explosives, and the western side of the pass was not just very steep, as in Arthur's account, it was an abyss. They froze in winter and starved most of the time, but cutting a road through the mountains took only a year.

Poor George did not survive to enjoy it. In 1866 the Sullivan gang, the Maungatapu murderers, mistook him for a gold buyer in the Grey Valley and killed him.

His road never really lost its character. A mountain crossing is always fragile and Arthur's Pass has remained daring ever since. When I was a child in the back seat of my parents' car, we crept over the pass in frightened silence, for anything could go wrong here and, by popular account, everything did. And does: breakdowns, collisions, slides, plunges, disappearances. Modern cars don't baulk at the grades, or the bends, or even the ice and snow, but on this road you don't take chances.

Horse-drawn coaches crossed the mountains until the 1920s. That old coach road can still be seen in several places along the route, although the modern road follows essentially the same path. The original road was poorly maintained and steadily deteriorated for years. After the Midland line to the West Coast opened in 1923 cars were often loaded onto railway wagons for a more reliable journey.

Porters Pass gives the first hint of what's to come after an easy run from Springfield. It goes up sharply. The old coach road turns off to the left near its foot, following an easier gradient which loops around and rejoins the new road near Lake Lyndon. The lake used to freeze each winter and families skated at weekends. Less so now.

The road sets off along the wide valley between the Torlesse and Craigieburn ranges, skifield roads and walking tracks leading off. It's a beautiful, easy drive, golden in summer and winter, mountain peaks aloof under Canterbury's huge skies.

Castle Hill Village was laid out in the 1970s as the only alpine village in this whole vast area other than Arthur's Pass itself. For all its mountain splendour it has developed only slowly.

The road climbs to Cave Stream, whose most famous feature is its 594-metre-long cave, the water carving through limestone formations that were the setting for the film *The Chronicles of Narnia: The Lion, the Witch and the Wardrobe*.

The film is less magical than the cave, which twists and turns around holes and through terraces and waterspouts inside the mountain and ends at a ladder alongside a three-metre-high waterfall, all in total darkness. Walking through this place by torchlight is a supernatural experience.

Castle Hill Station's old stone buildings appear under the knobbly rock formations that give the hill its look of medieval ruin. New houses too. High country stations — sometimes fiefdoms, always eyries — often had some towering figure in their history, but this old station was given new life and made famous at the same time by a city woman, Christine Fernyhough.

The road passes Cass, named for the Canterbury surveyor but best known for the little red railway shed with its lonely figure outside, painted by Rita Angus: in a 2006 television poll it was voted New Zealanders' favourite work of art.

Now the Waimakariri River sweeps alongside, so wide that trains on the far bank look like toys. The tussock has gone. The road is deep in mountain birch, first Lake Pearson then Lake Grasmere alongside.

Just past a tiny bach settlement, the Bealey, the long Bealey Bridge crosses the river. The gentle rocking motion of its spans is like crossing the river on a boat.

PREVIOUS SPREAD Approaching the pass.

RIGHT Winter snow, one lane cleared.

The Cobb & Co coaches which first made the regular run across the mountains had to splash through rivers. Even in summer it was dangerous. Many died in the river crossings along the road, Arthur Dobson noting in his *Memoirs* that 'the rivers flowing through the Canterbury Plains were at all times somewhat dangerous to cross, and particularly so in the summertime, when they were subject to floods caused by the north-west winds'.

Five horses pulled the coaches, changed every 24 kilometres along the way, a three-day journey on a lucky day. The Bealey was then almost as it is now, a group of cottages, with telegraph and police stations and the Glacier Hotel. A ferry near the present-day bridge took people across the river.

The Bealey Bridge is one-way but usually no one gets wet. The road passes Klondyke Corner and Greyneys Shelter then Arthur's Pass village pops out of the bush. This was once a construction village for workers on the Otira rail tunnel and some of its baches were their houses. Despite the cafes it still has that frontier-town aura, bustling with people passing through, or tramping, climbing or skiing, still with an air of excitement. Keas, the mountain parrots, pose for photographs and steal food from plates to the great delight of tourists. The old coach road walk follows a section of the coach track through town.

Its raw environment and its place names link the present to the past so that if it wasn't for the soy latte you might be anywhere in the last century and a half. You pass the Devils Punchbowl and leave by way of Jacks Hut, once a basic roadman's hut but a big improvement on the primitive shelters that housed the men building the road. You pass the Bealey Chasm and reach the pass itself, a gentle paradox with a memorial to Arthur Dobson. You pass Lake Misery and dive off Pegleg Flat to Deaths Corner at the top of the Otira Gorge where the old road sneaks off up the hill. Before 1999 this carried traffic to the west of the pass in loops and zigzags down a mountainside so unstable that road gangs were constantly shifting it, propping it up.

The road authorities could see they were going to lose the fight. They gave up and looked for a new route. It wasn't easy, for this was riven country. The Otira River ran down a chasm. The solution was to leave the land and fly. So the Otira Viaduct came into being. Construction workers soon knew how those 19th-century road gangs had suffered, and marvelled at their tenacity. They could commute, or live in houses bought by the construction company in Arthur's Pass village. But they still froze in winter, and often in summer too, and the rock was so hard it took a heavy toll on drilling gear.

The new viaduct opened in 1999. It carries traffic above the river in a beautiful curve so you seem to both float and fly alongside the mountain, far above the river. Shingle cliffs rear alongside, and you wonder how they kept the old road high on that unstable slope for so long.

The way down the mountains is a kind of road-fall. Beside you, invisible, the railway line runs right *through*

LEFT Arthur's Pass, 1959.

the mountain in a tunnel that took 15 years to cut.

You reach Starvation Point, then Windy Point, the two so close to each other that the workers who named them must have felt themselves between the devil and the deep blue sea, literally. The road travels under the rock shelter with its concrete roof, an open-sided tunnel etched into the mountainside. It carries the Reid Falls over the road, the tumbling water making you feel you're *inside* the waterfall, deep in the Otira Gorge.

The early Canterbury painter John Gibb depicted the gorge as foaming with white water amid dark, threatening forests, a mountain peak thrusting into truly horrible clouds and a Cobb & Co coach tiny in the might of it all.

He got it right.

You cross the river on the old bridge at the bottom of the gorge and, feeling lucky even in the 21st century, drive down to Otira, superb in summer when the rata is out, superbly cold in winter.

The old place was built as a railway town, largely in the 1930s. Now it is probably the most unusual town in New Zealand, for it is owned as a single entity. It seems endlessly on the market. It is regularly famous as optimistic new owners announce they have bought the town lock, stock and barrel, reveal ambitious plans for the place, eventually admit defeat and put up the 'For Sale' signs again. When I last drove through it the big old pub was still open and a dozen houses were occupied. A new owner had just bought the town. He was sounding . . . optimistic.

The drive has taken only an hour or so. You always end it with a mixture of relief and sadness. Yet, in a year when the rata is flowering and the sky is clear, it makes you feel the luckiest person in the world.

KURIPAPANGO

NAPIER

TAIHAPE

TAIHAPE TO NAPIER

THE GENTLE ANNIE

'... NOT COMMENDED FOR NERVOUS PEOPLE.'

Taihape was once a place in the bush, then a camp, then a town, then quite a large one. It survived the crises of the 1980s, when economic reforms torched small country towns, and has since found a happy balance as farming town and main highway stop.

It was scarcely populated before Europeans arrived, although its name means 'the place of Tai the Hunchback', who must have lived hereabouts.

William Colenso, the wandering missionary, arrived in Taihape in 1845. Its first European settlers came only in 1894 and they were from Canterbury, resettled under a government scheme to allow people without much money to acquire land. God knows how they felt when they arrived from the well-settled open south to find themselves in a small clearing amid thick bush which they then had to clear to make their farms.

Colenso described the terrain which, later, the Gentle Annie route was to run through, as 'being rather of a frightful kind ... And the solitude ... is

RIGHT A gentle part of the Gentle Annie road.

intense and almost unbearable.' But there was no easy escape if you lived in Taihape: the main trunk railway line reached the town only in 1904, and the sole access until then, the Gentle Annie route to Napier, was truly awful. It stayed that way for a very long time.

The Gentle Annie began as a packhorse and bullock track carrying wool from the huge inland stations here to Napier, a 10-day journey. Strings of packhorses could reach the hundreds. It was a long, dangerous journey especially over the Gentle Annie itself where a slip could, and sometimes did, end in a fall to the Ngaruroro Gorge far below.

The road progressed slowly until by 1893 a stage-coach could make the trip from Taihape to Napier in three days. The road began carrying motor traffic early in the 20th century, and became notorious even in a country where dangerous roads were the norm.

The *Observer* in 1931 carried an account from a party driving from Auckland to Napier by way of the Gentle Annie to assist relatives caught in the 1931 earthquake:

> *The descent of Gentle Annie, by a corkscrew road round slopes hundreds of feet in depth, was a hair-raising experience . . . the old-time squatters packed their wool out by this route. Now it is becoming a passable road for motorists, though not commended for nervous people.*

It remained infamous for decades, excluded from car-insurance policies, spoken of darkly by those who had braved the trip and wanted to impress their friends. As recently as 1980 the AA warned that 'Meeting another vehicle may involve backing up for as much as 1km to find a passing place.'

Until 2011 part of the road remained unsealed. Then the two local councils finished the work, taking out many of the bends and sharp bits. All the legends, myths, boasts and fears were sealed off with it.

Yet this is still a wild road.

You come across Taihape quite suddenly, set amid its pointy little hills. The town is the gumboot capital of the world, home of the annual gumboot day, immortalised by John Clarke in his Fred Dagg character. It doesn't look like a place for a wild night out but when I was in the army in Waiouru it was worth the 58-kilometre round trip for a session in one of its pubs. Wild nights are relative and a weeknight in Waiouru's winter was, well, wholesome.

Unlike smaller towns to the south, Taihape has settled into a steady prosperity, smaller than at its peak, bigger than its fellows. The main street has a busy cheer to it, although there's now a big gap in the main trunk line: in 1999 Tranz Rail, ever sensitive, demolished its wonderful old railway station.

Napier is 161 kilometres away according to the sign. The road starts innocently, past sheep yards and blossom trees, then takes immediately to those little hills, peaky as egg whites, and becomes a thread. Even now, with air conditioning and music, you can sympathise with Colenso: you don't know why, but it has a lonely feel. No cafés or petrol stations, no towns, passing lanes, espresso stops, hamburgers, laybys, pubs or even people for 152 kilometres.

The bigger part of this route is known officially as the Inland Patea Heritage Trail, once an ancient Maori track from the East Coast said to have been walked first by Tamatea Pokai Whenua, who arrived on the Takitimu canoe. That journey, with his son Kahungunu, is reflected in places along the way named for items he carried. A more permanent resident was Patea, whose wife's nagging over his hunting skills led to her own journey, over a cliff. Fleeing from her relatives he took up residence in what is now known as Patea Country, a vast tract amid the ranges.

Older maps showed you heading into a maze of curly roads but now it's hard to lose your way. Just

follow the sealed highway and take a packed lunch.

A bright red pond on a green sward. A young hawk rising in panic. White cliffs carved by rivers. A set from a cowboy film, although this has always been sheep country. Woolsheds whose architecture overwhelms farmhouses. No traffic this early spring.

Moawhango lies a little east, and you may spot the fine Whitikaupeka Maori church dating from 1904, the meeting house from even earlier.

A long time later, although it is less than a third of the way, you come to Erewhon Station. In the 1870s the station carried 80,000 sheep whose wool was sent to Napier by packhorse over the Gentle Annie, a stockman leading each team of 10, one animal in five carrying supplies. This trail was said to be the longest and busiest in New Zealand.

Then come Black Hill and Springvale stations and the Springvale suspension bridge over the Rangitikei, formerly the Erewhon bridge, finished in 1925 and still standing next to its modern (well, modern-ish) successor. The single-lane bridge was a symbol of the Gentle Annie's increasing economic significance: it

is lauded by engineers as a rare example of an early 20th-century suspension bridge and is listed as an historic place.

A little to the north is Ngamatea Station, at 29,000 hectares still the North Island's largest run and one of the main reasons for the Gentle Annie. Topknots of creamy-yellow limestone hunker on great cliffs of rock, vegetation clinging like hair. Then whoa! Something different — a vast green paddock holding hundreds of black Angus cattle.

Now you're rolling over a high plateau through purple scrub, the Kaimanawa Ranges to the north hidden by cloud.

John Mulgan's *Man Alone*, a creature of war and the Depression whose courage, ingenuity and self-sufficiency laid a template over the national character for three quarters of a century, was hunted through these ranges. He would still recognise the country instantly. Its wildness and loneliness endure.

A sudden change of character. Now you plunge deep into the bushy riven wilderness of the Kawekas, the range thrust high and still rising, its rock shattered and contorted. The Kaweka Forest Park took over where farming failed, the regenerating bush a symbol of good management.

The sharp drop, around halfway between Taihape and Napier, is the famed Gentle Annie. Tamed, it still snarls behind its bars. The road takes on that pock-marked look of New Zealand mountain passes. You begin meeting a few campervans, the new packhorses, labouring up and down, chary of that 100-metre drop to the green river.

But you stay on the road and instead drop in to Kuripapango, once the centre of what little civilisation the Gentle Annie could boast. It is named for a Maori warrior killed and eaten. The settlement lasted little longer. Once this place had two hotels, refuges from the awful road outside. It had a general store, stables, saddlers, blacksmith and bootmaker supplying all

Winter snow still makes Annie wild.

the essentials for the journey. It also claims credit for staging the first of another New Zealand favourite: dog trials.

But, oh dear. First the main bridge was washed away in a flood. Then the hotels, now combined into one, burned down. That put paid to the tourist trade. The coach service ended in 1913, the new main trunk railway diverted traffic, and today Kuripapango is a campsite. Yet a high single-span bridge tells the tale: this is deepest, darkest New Zealand.

The worst, or the best, is over. The road descends towards the Heretaunga Plains. The dark green lightens to grassland. The old Sherenden Hall. A passing glimpse of the symmetrical Mangawhare Station homestead built in 1879.

The road is another crossing, this time from raw interior into settled Hawke's Bay. For almost all its length there has been not a settlement nor a sign of one. None of the usual signs of New Zealand's past, no old shops, deserted schools, abandoned halls.

In the end they've put the Gentle into Annie at last. Yet she's still a rough diamond.

SPRINGS JUNCTION

HANMER SPRINGS

THE LEWIS PASS

'TRAFFIC ROLLS AS EASILY INTO NEWS BULLETINS AS IT ROLLS OFF THE ROAD.'

HOT-WATER HIGHWAY

On a fine day the Lewis Pass is beguiling, but on a bad one . . . well, there can be trouble right around the corner.

The Lewis is one of the three great passes through the Southern Alps. It is higher and busier than the Haast Pass, lower and less busy than Arthur's Pass. I've driven this road a hundred times and more, and for me it begins at the turn-off to Hanmer Springs, or more commonly *at* Hanmer Springs. Who would pass up the chance to lie in the hot water of those excellent pools looking over the tops of century-old redwoods to the snowy tops beyond?

Back on State Highway 7 the road runs alongside the Waiau River, the tussock hillsides purple with matagouri and red with fragrant sweet briar rosehips. It climbs around a bluffy section and passes two pretty little lakes which were once popular picnic spots but are now fenced off. Glynn Wye Station

RIGHT The Lewis Pass open to traffic after a snowstorm in June 2013.

FAR RIGHT Two boys admiring the view near the summit of the pass, 1953.

stands to one side before it drops to the wide bridge crossing the Hope River. Shaded buildings of the huge Poplars Station, half-hidden among trees, appear on the flat. Now running along the Boyle River, the road passes the strange-sounding Engineers Camp, a roadworkers' base and a scatter of houses where you speculate about the nightlife.

In fact, roadworkers based here probably sleep whenever they can, for they have plenty to do. This is a lovely drive on a lovely day, a dark one in the heavy rain that sometimes fills the pass, and a shifty one in the snow which quite often closes it or demands chains.

The accident risk is high: freight trucks, logging trucks, cars and motorbikes all roll as easily into news bulletins as they roll off the road. Slips and floods block the road and cut access to the northern West Coast.

Now the tarmac is rising gently. An inviting track leads off to the left where you can park and scare yourself on a swing bridge, then on you go.

The road is now deep in the Lewis River valley and thick forest presses in. A neat cottage owned by the Deerstalkers' Association is a marker for those in the know. One of the tracks leading down to the river is the way to a secret delight: a hot spring rising at the river's edge. Usually it is marked by a ring of rocks where the cognoscenti undress (quickly, for the Lewis sandflies are among the most attentive in the country) and sink into the hot water. Alas, a rockfall put this free luxury out of action in 2011. But who knows when it might reappear?

You pass the buildings of the Boyle River outdoor centre and now you're into the pass proper.

The Ngai Tahu travelled over this pass for much the same purpose as it is used now: passage between the West Coast and Canterbury, and transporting goods, in their case the precious pounamu, or greenstone.

The first European to discover the pass, officially at least, was Henry Lewis in 1860. The name became permanent but not a lot is remembered about Henry otherwise. He was a surveyor with the Nelson Provincial Survey Department and seems to have been one of those excellent functionaries who do their job well, collect their gold watches and retire. In 1889 newspapers of the day reported that Lewis died at 77, 'well known and highly esteemed'.

The pass he discovered now leads the road steadily upwards. You come to a kiosk and a walk around a nice little lake and think you're at the top but the summit is a short distance further on, 865 metres above sea level and unremarkable.

But now the road behaves more like an alpine pass. It creeps along cliff faces, runs over several one-way bridges, drops away frighteningly to the Maruia River far below, and offers splendid views of mountains and valleys wherever you can find space to stop.

At the bottom you come upon the Maruia Springs Thermal Resort. The road is easy from here to Springs Junction, a series of long straights and smooth bends running through huge trees, lots of beautiful parking places, beloved of television commercials featuring shiny cars.

Once I drove through here in a completely different setting. The beech forest that year had seeded hugely, an event known as a mast year. Thousands of rats fed on the seeds. Hundreds of them had been run over and other rats were feeding on the carcasses, one of the reasons why rats are not loved. It was a disgusting and rather frightening sight. But I haven't seen the phenomenon since, despite several mast years, and in the meantime the hot rockpools at Maruia Springs summon with their siren call.

THE LINDIS

'WHEN IT'S GOOD IT'S BEAUTIFUL, AND WHEN IT'S BAD IT'S HORRID.'

A thousand landscape paintings show the Lindis robed in gold. Soft folds of hills fall to the valley floor. So it appears for much of the year. For the rest, it's hard and cold.

This is an extravagant land. Near Tarras the highways fork: one goes on past Lake Dunstan to Cromwell, the other slips around the end of the Pisa Range, crosses the Clutha River and runs on to Wanaka. Both routes are spectacular.

The road north from Tarras leads through the Lindis Valley and crosses the fabled Lindis Pass.

The pass is rather like the paintings: when it's good it's beautiful, and when it's bad it's horrid. I drove through it one wild winter's day when dozens of cars were stuck in the snow and ice, so many beside the road that it looked like High Street on a Friday. The pass was once legendary, its reputation as fierce as the Otira's. It is tamer now, but every winter its claws show.

Tarras began life as a tiny town on the fringe of the mighty Morven Hills Station, the huge farm which dictated the way of life around here. It is still a tiny town, with a couple of shops in stone buildings,

a school, a few houses and the war memorial hall and community centre, its grandest structure.

A sheep sign and a road cone show that the once-familiar sight of a mob of woollies being run along the tarmac is still in vogue here. There's no sign of the sheep but something else is taking over the road: a house on the back of a transporter belts along at 80 km/h. The shadowed hills are instantly recognisable. This is the Lindis, sure enough.

A shingle road leaves the highway and angles off to the left. Old Faithful Road. The highway here is lovely, straightening and leading through willows. The detour along old Faithful is worth it, though. It's narrow, steep, runs through farmland and just as it would have rejoined the main road had the bridge over the river still been intact, it stops at a ruin.

This is the old Lindis Pass Hotel, a relic of the first gold rush here in 1861. It was, in fact, Otago's first goldfield. Samuel McIntyre, a roadworker, noticed that the terrain was similar to the Californian goldfields, where he'd mined for gold. Sure enough, there it was. Within days he and his mates had *four pounds* of the precious metal. A few weeks later 400 diggers were working the field. Yet no one, apparently, got rich.

A month after the Lindis reached its peak Gabriel Read discovered gold at Gabriels Gully in Central Otago, starting a truly enormous gold rush. Within two months the Lindis was deserted.

The Lindis Pass Hotel was thrown up during the excitement and rebuilt in stone 10 years later. It became a boarding house, store, post office, school and private home and was finally abandoned in 1951.

Remains of gold workings lie nearby, along with Wattie Thompson's old concrete hut. Wattie was the area's last goldminer. He worked Camp Creek after World War II but his claim was wiped out by a flash flood in 1971.

Legend says a farmer stripped off the hotel's corrugated iron roof for his woolshed and without it the stone walls began to crumble. It became a picturesque ruin, even the set for a television beer commercial. It would have been just a pile of stones if the Department of Conservation hadn't stepped in. DOC took over the building in 2005. Stonemasons rebuilt a collapsed wall, stabilised others and in 2011 DOC unveiled a fully restored, genuine, ruined gold-rush hotel, still without its roof, windows and doors but good for another century.

Past the old hotel the main highway starts flexing its muscles. It dodges around an enormous bluff standing like a fortress on the road. This was an old Maori trail, used by the Ngai Tahu as a summer route between the Waitaki and the lakes. It's easy to imagine here the party of Ngai Tahu fleeing noiselessly, hiding their tracks as they escaped from the Ngati Tama war chief and Te Rauparaha ally Te Puoho in 1836. Te Puoho had decided to obliterate the Ngai Tahu and led a war party down the West Coast and over the Haast Pass to Wanaka and Hawea, where he promptly attacked the locals. Survivors fled back through the Lindis along the path you're driving now. The Ngai

Tahu paid Te Puoho back, killing him in Southland.

Now the highway dispenses with bends for a while and becomes a long straight along a river flat. At the end of it is an enormous stone woolshed. This, at last, is the Morven Hills Station, which once roamed over the countryside much further than the eye could see.

The first European across the pass was the Otago surveyor John Turnbull Thomson in 1857. Thomson named it after Lindisfarne Island, near his home in Northumberland. He went on to become New Zealand's surveyor-general.

John McLean followed on his heels. McLean is said to have been guided over the Lindis in 1858 by the Ngai Tahu chief Te Huruhuru, who was probably a survivor of the Te Puoho raid and called the pass Okahu. McLean saw a huge plain stretching towards Wanaka and immediately sought a licence at the usual peppercorn rental, for this was classified as 'waste land'. Runholders had to stock their land within a year and McLean didn't have enough for his vast holding. The story goes that he plied the stock inspector with whisky while station-hands ran the same sheep from block to block.

He and his two brothers owned great tracts of New Zealand already, and at their peak their holdings ran to far more than 200,000 hectares; figures vary. They sold Morven Hills in 1874. John went on to become a member of the New Zealand Legislative Council. His brother Allan, who farmed Morven Hills with him, was famous for his plum-coloured suits and his white coach, known as the 'Yankee Express'. His giant home in Christchurch, McLean's Mansion, survived the 2011 earthquakes — just. Until 1955, under the terms of his will, it was a home for women of refinement but reduced circumstances.

Now you can see their Morven Hills legacy from the road. John's homestead, still occupied, is partly hidden by the stables. Two huts — one first a school, then blacksmith's shop, then store — still stand, and

PREVIOUS SPREAD
Through the valley
of golden folds.

ABOVE Approaching the Lindis.

the long cookhouse lies behind. As does the woolshed, built around 1880, which holds 1500 sheep and once had 34 stands, or shearers' positions.

Past Morven Hills the road begins taking on that serious look of New Zealand passes. The road remains the same, two-lane tarseal, but the engine note changes, the sky seems darker, and even the tussock has a warning look. Quite suddenly, you're there, on the second-highest point of the State Highway network, at the divide between two sensational pieces of New Zealand, Central Otago on one side, the Mackenzie Country on the other.

The pass itself is quite gentle. When you reach the summit, 971 metres, you may wonder what the fuss is about. In summer, that is. In winter, all sorts of mayhem can happen up here. Drivers stranded in the ice. Cars wrecked by fallen rocks. Or, as in this letter from an indignant driver to the *Southland Times*:

I said to my daughter there'll be trouble at the summit if not before and sure enough there was.

Once the 2wd cars slowed or stopped they lost traction and could not move.

Those of us in 4wd then proceeded to drive around the stationary cars on the wrong side of the road while also avoiding the vehicles coming the other way. At the summit there were several vehicles, cars, buses, someone towing a boat!!, either stranded or putting on chains. I was further amazed to see three vintage cars attempting to come over the pass from the other side.

Even, in 2000, a plane crash killing six as the pilot, flying below the mist and cloud, tracked the highway and flew into the hillside near the top.

A memorial stands near the summit, although not to Ngai Tahu, or Thomson, or McLean. It marks the first liberation of red deer in Otago, shipped from Scotland to Port Chalmers, brought by paddle steamer up the coast and taken by bullock wagon to the Lindis where they expanded into an expensive pest. A pass with a past.

● TURANGI

WAIOURU ●

UNDER FIRE MOUNTAIN

THE DESERT ROAD

'THE HIGHEST EXCITEMENT/ADVENTURE/DISASTER RATIO IN ALL NEW ZEALAND.'

Two memories of the Desert Road stay with me.

In the first I'm staring at it from a camp high in the hills. Not so much a camp as just a place in the starved scrub. These were the days of National Service, when unlucky young men whose birthdays were drawn in a ballot were trundled into the army for a few months. I was doubly unlucky. The army was one thing, but the military camp at Waiouru was several planets away from student life. The bleak dawn was so ferociously cold that we all believed hell *had* frozen over that night. How we wanted to be on the Desert Road, heading north or south, anywhere as long as it was away from this place, with the heater on full.

In the second I'm on the Desert Road in a long line of trucks and cars all stalled in the snow, with a cop leaning through the window saying we weren't going to be anywhere else soon. How we wanted to be *off* the Desert Road.

Oh, and a third. In the mid-1990s Ruapehu erupted, again. The ski season came to a sudden end. Volcanic dust filled the air and cancelled flights. Ash ruined turbines in the Rangipo power station. Smoke and flame shot from the mountaintop. The Desert Road was closed, of course. It closes often. Traffic was routed around the other side of the mountain, through National Park and Ohakune. But there we were, shut in by bush, bends and buttresses. On the other side we imagined smoke and fire and hot red lava burning down the mountainside. How we wanted to be *on* the Desert Road.

These stories have one thing in common. On the road or off it, you need to be on your way smartly. If something is not happening while you're on the road, something is going to happen. Anything from a truck crash to the planet blowing off steam. Nothing minor.

The road is only 63 kilometres long, but you always give a sigh of relief on the 63rd. It's the highest point in the state highway network. It also has the highest excitement/adventure/disaster per kilometre ratio in all New Zealand. You feel alone here, and you are.

There's a good reason why no one lives along its length except the residents of Rangipo Prison, who don't have a choice. The road traverses the Rangipo Desert. The landscape was boiled to a crisp by

thousands of years of volcanic eruptions. Nothing survives here but low bush and wild horses. The Black Gate of Mordor scenes for *The Lord of the Rings* were shot here.

The weather runs to extremes. Not so much runs as races. Five soldiers and a naval rating died in 1990 when they were caught in an awful storm on Ruapehu's flanks. This country is beautiful but uninhabitable. You're wise to have business that takes you elsewhere, urgent business. But the truth is that love it or hate it you have to live with it. There's no escaping the Desert Road.

The road didn't exist until quite recently in New Zealand's motoring history. It began as a rough track for an intermittent coach service between Taihape and Taupo while the main body of traffic ignored the desert and detoured through Napier and later through Ohakune. World War II was its driving force. The Army loved the desolation and set up the biggest camp in the country at Waiouru. The road improved, a little. Clouds of pumice dust still clogged radiators and suffocated passengers. Driving from Taihape to Taupo could take a whole day.

Royalty achieved what world war could not. When the nation was tidied up for the young Queen's visit with the Duke of Edinburgh in 1953-54 the road was widened — and sealed.

Unlike most high roads in New Zealand this one is an easy drive. It runs long, quite straight and uphill from Turangi until it reaches the Three Sisters, where it convulses. It dives into gullies, skirts hillsides and dodges like one of the wild horses in the hills behind. You're inside the landscape here. An insect boring through an ancient tree must feel like this, crossing rings laid down over centuries. Layers of lahars and ash twist and swirl.

You emerge near the top and it's glorious on a fine day. Yet, are you sure you're in New Zealand? Where's the green? Where's the lightness of being?

This landscape is deep and sombre. Its folds don't invite. They threaten. Ruapehu imposes, her warriors Ngauruhoe burping steam and Tongariro stunted and muscular. The three volcanoes and the central plateau, almost everything you can see, were given to the nation by Horonuku Te Heuheu Tukino, paramount leader of Ngati Tuwharetoa.

The drive from here to Waiouru is wide and easy. The feeling it gives is not. I've never driven this road without seeing a traffic patrol car, usually with its lights flashing beside a despondent driver. I know why people speed. Best get through while the going's good.

PREVIOUS SPREAD
Heavy haulage on the Desert Road.

ABOVE Mount Ruapehu – fire mountain.

RIGHT Mist lowers over the volcanic peaks.

THE OLD LION

CROWN RANGE

'IF YOU TAKE IT FOR GRANTED ITS BITE IS FEROCIOUS.'

The Crown Range is a road with a past. Once you couldn't take a rental car over it or you'd lose your insurance. Once, you *could* take your life in your hands over that road. Once . . .

It is a tamed beast now, but if you take it for granted its bite is still ferocious. No false pretences for this road. It zigzags from the main highway out of Queenstown in a series of hairpin bends, climbing steeply. Spring's icy cold is sweetened with the smell of red rosehips. But when you emerge onto the Crown Terrace, why, you're above the civilised bustle of the Queenstown road, alone with the mountains and the golden brown.

The terraces step above the lake like viewing platforms, a broad flat land spread beneath the peaks, an entrée, for you must tackle those peaks to reach Wanaka. You can see Arrowtown from here, and the Remarkables' jagged tops saw at the sky. A sign says the Crown Range road is open and the gate is swung back. Glencoe Station lies beside you.

The road slips around a steep bluff into steeper country, climbing all the way. Snow appears beside the tarmac, just to remind you of its wintry reputation.

Wooden barriers hold off falling rocks. Every bend hails a new view now, of Queenstown in the distance, of vineyards far below in the Gibbston Valley, of new peaks in a heraldry of their own. Eastburn Road runs off to Eastburn Station, running all the way to Cardrona. Snow poles appear as the road eases around basins and suddenly you're at the summit, the Crown Saddle, 1076 metres.

You stand there proudly, for you're on the highest paved road in all the land, if only two metres above the Desert Road through the central North Island.

William Rees and Nicholas von Tunzelmann, who were both runholders and explorers, became the first Europeans to cross the pass in February 1860. They were searching for sheep country and would have stopped just where you are now, imagining sheep dotting the tussock and composing Victorian elegies to the landscape, 'great mountains held us in thrall' and so on. The landscape was not quite to their taste, of course, and they set about improving it by burning the matagouri and speargrass. Only a year later the first sheep were run across the pass to Rees's station at Wakatipu, close to the town which

The Cardrona River makes its debut as you leave the pass for Wanaka. It is flighty, at first, a happy mountain stream trickling silver, flitting from one side of the road to the other in crossings so frequent they don't have names, only numbers: Cardrona 3, 4, 5 and so on. The road fills in where gully used to be, until the river grows from a thread to a skein to strong enough to brook no interference.

A sign warns of an accident black spot, although this one looks little different from the rest. Now you are at the bottom of a valley, the river bustling importantly alongside.

The old Cardrona Hotel appears, built in 1863 and sagging slightly, celebrated in songs, replicated even in inner-city Auckland. Several thousand people lived here then and the school was the biggest around. The gold rush may have been shortlived, but there's a new rush now, ski-ing and tourism. One hundred and fifty years on, the pub flourishes still.

Something has changed, however. Right up to a few years ago, scarcely anything other than the hotel stood at Cardrona. Central Otago and the Lakes are littered with ghost towns that once boomed. Cardrona is heading the other way. Now the hotel is the centre of a modern village. An old cob cottage is dwarfed by its new neighbours. Homes and holiday homes spring white and bright in the schisty landscape. The Cardrona ski-field entrance shouts beyond. Even the bridge numbers reach double figures as Cardrona swells to match its surroundings.

It becomes an easy journey along a wide road. A green valley leads down to Wanaka, where the fat town grazes beside the lake. SUVs are the cars of choice.

Queenstown is just a hop, if a high one. The Crown Range road is an old lion, but it still gets the occasional thorn in its foot.

he founded, Queenstown. He introduced both sheep and the game of cricket to the Wakatipu. Family names dot maps of the region.

Then came a gold rush. Or rushes. Gold was discovered at Cardrona on the Wanaka side of the road in 1863, and the miners rushed over the Saddle. The Arrow and Skippers discoveries followed a few years later, and miners rushed back the other way.

Tourists were crossing the pass by 1877, so it was a busy enough place even then. By the new millennium, the road was sealed and now it is a shortcut between Wanaka and Queenstown. Yet the atmosphere survives well at these high altitudes, for its essential nature is untouched. On 21 July 2014, 14 years after it was paved, a police bulletin instructed drivers to fit chains for the crossing after several drivers spun out of control and crashed. Just to make sure, patrol cars stopped cars at the top of the zigzag: no chains, no go.

Slabs of schist line the road downhill from the pass, creeping down gullies and past chain bays.

DANSEYS PASS

'A 19TH-CENTURY GOLDMINER HERE WOULD WONDER WHAT THE 21ST CENTURY WAS ALL ABOUT.'

A VANISHED WORLD

This is a crossing between two worlds. One is the Waitaki Valley, bright, wide, full of lakes and the mighty river, and not heavily travelled for there are faster ways into the Mackenzie Country.

The other is the Maniototo, that great russet expanse of bare hills and old stories. They are linked by Danseys Pass, a chameleon road whose character changes to fit the country it traverses through the ranges. It is easily closed by snow and ice, although that's hard to believe on a fine spring day.

The Waitaki has always been ogled by electricity generators. Baby-boomers were raised on stories of Lake Benmore and Lake Aviemore where dams were proud symbols of New Zealand's progress through the 20th century. Most recently an ambitious scheme to divert the river through canals and generators caused uproar before it was dropped.

Farmers have always prospered here and now it's a new wine region, vintners hustling in. Daffodils are everywhere this spring, and blossom. It feels like a garden so benign that anything could grow.

The lower reaches have been branded the 'vanished world' by tourist interests but a new world is rising. Several roads lead south from the Waitaki Valley and connect to the Danseys Pass route. All are intriguing. The most direct runs off State Highway 83, the Waitaki Valley road, just before Duntroon.

Awamoko and Georgetown have already put their stamp on the routes, with fine old stone buildings. Duntroon is a kind of signpost. Once, it was an outlier of the huge Otekaike Station owned by Robert Campbell, an old Etonian who established a fiefdom in the Waitaki Valley. Campbell died in 1889 aged only 47, and his young widow Emma a year later, but his legacy lives on. His 35-room mansion, built of Oamaru stone in 1876, set the template for architecture in the valley.

Campbell's station was later sold to the government and broken up. His grand house became a special home for boys in 1908 and grew into a village itself. It was closed in 1987 and sold, but everything still stands. The homestead looks splendid if severe and as you peer at it from the road you wonder what the boys thought of it, what bleak lives they led.

The Danseys Pass road crosses the old bridle path, once the main route for the crossing. The path runs up the Otekaike Valley past Campbell's homestead. His two homesteads, in fact. He thought the first too small after he married Emma Hawdon in 1868. That house still stands as a farm homestead partly hidden in a grove of trees. By modern standards it is both grand and elegant, yet it is dwarfed by the stone edifice Campell replaced it with.

William Dansey bought the Otekaike run before Campbell, in 1857, after searching the lower North Island, and the South, for land. His cottage still stands in the grounds of Campbell's elaborate mansion, below the graves of his two young children who died after being poisoned, possibly by tutu or deadly nightshade berries. With three others he walked through the pass in 1855–56 and was probably the first European to see the Maniototo.

St Martin's Anglican church in Duntroon further down the valley from Otekaike follows the style of Campbell's second house: built of the same limestone, it is a grand place in this tiny village. Churches outlive fashion and economic shifts and live to tell to the tale.

Not far from the church (for everything in the little town is close) stands the old Nicol's blacksmith shop, now an historic place but still in good working condition after a century. Much older are the Maori rock drawings under a limestone overhang along the turn-off to Danseys Pass. Maori trails criss-cross the country. Rock art decorates many limestone shelters in this region. This is one of the better-known and more accessible, an account of the time in charcoal and ochre still vibrant enough to prickle your neck.

A little further on you can take a left turn for Ngapara and discover the Elephant Rocks. An ancient seabed lies here, limestone trapping the bones of sharks, penguins, dolphins and whales and preserving them for 25 million years as fossils. The limestone has been cut and brushed by wind and rain into shapes

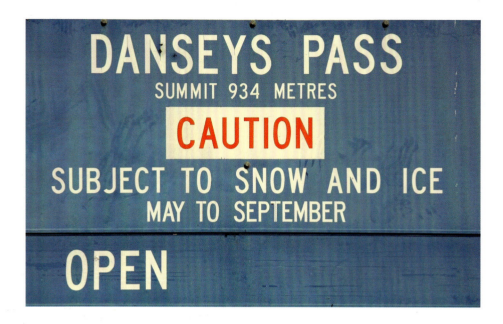

so fantastic that naming them after the animals of another country is boring understatement. Creamy-yellow limestone has weathered into dinosaurs, pedestals, toadstools, bollards, umbrellas, all from the reefs and lines of the old seafloor.

There's even a stone village, like a pueblo, which looks like one of Peter Jackson's sets from *The Lord of the Rings* but in fact was built for the film *Kingdom Come*, which was never made. In 2012 it was reported that the film might be resurrected and the village used, and that resource consents had been applied for, but there was no sign of life when I called in two years later. The area was also the setting for the battle scene in *The Chronicles of Narnia: The Lion, the Witch and the Wardrobe*. Film-makers love it.

Now you sit on a smooth rock in perfect silence and smell the clean air, hills flowing down to the sea in one direction and rising to mountains in the other.

So many exciting discoveries have been made in this district that several farms have been opened up to visitors following a well-defined fossil trail. Only a kilometre from the Elephant Rocks at an area

signposted Anatini are baleen whale fossils.

We go on to Ngapara for no good reason other than it's a very nice old town whose limestone buildings, flour mill, lodge, old hotel, church and houses have preserved it where many New Zealand small towns have just rotted away. According to one old account, 'The village was a busy place — the train went into town and back every day and brought the paper and letters and parcels. Over at the mill, old Nugget, everybody's friend, strained in the harness as he hauled railway trucks laden with bags of flour across to the turntable on the main line. And farmers arrived with grain in wagons drawn by horses or by traction engines . . .'

You drive back to the Danseys Pass road in a proper mood, for this really is a trip through living history. The road takes you past the old Maerewhenua Diggings, once the goldfields' edge. Goldminers poured through the pass in the mid-19th century, their water-races scoring the hillsides. The road is still lonely. It is often too narrow for a centre line on its paved section. Hacked into the hillside it follows a gully uphill, grass lying flat from the winter snow, becoming steeper and harder in the best pass tradition. It has a dreamy quality, although too much dreaming here could be fatal as it weaves through clefts, now all but one-way.

The seal gives up and the road becomes a brown mud track. Another patch of tarmac, teasing, then on to shingle, the verdant Waitaki now far behind, the Maniototo's stark beauty well ahead. This country is simply raw. Yet it soon drops the Waitaki's hue and takes on the Maniototo's cry.

A purple gateway announces a brief return to civilisation, a lavender shop delicate in the wilderness. A ford masquerades as a bridge. Through tight valleys the road presses on, now just a track. A blue Ford whizzes by without slowing, proving at least that the road is wide enough for two, even if one has its wheels over the edge. A last saddle, slashes of snow filling mountainside creases, the rutted road shaking the car like a mad terrier.

ABOVE The mighty brown hills of the pass.

INSET Road to Duntroon, c. 1900.

We are lost in mighty brown hills.

A sign warns of bends for the next 10 kilometres. What? Were the last 10 just a rehearsal? The carriageway is now down to bare rock in places, the insides of sharp bends shored up with schisty rock. A 19th-century goldminer here might have wondered what the 20th century was all about. I am resigned to being lost in space when I come across a patch of trees in a landscape where there have been none. Under them stands the long, low Danseys Pass Hotel.

The hotel has been a haven, refuge, shelter, a pause in the pass's monochromatic set, for a century and a half. If it is inviting now, imagine the joy miners must have felt after trudging through the hard, icy pass. In fact, it is said that miners worked on the hotel in return for beer. They planted the trees of their home countries in the German Creek reserve behind the hotel.

The hotel is the only survivor of the boomtown housing 2000 people which sprang up around the Kyeburn Diggings. The landscape seems to have been turned over by a giant plough and the town has almost disappeared. Only the cemetery remains. A sign before the graves announces charges: a single interment in open ground one pound, or ten shillings for children. Sinking a grave six feet, one pound, each extra foot another five shillings.

From here we can travel at 100 km/h but half that sounds reasonable, even if the newly graded road feels like carpet. Larches, pale green in spring, welcome us to Naseby along with its long-standing sign: '2000 feet above worry level.'

The old goldmining town stands much as it always did, scorching in summer, freezing in winter. Naseby sounds nasal but it's better than one of its previous names, Hogburn. Its 1860s population of 4000 has dropped to 100. Once the smallest borough in the country, it is still the prettiest, perfectly formed, with many of its oldest houses and buildings in good working order. Its most modern attraction, an international curling rink, caters for one of the nation's most mysterious sports. But I prefer its two ancient pubs. By the fire. Tucked away from the wild country outside.

UPPER TAKAKA

RIWAKA

OVER THE MARBLE MOUNTAIN

TAKAKA HILL

'KARST SHAPES MARCH OUT OF THE MISTS IN SOME MAD GOBLIN JAMBOREE.'

The Takaka Hill demands staying power. Sometimes it seems to go on forever. It is an endurance event compared with the mere cross-country of lesser passes, the more so because it leaves the benign green garden plains of Nelson in a flash. Before you can say apples, you are in a full-lock hairpin bend and it is only the first of many.

You can do the arithmetic on the sign at the bottom. Riwaka, near Motueka, to Takaka, Golden Bay. The hill should be only 25 kilometres long. A trifle, you think. You drive through orchards, apples red on trees looking spruce and orderly, and suddenly in front of you is a beguiling rise, the road bending out of sight.

You swing the wheel hard over this way, and that, then this way again. Not far up is a place where you can pass, perhaps: it's short, it's on a corner, and other cars, drivers now convinced they should have stayed home with *Coronation Street*, hardly ever pull over. But if you don't take your life in your hands and pass, you may be in for a long slow haul. Passing lanes are few on this hill, and the next is a few kilometres away.

All of them are designed for the nippy.

Hang on, though: perhaps it really is better to travel slowly than to arrive. You can't see beyond the next bend, let alone where you're going, and only rarely do you see where you've been, but you're surrounded by bush, and birds, and it's warm (because you're in the sunniest part of New Zealand), and life moves into sharp focus, not least because if it doesn't, well, the edge is right *there*.

It's said there are 365 bends on this hill, one for every day of the year. I haven't counted them, but I believe it. The first part is the worst, (or best, depending on what you like). Just when you're punting on whether the steering will fall off before your arms do, it straightens out — only a little, mind you, and you'd never think so anywhere else.

This was once the bridle track between Nelson and Golden Bay, first roughly mapped by George Murray over the Pikikiruna Range in 1844. The steep, difficult Pikikiruna track was cut in 1857 and turned slowly into a bridle track in 1878, then a road around 1900, following the track in places. The present road

extremely difficult terrain. That first bend, known as Drummonds Road, always gave road workers trouble, threatening to drop onto Riwaka Valley Road below. It sets the pattern.

The most infamous corner is the Eureka Bend on the Golden Bay side of the hill. It's one of the three great hairpin bends on that side which are so tight that from above they look like an earthquake graph. When the unstable rock of the bend slips, as it did in the first decade of the new millennium, chaos follows. This is the only way in or out of Golden Bay for road traffic, although two of New Zealand's great walks lead away, the Abel Tasman Coast Track at one end and the Heaphy Track at the other.

After that big slip, everything from cars to freight trucks to supermarket supplies halted. Golden Bay was cut off. Following the second big slip of the decade a trembling Bailey bridge carted traffic over the carnage until more permanent repairs were made. Letters to the local newspaper prophesied a return to the good old days of self-sufficiency and sea transport. Local businesses canvassed farm tracks and barges. But for now the road is open and it is a journey as much as a drive.

This place is not called the Marble Mountain for nothing. Marble quarried here made buildings in cities around the country including Parliament Buildings and Nelson Cathedral. A limeworks not far from those quarries signals the end of the worst bends on the way up.

At every bend now — yes, even dozens of them — there's a new view: Tasman Bay with Nelson shimmering in the distance, the toffee-apple red covering orchardists' crops, the brilliant Adele Island rearing from sea of that jade peculiar to the bay, the bush, the eccentric houses of recluses peering from it.

It's hard on cars. Once I was weaving my vintage Jaguar through the twists when I saw a wire wheel overtaking me on its own, a split-second before my

follows both bridle track and coach road in only one short stretch, but anyone who drove over it before it was widened in the 1960s would recognise it now: a few more passing lanes, a bit more seal, but the same number of twists and turns and just as steep.

Summers in the 1950s and 1960s would find the roadside littered with cars that had expired in gouts of steam, or broken cogs, or had stopped to eject hordes of kids bringing up their milkshakes in an epidemic of car-sickness. My dad used to plough over the hill with the Ford Zephyr groaning under five kids and an overloaded trailer. Behind us stretched a woeful parade of caravans and trailers, so that the whole spectacle looked like a refugee column.

In a sense it was: steady jobs and 40-hour weeks were something to escape from, then. People headed for Pohara beach, or Totaranui, that gorgeous gem of a beach whose access road was so tight and skinny that planks were laid on the inside of hairpins to take the trailer wheels.

Japanese cars and imports ended the carnage on Takaka Hill. A journey which could take all day then can now be accomplished from bottom to top in 22 minutes.

The hill's reputation remains raffish. This is

PREVIOUS SPREAD
Takaka Hill road.

LEFT Snow on the summit of Takaka Hill, c. 1920s.

now three-wheeled car collapsed.

As the road nears the summit the landscape fills
with eerie shapes, marble and limestone hollowed,
sculpted, tall as giants and small as goblins.

The road eases up a little. This country is familiar
to anyone who has seen *The Lord of the Rings*. You can
not only go over the mountain on this road, but into
it through the Ngarua Caves with their ancient moa
bones; or for cavers who revel in the underground
networks, down the 183-metre deep Harwood's Hole,
where vertigo battles that insane urge to jump.

Lookout points are everywhere, all of them worth
the stop, but when you reach the top of the Marble

Mountain, 791 metres, you get the best of them all.
Golden Bay is laid out before you, deep green running
out to smoky mountains then the brightest of seas.
I have driven in and out of Golden Bay all my life,
hundreds of times over the years, and it's never the
same drive twice. Sometimes, when the karst shapes
march out of the mists in some mad goblin jamboree,
I cannot imagine anywhere in the world quite like it.

Three hairpins lead to the bottom where once you
could celebrate in the enticing Rat Trap Hotel and get
the kids in the car park a raspberry and lemonade.
Built in 1903, burned down 1994. Amen, you say, to
both mountain and pub.

ARIKI

THE SHENANDOAH TRAIL

SPRINGS JUNCTION

SPRINGS JUNCTION TO MURCHISON

'A LUMPY, GRUMPY OLD BOY IN ROCK.'

The Shenandoah Highway is an enigmatic road. It begins at Springs Junction, although you will not find any springs there. They're located at Maruia Springs, 15 kilometres to the east. The road is said to be named after the Shenandoah River, the mighty waterway flowing through Virginia and West Virginia in the United States.

> *Oh Shenandoah,*
> *I long to hear you,*
> *Away you rolling river.*

The Shenandoah road flicks by and over the Shenandoah River but only the bridge names give it away: this is a bush stream rather than an Appalachian marvel.

It was named by George Fairweather Moonlight, the Scottish goldminer who left his name on creeks and places through Central Otago and the West Coast: at one time the Buller area became known as Moonlight country. The Pessini gold nugget, one of New Zealand's biggest ever, was found in Moonlight Creek. Moonlight built an accommodation house and store in the Maruia Valley, spoke with an American accent, dressed in American clothes and gave streams American names such as Shenandoah and Rappahannock.

Now this road displays the district's new gold, dairy farming. Expansive, expensive milking sheds sit in pastures reclaimed from the bush: rather ironically,

ABOVE Swing bridge across the Maruia River, c. 1910s.

for the Maruia Declaration which attracted more than 340,000 signatures and became a blueprint for native forest conservation originated around a campfire on the banks of the Maruia River.

A long straight heading north from Springs Junction crosses the Maruia River on a lengthy, one-way bridge where the road bends at both ends so it's hard to see what is coming the other way. It rolls easily north along what often resembles an avenue, so gracefully are the trees placed. This is misleading. The highway is 61 kilometres long. It runs beside the Maruia for much of that distance, squeezed by high ranges thick with bush. It is sparsely populated, lonely both by day and night. You can drive along this highway in the dark and see scarcely a light.

The nearest thing to a settlement here is Maruia (the name goes a long way, literally). Here, in a nice sweep of road, sits the historic Reids store, now well restored and reborn as a cafe, a popular spot in a journey where it's a long way between good coffees.

The road wends its pleasant way north until it kinks at a place called Burnbrae on the map but distinguishable to drivers by a cluster of farms at an intersection. Here comes the Shenandoah Saddle. The road rises quite gently, becomes hemmed by native forest, and suddenly a sign announces that you're at the top. This is surprising, because South Island saddles and passes usually involve a lot of grunting by both you and your car.

The downside is a little more spectacular, especially a bend near the bottom which can trap those who thought it time for a little speed.

Then the Shenandoah bridges, more forest, Pea Soup Creek (presumably a hangover from goldmining days) and a sign announcing a fine view of the Old Man Range. You'll need to look over your shoulder, for it lies to the south, a lumpy, grumpy old boy in rock silhouetted high in the sky. But the main attraction on this stretch of road is the Maruia Falls. The falls

did not exist before the 1929 Murchison Earthquake. The magnitude 7.8 quake killed 17 people, destroyed houses and roads, shook the sides off mountains and created the Maruia Falls in an instant. Now they lie beside the Shenandoah Highway, hypnotically powerful.

Shenandoah itself is another dot on the map, otherwise invisible to the naked eye.

The road ends at the junction with State Highway 6, west to Murchison, east to Inangahua. But if you've time on your hands or haven't had enough yet and want another way to Murchison, you might turn back to those farms at Burnbrae, where a shingle road leads off to the east. It crosses the Maruia Saddle and drops alongside the Warbeck Stream to the Matakitaki River where goldmining is still alive and well. A stone bridge takes it over the river and the gorge below is worth the trip alone.

I first drove this narrow road in a car old even for the time, when the Shenandoah Highway itself was mostly shingle. I remember not so much mountains or rivers or spectacular scenery as the steep hill running down to a one-way bridge. As I went down it was obvious my brakes weren't up to it. A farmer driving a tractor and trailer across the bridge realised it too. We both knew we were about to meet very soon, cataclysmically. He backed smartly, although I did not have time to admire his reversing skills. He shot back, I shot past: 'Sorry!'

He merely raised a finger in that way of farmers suffering fools.

TAUPO

TARAWERA

NAPIER

BATTLE ROAD

NAPIER TO TAUPO

'A NERVOUS PASSENGER MIGHT PREFER TO WALK.'

The Napier to Taupo road is eccentric. Sometimes it seems innocent enough, its peculiarities nicely ironed out. But here are two extracts from news bulletins showing its dark side:

The New Zealand Transport Agency says motorists should make sure they leave with a full tank of petrol, warm clothes and blankets, food, water, and a survival kit in case they get stuck.

The Napier to Taupo road in the central North Island has reopened, with a civil defence state of emergency lifted after motorists had to be rescued from snow-stranded vehicles on Sunday.

The road was dramatic from the start. In the late 1860s a line of stockades was built along the route, at Opepe, Runanga, Tarawera, Te Haroto, Titiokura. The idea was to protect the road from the Pai Marire or Hau Hau insurgency, sometimes learning from Maori and using their system of pa palisades. Ironically, the Pakeha road lay along a track used by the Tuwharetoa of Taupo to collect seafood on the Hawke's Bay coast.

The good Reverend William Colenso, the peripatetic Anglican missionary, blazed the trail for Europeans when he walked from Napier to Tarawera in 1847. By 1874 the road was carrying coach-and-horses, a two-day trip between Napier and Taupo. That sentence excludes the qualifications: endless fords, 43 across the Esk River alone, six teams of five horses for the trip along a steep and often icy road.

Lord Burford rode the route in 1891 in just under eight hours for a bet. (Clearly Burford was a sporting gent, for upon hearing in January 1893 that a 'deaf and dumb native', Wharerangi Matuahu, had hopped, stepped and jumped 14 metres at the Christmas sports in Taupo, he 'induced' him to jump again. According to the *New Zealand Herald* of the day, 'He was not in the humour and had to be almost forced to jump,' when he managed a mere 13.2 metres.) An account of the journey published in Napier's *Evening News* in 1887 recorded the following exchange:

'It blows here sometimes' I enquiringly suggest to Mr Bodger. 'By Jove, yes. It does blow, sometimes; stops coach and horses altogether, when it does its level best.'

The first car over the road was a Locomobile steam car in 1903. The Hawke's Bay Motor Company operated a coach service from 1906, using horses at first because the road was too hard for motors, then put a Cadillac car on the road in 1913 and cut the trip time to only eight hours.

By the 1950s the journey had become less perilous but was still a four-hour test of a car's durability, with a trail of broken bits along the unsealed two-thirds of its length. Even now, when the road has been sealed, realigned, widened, straightened, renamed the Thermal Explorer Heritage Trail and the two-day trip is reduced to around two hours, it can throw up this kind of report:

Police say the Napier-Taupo road will remain closed until further notice, after hundreds of drivers were forced to abandon their vehicles following an unseasonal heavy snowfall. More than 700 people were evacuated after their cars became stuck in metre-deep snow.

No hint of all this as you pass through the vineyards around Eskdale and not even the sign 'No fuel for 130 kilometres' can upset the quiet beauty of the place.

Te Pohue appears as a collection of huts around a small lake, a school and a hotel. The coach had its first stop here, having released a pigeon in Napier to tell the hotel how many for lunch. Even now the road seems to slither down Titiokura to the steep canyon of the Mohaka River and its tiny settlement and marae and bright blue schoolhouse. The 1887 account tells how this trip once was:

A steep sidling on the face of a papa bluff a few hundred feet high . . . A nervous passenger might prefer to walk down. We skidded down the papa roadway, slippery with the rain, rattled over the river on a good bridge, and pulled up for a few

minutes at Doney's accommodation house, a hundred feet above the water.

Now you whisk over and by, and on to Te Haroto, once a big timber town and still beset by pines. The marae is what it always was, home to the Ngati Hineuri, who once sheltered Te Kooti under the noses of the garrison in its stockade.

Then Tarawera, for years the first overnight stop for the coach, and always an important pause for Maori on their way to and from Taupo. It was also the base for the Hau Hau attack on Napier in 1866 where they were routed and lost 21 dead and 30 wounded (some of whom died later), around half their force. Tarawera is better remembered for its hot springs. In 1907 the writer Katherine Mansfield was enlivened by 'the air and the danger' and lolled in the hot water 'like oil and quite delicious, we of course in our nakeds'.

This was always the most gruelling section of road. It includes the steep Turangakumu ascent, the name meaning 'raising up of the buttocks' by bird-snaring parties as they bent over to climb. The road winds through the Waipunga Gorge, finished only in 1972, running through deep forest with cliffs leaning over. The Waipunga Falls lie near the highway.

Now you're driving down to the great forests and conservation areas of the Kaingaroa Plains created by the huge Taupo eruption of 186 AD, remote, cold, and altogether a proper setting for two strange episodes in New Zealand's history.

Eighteen-year-old Mona Blades was hitch-hiking from Hamilton to Hastings when she climbed into an orange Datsun car on 31 May 1975 and disappeared forever. She was last seen in the back of the car by a fencing contractor on Matea Road. When he drove back a little later the car was empty. Despite a huge police search Mona was never seen again, nor was anyone charged. The case surfaces every now and then, but it remains one of the country's unsolved murders.

PREVIOUS SPREAD The main highway between Taupo and Napier, State Highway 5.

Turangahunui
Saddle near
Tarawera, 1953.

The other episode involved George Wilder, the great prison escaper. In the second of his three jail breaks Wilder, by now a folk hero, had been on the run for 172 days when he was found in a hut at Rununga Bush near Rangitaiki. As usual, he went quietly. Rangitaiki's hotel burned down in 1988 and the place's best feature now is its lodge.

Now you're getting close to Taupo but there's a last stop: Opepe. Two Maori tracks crossed here, the Taupo to Napier and the Urewera to Tokaanu. In 1869 14 men from the Bay of Plenty were camped there, did not post sentries and were surprised by a group of Hau Hau. They fled for the bush but only five survived. The other nine are buried in the tiny cemetery here, their names inscribed on a totara headboard. A stockade was promptly built on the site, garrisoned by up to 140 men. It was manned until 1886. Another track leads to a huge totara log hollowed for a water trough fed by a spring, which served the camp. It's quiet and far away from that violent night.

Lake Taupo lies silver in the sun, cause and reward of the journeys of centuries. From this place you can look over the grand triptych of Ngauruhoe, Tongariro and Ruapehu, be awed, and delighted.

CHAPTER TWO

LONG AND WINDING ROADS

DRIVING ROUTES

1. SOUTH WESTLAND HIGHWAY
2. FRENCH PASS
3. THE KAIKOURA COAST
4. THE HOMER TUNNEL
5. THE HERBERTVILLE HIGHWAY
6. QUEEN CHARLOTTE DRIVE
7. WAIROA TO MURUPARA
8. MANGATUPOTO TO STRATFORD

LEFT Queen Charlotte Drive, Marlborough Sounds.

HOKITIKA

FOX GLACIER

JACKSON BAY

THE WILDEST ROAD

SOUTH WESTLAND HIGHWAY

'IF YOU SAY DIFFERENT YOU'LL HAVE A MILLION SOUTH ISLANDERS AND SEVERAL MILLION TOURISTS TO ANSWER TO.'

The South Westland Highway joins the wildest, most remote country in New Zealand. It is part of the longest highway in the country, its competition, State Highway 1, being in two halves.

This long, long road, State Highway 6, begins in Blenheim, loops over the top of the South Island, ducks through the Buller Gorge to the West Coast, runs almost the entire length of the Coast, climbs away over the Haast Pass, dances alongside three great lakes — Hawea, Wanaka and Wakatipu — and is stopped from going on to Bluff at Invercargill, usurped by its rival, State Highway 1. Certainly it is the most spectacular highway in the nation, and if you disagree you'll have a million South Islanders and several million tourists to answer to.

The Great West Coast Highway is such an outstanding part of that road that the only question in West Coasters' minds is whether the northern part of

the route is as good as the southern or, the odd radical might say, better.

If I had the casting vote I'd say the Punakaiki Coast is brilliant. It has everything from blowholes to boodles of bays. But for sheer endurance, hour on hour of adjectives heading for serious overuse syndrome, I'd pick the south. Past and present are indistinguishable here. Eleanor Catton's Hokitika in *The Luminaries* is still recognisable: the ships have gone along with the gold, but a certain atmosphere endures.

A little further south the late proprietor of the Lake Mahinapua Hotel, Les Lisle, was able to *sell* that atmosphere in a Mainland Cheese television commercial whose theme was 'some things never change'. Nor do they. Lake Mahinapua still glimmers under its forest fringe, quieter now than a century and a half ago when steamers and barges carried gold-seekers up and down its length. Les Lisle himself,

famous for huge whitebait patties and a very long beard, lived most of one century and made inroads into the next before dying in 2013 at the age of 88, only 20 years or so younger than his pub.

This is gold country. I once wrote an article about a man who lived not far from Hokitika and found gold in his backyard, lots of it. By day he fixed pipes, for he was a successful plumber. By night he scooped up tonnes of earth and rocks with his digger while his wife sorted the flakes and nuggets. That really *is* moonlighting.

The streets of Ross aren't paved with gold. But legend has it that below the town lie millions. Depending on the person, and the hour, and the bar, it can grow to billions. The Hon Roddy, New Zealand's biggest-ever nugget at 3.1 kilograms, was found not far from here. This is one of the Coast's paradoxes: the immense wealth that has been dug out of the place and evidently remains to be found, and

the frugal quality of every town you drive through.

Should you not want to drive on, however, there are plenty of places where you can get a pan and have a crack at striking it rich yourself. Personally, I've always regarded myself as more gainfully employed spending the time in the bar at Ross's veranda-ed Empire Hotel, having a beer under the baleful eye of a stag's head.

The road here heads for the hills with the determination of the miners it once served. You marvel at Lake Ianthe, for despite Lake Mahinapua you haven't seen enough lakes to be blasé. Yet.

A sharp right over the Wanganui River and you're at Harihari. Or Hari Hari. The town is different. Its kind of gold was timber. This was once the kind of mill town that conservationists ground their teeth over. Locals disliked greens even more than the people who are changing the name of their town. They seem to be losing on both counts. Various meanings are attached to the name, and spellings too: it was

PREVIOUS SPREAD Wild ride on a wild coast.

ABOVE No Fuel sign on the South Westland Highway.

originally Hari Hari, but officialdom has enraged local people by moving steadily towards Harihari. As for the forest, it's now protected.

Hari Hari's big day was 7 January 1931. The Australian pilot Guy Menzies left Sydney intent on making the first solo flight across the Tasman. He headed for Blenheim, but the wind blew him south and there he was, circling above a nice, green, flat pasture in a strange land full of mountains and rivers. He landed. It wasn't a paddock. It was a swamp (the Coast has a lot of those too). The plane flipped. Menzies lived.

On 7 January 2007, the 75th anniversary, the Australian businessman Dick Smith repeated the flight in a single-engined Cessna. He landed on a specially extended runway almost to the minute, and right way up. The gathering later repaired to Menzies' swamp, and, according to the *Greymouth Evening Star,* 'Only on the West Coast would you find a brass band sitting on the edge of a paddock, in full uniform, with instruments and music stands, welcoming dignitaries and visitors to Menzies' landing spot in a Harihari swamp.'

Many inviting roads lead off this highway and the road from Hari Hari is one of them. It runs off down the valley past the La Fontaine Stream where Menzies landed and ends at the Wanganui Bluff at the river mouth. I'd call it spectacular but by the end of this stretch of road the word would become threadbare.

The main road trips along the foot of a range to Whataroa. It's hard to believe, but here you're only a short distance from the headwaters of the Rangitata River in south Canterbury as the crow flies, although a crow is the only creature that will do the trip in less than a week because the Southern Alps lie between.

The main business here is a rather more graceful bird. The kotuku, or white heron, is an Australian import, as you can tell from its accent, a harsh croak. In New Zealand it breeds in only one place and here

you're all but standing on it. Their nests are untidy affairs, a tangle of sticks hanging over the Waitangiroto River, but tourists, even Australians, love them.

Their long, elegant white feathers were loved by Maori too. Early settlers, not well remembered for conservation, valued them so highly that by 1941 there were only four nests left. Now they breed in a carefully managed reserve and their population has climbed slowly to between 100 and 120 birds. They appear in swamps and estuaries all over New Zealand but they're still so rare that seeing one can seem miraculous (except in Christchurch, where they're accused of pinching goldfish).

When they're breeding they favour the Okarito lagoon, the biggest in the country still in original condition. The 10-kilometre road to Okarito branches off at The Forks just past Whataroa.

Okarito was once an important seasonal settlement for Maori, then a goldmining boom town with an important port. Its population reached 1500 and grandiose plans even included a university. Only Donovan's store survives. It's a quiet little place now and its tiny population likes it that way.

As the road treads south the forest simply becomes heavier, so primeval that if you stop the silence seems to press on your brain, and you're inexplicably keen to get on your way. You pass the mirror-like Lake Mapourika opening up beside you like an inland sea. The Franz Josef glacier rises from the bush, the sublime Alps rearing behind. It was named by the geologist Julius von Haast after the Austrian emperor but no Germanic quality remains. The glacier rolls from the Alps in such a huge jumble that the first European description of it came from a steamship at sea.

The glacier teases. It retreated from the 1940s, advanced from 1984 and as rapidly retreated from 2008. Given the global warming outlook the best time to see it is, well, right now.

All the while, as you round a bend or start on a fresh straight or climb a hill, there are glimpses of those huge peaks, the bulk of them tipped white. The road kinks southward to Fox Glacier, which bursts upon you like a carnival in the wilderness. It's as bright as the forest is sombre. Cafés beckon, bars cheer, hotels and motels shout how lucky you will be if you stop right here. Which, if glaciers are on your mind, you probably will.

The Fox glacier was named after a New Zealand prime minister, possibly an advance on an Austrian emperor. That is the only advance, though. Tourist businesses will tell you that both glaciers are moving at 10 times the normal speed, backwards. With the Fox, too, that's a retreat worthy of the French. This time, glaciologists are pessimistic. Some of them are digging out the last rites. Your chance of seeing a glacier is melting away. The Fox's terminal face was once an easy walk from the village, but now, best think about a helicopter.

On the other side, there's a road to Gillespies Beach which is neither retreating nor advancing and remains much as it always was, shingly, strewn with driftwood, open to the pounding Tasman. It

was named by a gold prospector called Gillespie who struck it rich in 1865. Yes, a boom town sprang up, died, hiccupped for a few years before 1946 when a gold dredge worked over the beach sands, and disappeared leaving only a cemetery and bits of machinery. But as you stand there, ozone zinging around your ears, lonely as a penguin, you feel as lucky as Gillespie.

Bruce Bay down the road is like Gillespies but bigger, its end vanishing into the haze hanging over the forest. Giant rimu line the beach, which is covered by equally big chunks of driftwood, as if forest untouched for hundreds of years had been swept into the sea by a flood. That is probably what happened.

The tiny settlement of Bruce Bay is dwarfed by its beach and if you ever need reminding of your true significance in the world, just stand here. Maui, the Polynesian explorer, is said to have landed here at the end of his epic voyage, but the beach is named after a paddle steamer instead.

You head back into the mountains, past Lake Paringa then Lake Moeraki (ho-hum, more magnificent lakes, you say), and suddenly you're back on the coast and driving down to Haast.

At the Haast River a road branches off. The main highway takes you on to the Haast Pass, and that's a story in itself. But you want the end of the road, the very end. So you turn right.

A long straight road right on the sea takes you to Okuru. In spring, whitebaiters throng the Okuru River; the stands grow more expensive as they get closer to the mouth. The season usually peaks in October; a good time to approach whitebaiters around their jetties and nets and huts. A pattie for tea.

Turn right at the Arawata River, haunt of William O'Leary, aka the famous Arawata Bill, hero of Denis Glover's poem of the same name. He spent much of his life in the river valley prospecting for gold and rubies. He found neither (although he claimed to have

ABOVE South Westland:
cliffs, rocks, sea,
bush, mist.

found the rubies), never married and, when confined to an old people's home in Dunedin, tried to escape back to his river. He died aged 82.

All of this is easy to believe here, amid the unchanging, where the past is the present.

The main road runs on to Jackson Bay and stops. This was once a big Maori settlement of perhaps 3000. Disease and fierce clashes with early sealers reduced their numbers to less than 200 by 1857. Optimistic, and absent, Pakeha planned a model settlement, judging the mountains and bush (again, presumably from afar) to be good agricultural land. Between 1875 and 1878 an international town of 400 people was established. The country beat them, of course, and they vanished, leaving only an old cemetery mouldering in the forest. Timber-milling flourished

for a while but now there's just a wharf to mark that. A few fishing boats are moored in the bay, a scatter of houses and sheds on shore, and a stillness.

A few optimists still eye the area, this time for a road south. If, instead of turning right at the Arawata River you drove straight ahead, you'd plod along the Jackson River Valley until you met the Cascade and you'd be on the route of one of New Zealand's least likely road proposals. This one has been around since the 1870s and has popped up regularly since. It would run from here to Hollyford and join up with the road to Milford Sound. It would intrude on two national parks and a world heritage area. None of that dissuades the West Coast interests still backing the plan.

No government to date has been enthusiastic. So far, the country remains inviolate.

FRENCH PASS

ELAINE BAY

OKIWI BAY

RAI VALLEY

FRENCH PASS

'A FEELING OF INTRUDING INTO COUNTRY WHERE ROADS JUST DO NOT FIT.'

The road to French Pass is one of the country's newest and least-known roads. Newest because it was finished only in 1957. Least known because it's difficult and dangerous, and the village at its end has a permanent population, at last count, of nine.

The top right-hand corner of the South Island frays into the Marlborough Sounds, whose drowned valleys account for a fifth of the nation's coastline. Most bays are still accessible only by boat, or walking track, and the Sounds have the feel of life once removed.

The French Pass road before 1957 was at best an old bridle track. The pass was one of the last areas in New Zealand to be opened to road traffic. Even now the journey has a feeling of intruding into country where roads just do not fit. It runs off the main road between Blenheim and Nelson near the small town of Rai Valley which, in all the years I've driven through it, has scarcely changed. The road is placid at first, running through farmland, but soon hints at what is to come. It crabs through hairpins, up a ridge and drops sharply into Okiwi Bay, setting the pattern: sharp bends, steep hills, beautiful bays.

Okiwi Bay is a classic Sounds bay even if it isn't in the Sounds, technically, for Croisilles Harbour opens into Tasman Bay. Pert little baches and homes cluster in ponga, fuschia, totara, pohutukawa, beech, nikau, around a beach where people can swim or launch their boats. Some people live here permanently, for this bay is within easy reach of Nelson — easy, that is, if you don't mind driving over the three big hills between.

A neat hairpin bend leads you out of Okiwi Bay, training you for what is to come: a whole lot more hairpins. The road climbs then edges along a narrow ridge which will become much narrower before you reach its end.

A short side road drops into Elaine Bay in Tennyson Inlet. It's in the Sounds, yet so close to Croisilles that a good fielder on a fine day could just about throw a ball between them. Elaine Bay opens the door to the Sounds' new industry, aquaculture: mussel and salmon farming. Farmers expect aquaculture to be a billion-dollar industry by 2025, mussels the biggest part of it. Rows of floats supporting mussel lines crowd bays all through the Sounds. Mussel boats moor in the little harbour formed by this bay. Beyond it the islets and

inlets go on forever. The sun shines, the sea sparkles. It's hard to be cross.

Now there's bush. It's a mixed blessing. The bush is nice but it hides the view. The sea pops through the gaps and, whoa, how steeply the land falls, and how far down the water. The road emerges at a strange landform which, on the map, looks rather like an italic *H*. The crossbar connects an island-like feature jutting towards Cook Strait. A road runs along here, all the way to a deep bay called Port Ligar.

The last time I drove along this road *Country Calendar* had recently featured Port Ligar farmers whose family had farmed their remote country for generations. Not long after the programme was filmed the father of the family was passing another vehicle on a road so tight that a wheel of his truck was on the verge. The edge crumbled and he was killed as his vehicle tumbled down the steep hillside. It was a terrible tragedy for the family, and for the Sounds, where he was well known and respected. For drivers like me, it was an awful lesson in just how deadly the road could be, even for people who'd driven over it all their lives.

If you'd never heard this story, the landscape would warn you now. You pass the turn-off to Port Ligar, and your next stop is French Pass. It has to be, for the road is too narrow to turn around. You take the steering wheel in an iron grip and, oh how hard you concentrate. The shingle road seems bare. It is. The ridge seems sharp, falling into the sea on both sides. It is, and does.

The bends are so abrupt you have the unnerving

PREVIOUS SPREAD
Twisting along the ridge to the pass.

ABOVE The feeling of driving into space.

sensation of driving into space as you turn.

Suddenly you make a sharp right turn and drop into French Pass. You take a deep breath and look around. In summer it is full of visitors, in winter deserted. It seems quite a big place, until you look more closely.

The school is closed, although still used by school groups. Some 40 children once lined up at the classroom each morning. There is a garage, a little store in summer, some accommodation. A ferry runs to D'Urville Island. The nurse's house is empty.

The Post Office, Money Order and Savings Bank has gone, possibly to the postmaster's relief: Wallace Webber had to collect the mail for the district once a week from passing Union Steam Ship Company vessels, a difficult and dangerous job in the tide races of the pass. The job passed to his son George, who was collecting the mail in the whaleboat when the steamer *Mapourika* was slewed so viciously by the tide that it cut his boat in two. George managed to rescue the mailbags and dried the mail in the steamer's boiler room. The mail got through, even if some of the letters were unreadable. Mail delivery in the Marlborough Sounds is still an adventurous business.

George Webber was one of the first to see the famous dolphin Pelorus Jack, which arrived in 1888 and played around the steamers delivering the mail. For 25 years Pelorus Jack accompanied ships travelling between Wellington and Nelson in the approaches to the pass. It would race up to them in great leaps, delighting passengers and crew. Webber sometimes had to use an oar to fend the dolphin off his vessel: he estimated Pelorus Jack to be almost as big as the boat. It became a tourist attraction and national legend and was protected by a special Act of Parliament. But Pelorus Jack disappeared in 1913 and was never seen again.

French Pass lies between this slender tip of the mainland and D'Urville Island. It joins Tasman Bay

to Pelorus Sound and Cook Strait and is still well used by pleasure craft and shipping. With a huge body of water on either side, each wanting to squeeze through the pass in the direction the tide is pushing it, the passage is spectacular in full flood. It looks like a serious river rapid: an apt image, for the sea literally runs downhill. The tides create whirlpools, powerful eddies, water-races. Sailors treat it with great respect. You can walk down to the old lighthouse on a steep flight of stairs and see just what worries them.

The French explorer Jules Sébastien César Dumont d'Urville was one such. His voyage of exploration aboard the *Astrolabe* almost ended in the pass in 1827. D'Urville eyed it warily, finding it 'like a seething sheet and the water washed into the basin forming whirlpools of incredible violence'. But he resolved to go through. Day after day he tried and failed, and on the final day he was all but wrecked. His ship was swept onto the rocks but scraped over, leaving bits of its keel floating alongside.

He left his name on the island and his nationality on the pass. But you're not sailing today. You have the car. You sigh with relief and try not to think about the drive back.

RIGHT The wharf at French Pass, Marlborough, c. 1912.

THE KEKERENGU STORE

KAIKOURA

OARO

THE KAIKOURA COAST

'BESIDE THE BLUE PACIFIC, LAZING, STRETCHING FOREVER.'

BLOOD ROAD

If you concentrate, you can count four humps in the Hundalees. On the fourth, the highest, you look down a long valley, still heavy with bush, kowhai gushing yellow in spring.

The road through the Hundalees was once one of those fabled stretches of New Zealand highway, a place where people came to grief in breakdowns or crashes. Perhaps it was simply a contrast with the easy North Canterbury roads, State Highway 1 slipping smoothly through its curves. Yet it was a tough little number, grunting grades and tight bends, and it always seemed dark. Even now, eased, it is slow.

On that fourth summit you were in the clear. The world was full of light. The valley led down to the sea which always shone. It always does, no matter what the weather. It seemed to go on forever, bouncing blue, even the rocks white, and Kaikoura, you decided, must be the happiest place in the world.

So it seems, still. The road runs down to Oaro with its little clutter of baches where the railway line leaves the highway to pursue its own course around the coast. Suddenly you're in another world. The Kaikoura Ranges shelter the coast. Bush-clad rock drops to the

road; often, in bad weather, drops *on* the road. And on the other side of the road is the blue Pacific, lazing, stretching forever, lapping against great black rocks, tiny islands white with guano.

Only the Punakaiki coast matches this road for splendour, and this coast is gentler.

Its history is ferocious, however. The coast here was covered in Maori tracks. Barry Brailsford's book *The Tattooed Land* shows pa spaced every few kilometres all the way north to Clarence. Ngai Tahu and Ngati Mamoe fought over the territory, and the Ngai Tahu were swindled out of their land by James Mackay on behalf of the Crown which, having bought the entire West Coast for £200, apologised to the young colony for spending an extra £100, or £300 total, on all iwi land north of the Hurunui.

But the famous raid by Te Rauparaha in 1829 dominated all. The King of Kapiti attacked the main Ngai Tahu pa at Kaikoura and killed 1400 inhabitants. Survivors fled south to Omihi which proved a fragile refuge: his warriors killed most of the pa's occupants there too, refugees fleeing into the mountains or south to Kaiapohia. The population of the Kaikoura coast was all but wiped out.

No sign of blood or treachery 185 years later. The Waitangi Tribunal recompensed Ngai Tahu for the Mackay Purchase and Omihi's scars are covered by a camping ground and a café. But history lies heavy in the air, thick on the ground in old pa, relics, wrecks.

The road bounds along the coast just above the water, white and yellow rock daisies clinging to the cliffs. Few places in the world offer such easy access to wildlife. Seals loaf in the kelp, seabirds from Royal Albatross downwards skim the water, dusky dolphins sport in great schools, sperm whales dive up to two kilometres into the Kaikoura canyon which in places is just 500 metres from the coast.

The road dives too, into two sets of tunnels carved through rocky headlands. Beside one is a pool where you can jump into clear seawater left by the tide, among the anemones and vivid seaweed. Crayfish once hid there, for the name Kaikoura refers to crayfish, but they're not as plentiful now. Car horns bounce off the tunnel walls, echoing generations of children shouting, 'Honk the horn, Dad!' Nowhere to pass and only the determined can stop, but if you do, this wild seascape is worth it.

The road reaches the Kahutara River where the water rushes into the sea, creating the kinds of waves beloved of surfers, then evens out, passing Puketa where whale-spotting aeroplanes sit on the airfield. Whale-watching is one of Kaikoura's main industries, boats owned by Ngai Tahu leaving South Bay. Their base is not far from the rock where James Mackay sat for a month as he bargained for land, a sharp and uncomfortable seat named Te Turu o Make, Mackay's stool.

Kaikoura, like its coast, is always bright and busy. I drive through the town to the Pier Hotel beside the main fishing wharf where you can sip a beer and look through the bar window to one of the country's most glorious views. Across the bay and the fishing boats lie Fyffe and Manakau and their mountain companions on the seaward Kaikouras.

It's an easy journey around to the Kaikoura peninsula with its pa and its gannets and its wide rock terrace reaching into the sea. Fyffe was the name of Kaikoura's first European family and their house stands on its whalebone foundations on the road leading round to the point.

On the nearby foreshore stands a chimney, all that is left of the Customs house from the old port. A shore whaling station was working here by 1843, growing to three. Kaikoura had become a port by 1859 and a town by 1861. Its dangerous coast made even this tricky port preferable to the cliffs and river crossings to the south and north. The town was the only place of any size between Blenheim and Rangiora, a stop on the bridle track which by 1891 had become a coach road. The railway was finished a full century after the town's beginnings, in 1945, a huge project with 21 tunnels. The port closed only in 1949, when the road became faster and safer than sea, yet even now it is quite regularly blocked by huge slips. One of the great things about this road is that they'll never be able to tame it.

None of this speaks of its magic. Here's the account of an early, rather awed, motorist:

The high snow peaks burn with sudden fire; the glow dies away; the rugged heights become deeply, darkly blue, remote, like the indigo depths that lie beneath storm-shadowed seas . . . Now we are out on the coast again, running through a magnificent seaside park, with the blue Pacific stretching away into a pearl-pink haze on the horizon.

I usually abandon State Highway 1 at the northern end of town and run along the old coast road, leaving Kaikoura's white cliffs blazing in the sun behind. It is gentle here, cared for, and there's a nice old dairy factory converted to a house, and the road deposits you

ABOVE Road tunnels, one of two sets carved through bluffs.

back on the highway just before Mangamaunu, where you can still see traces of the old village and school. Henry Lawson, who ranks alongside Banjo Paterson among the great Australian writers and poets, taught here in 1897. His enthusiasm for teaching Maori — disconsolate, dispossessed and decimated — waned after only eight months. Mangamaunu remains famous among surfers, and State Highway 1 has been widened here to give them room to park.

Now the road creeps into bays, around points, past stalls selling crayfish. Seals are everywhere, especially at Ohau Point where cars are warned to watch for seals on the road, but I find tourists more dangerous.

Just past the point a walking track leads under the railway line and up a stream to one of the most startling places on this wild road: a deep pool fed by a perfect white waterfall. The pool is the playground of young seals, their numbers depending on the time of year. They begin leaving in spring. The seal

pups writhe around each other, graceful, unafraid of their audience.

The road grows easier now, running past Clarence at the Clarence river-mouth, the most interesting part ending at Kekerengu. The place was named after a Ngati Ira chief who liked to live dangerously. Having been forgiven for dallying with one of the fierce Ngati Toa chief Te Rangihaeata's wives, he then seduced another. He fled to Kaikoura and some say he was put to death at Kekerengu for the trouble he caused.

Inland lies a little village. Joseph Tetley established a huge sheep station here, prospered, failed, fled. Two cob accommodation buildings from the old station survive, and houses trail up the valley, but the real gem here is the tiny church, scarcely bigger than a bus alongside its cemetery, filled with stories.

A big café marks the place on the highway. It's a good place to have a cup of coffee and watch the seals on the black reef.

MILFORD SOUND

HOMER TUNNEL

TE ANAU

INSIDE THE MOUNTAIN

THE HOMER TUNNEL

'THIS WHOLE PLACE IS A ROCKFALL, THE DIFFERENCE BEING THAT QUITE A LOT OF IT HASN'T FALLEN YET.'

In 1889 colonial New Zealand was a young country, flexing its muscles. Crowds thronged the New Zealand and South Seas Exhibition in Dunedin. The Free Kindergarten movement started. The first recognised Leader of the Opposition took his seat in Parliament. The first balloon ascent was made. Julius Vogel, the former Premier, wrote New Zealand's first science fiction novel, *Anno Domini 2000; or, Woman's Destiny*.

William Henry Homer and George Barber discovered the Homer Saddle that year. They suggested a tunnel. The idea was remarkable for two reasons. First, Fiordland was even more of a wilderness than it is now, and technology did not extend far beyond picks and shovels. Second, the road would go to Milford Sound and stop. It was a road to nowhere.

The idea lay dormant for the next four decades. Poverty revived it.

The nation was in the middle of the Great Depression. A project of the tunnel's size would mop up the unemployed. Tourists would pay handsomely for access to the majestic Milford Sound. Presto! The country's poorest and richest would benefit.

In 1935 work on the tunnel began. Essentially, men were given a pick, pointed at the rock wall of the Darran Mountains, and told to go dig a hole. Only five of them at first, then a growing number, then wives and families.

Their surroundings were magnificent: the Upper Hollyford Valley on the eastern side of the mountain range and the Cleddau Valley on the western side. But the country had been carved by glaciers and covered in rainforest. Heavy rain saturated the valleys, avalanches roared off vertical rock walls, ice covered everything. Men lived in tents and makeshift cottages and battled granite every day of their working lives. Their pay was as bad as their working conditions. At least they had fresh bread: the remains of an old concrete baker's oven still stands beside the road.

The Upper Hollyford and Cleddau valleys are superbly enclosed by near-vertical rock walls up to 800 metres high. But they were prone to avalanches. In heavy snowfalls dry avalanches, near-silent, poured from vast snowfields high above the valley floors, so far above they were invisible, sneaking down on the

Work on the Homer Tunnel resumed in 1953. The first private cars drove through it in 1954. Now it is the only one of the Fiordland sounds which people can drive to in their own cars: Doubtful Sound has a road into it, but the public first has to cross Lake Manapouri by boat to West Arm.

This is a journey of around two hours from Te Anau, depending on how spellbound by the scenery you are, and whether you take a side trip: one leaves the main road and follows the Hollyford River towards the coast, expiring in a deep, lonely valley. Make sure your petrol tank is full and put aside the whole day.

The road rolls easily at first, leaving farmland for a much older New Zealand, scarcely changed over the centuries. Sometimes you are in open country, mountains hedging its edge. At others you drive through beech forest and the mountains seem to be at the end of a tunnel. But they're always there, capped white even in summer. Thousands of tourists travel this road but outside the busy periods you feel alone.

A sign announces that you're in the Fiordland National Park, a World Heritage area, but it seems superfluous, for what else could this be? You're in untrammelled country, forest, swamps, rivers, lakes, mountains, the works. No more 'for sale' signs, except perhaps in the office of the Minister of Mines.

The Eglinton Valley opens before you, wide, flat, green. The Mirror Lakes. Patches of white clematis high in the trees, pure against dark beech, like lights. Avalanches keep the valley floors clear. If it's misty, you're lucky. Rain blots the view, and there's quite a lot of rain here.

The road narrows, lots of one-way sections, but you're transfixed by rock walls falling hundreds of metres to the river beside you. The road hooks around the angry snout of a rockfall.

This whole place is a rockfall, the difference being that quite a lot of it hasn't fallen yet.

The road begins to climb. It reaches 940 metres

working men whose last-minute warning was a blast of compressed air. Sometimes it was the last thing they ever heard: a bronze plaque beside the road records the death of Percy Overton, aged 26, killed when an avalanche engulfed the tunnel entrance. Several other men were injured.

Despite the reinforced concrete shelter built subsequently, others were killed: Donald Hulse, the engineer in charge, and Thomas Smith, works overseer, died in 1937.

Work slowed. The mountain was pierced ('hole-through') only in 1940. A huge avalanche destroyed even the 'avalanche-proof' concrete approach shelter in 1945, but no one was injured for World War II had suspended work.

Many workers must have celebrated when war broke out. They risked death and injury on the battlefields, but they risked both every working day. As fighting men they were better fed, better paid and the weather was a big improvement.

at its highest point. You're in avalanche country, and it's still dangerous: a massive avalanche killed a road maintenance supervisor in 1983. The danger zone starts at Falls Creek and doesn't end until you're at the Chasm on the Milford side of the tunnel.

Avalanches within these bounds close the road an average eight days a year but in a bad year, they can be much worse. A storm in September 2013, already a year of bad rockfalls, brought down 20 avalanches in a day, blocking the road for most of a week after a year in which it had been closed for more than 70 days. Tourists were trapped in Milford. Road closures like these cost the tourist industry millions each year in cancelled tours, flights, cruises.

This is one of the country's leading tourist attractions. The industry is the reason for the road's existence. It supports a huge superstructure of hotels, lodges, airlines, shops, a workforce in Milford and Te Anau and Queenstown. Closures are inevitable in such wild country but they're very expensive, and avalanches have another quality: they're all but unpredictable. You'd need to be either insensible or stupid not to recognise the truly wild nature of the country you're in.

Transit New Zealand runs a control programme which uses sophisticated equipment to monitor avalanches, both sensing danger and using explosives to set off controlled falls while restricting traffic or closing the road. The avalanche risk is predicted and drivers make their own decisions, although kiosks in the depths of winter tell motorists how to drive safely and check their chains. Signs warn of the avalanche risk: low, when the road is open; moderate, when the road could be closed at short notice; and high, when it's closed.

The road slithers up towards the Homer Saddle, climbing so steadily that quite suddenly, without any more fuss than a green light, you're inside the Homer Tunnel.

What does it look like? A mountain from the inside. No lining, no tiles, no embellishments, just rock, jagged and black. It's dark. You remember that three buses have caught fire just about here, although no one was seriously injured. You follow the lights of the car ahead and wonder how the driver is finding his way; yet if you're at the head of the queue it's simple enough.

It's quite short but still, you welcome the light at the end of the tunnel.

You emerge into bleakness, startling, superb. Sheets of bare rock flake off the mountains, sheer, nothing for the most tenacious root to grab. The mist parts around the peaks, like a salesman revealing gems. Mighty waterfalls are scaled down to threads on their faces. Far below, the river forms turquoise pools. Tracks lead off into the wilderness. One of them goes to the Chasm itself although by now you'll have more than an inkling of what it is like.

No matter how many times you've seen Milford Sound, Piopiotahi, and for most of us that's perhaps once or twice in a lifetime, it thwacks your senses. Still water and Mitre Peak. It's so huge. You're so small.

A cruise ship manoeuvres in the Sound. In Auckland they look big. Here, the ship seems tiny.

Hardly anyone lives in the sound. It's for tourists, who gasp.

There are other ways of getting to Milford Sound. You can walk over the famous Track. You can fly in. You can come by boat. Other routes have been proposed, and so far rejected. The most ambitious was a new tunnel planned by South Island business interests running through the Routeburn at the top of Lake Wakatipu and joining the road, cutting travel time. The 11.3-kilometre tunnel would run through two national parks, Mount Aspiring and Fiordland, and a World Heritage area. Not to mention affecting the famous Routeburn Track.

In exchange, the Milford working day would be

lengthened. With no room to accommodate the hundreds of thousands of tourists who visit the Sound each year, for most it's a day trip only. Tourists have to cram their day into a few hours. By cutting down the time taken to get into Milford, the tourist infrastructure, the cafés, cruise vessels, guided tours and so on would work more efficiently, under a more evenly spread load. Environment groups and the wider public protested vigorously. In 2013 the conservation Minister, Nick Smith, rejected the tunnel plan.

The legacy of all this is a road that exists for no other reason than the beauty of its surroundings. It earns its living in every way.

Despite the attraction and the rarity of experience, the big iron gate which closes the road stuck in my mind. I could not escape the thought: let's get out of here before something falls.

ABOVE Avalanche warning sign on the road to Milford Sound.

RIGHT Sheer rock walls loom above the road, Cleddau Valley.

MASTERTON ● — ALFREDTON ● — PONGAROA ● — WIMBLEDON TAVERN ● — HERBERTVILLE ●

TO THE BACK OF BEYOND

THE HERBERTVILLE HIGHWAY

'AND WHAT BETTER PLACE TO ESCAPE TO?'

This is a long and often tricky drive leading to, well, nowhere much. It might even set a record for the number of bends in a state highway, a hotly-contested title. Few straights relieve it, and if you're stuck behind someone, get used to it. In the end, where does it go? To the back of beyond, but it's an intriguing journey.

The road runs out of Masterton along the Whangaehu River and is given the rather grandiose title State Highway 52: grandiose because its red line on the road map has that ominous chequered appearance in parts, indicating that it falls below standard. This only makes it more attractive to the saloon-car adventurer.

You drive for some 46 kilometres before coming across any kind of settlement. It's Alfredton, at the end of a mischievous little stretch of road. Alfredton has a pretty church, listed by the Historic Places Trust and worth looking at; also a school, hall, domain and, luxurious touch, golf course. It was grandly named after Prince Alfred, Duke of Saxe-Coburg and Gotha, second son and fourth child of Queen Victoria, who may or may not have known about his namesake on the other side of the world.

Another dotted stretch of highway and you're at Tiraumea, which has a hall with public toilets and little else, then Pongaroa, a rural metropolis by comparison. A monument here tells you of the local boy made good, Dr Maurice Wilkins, who went on to unravel the puzzle of DNA and win a Nobel

ABOVE The Herbertville Highway.

prize. This was once an ambitious town, when the Masterton to Napier railway was to have gone through it. The township grew to match its citizens' expectations. Alas, the railway went the other way, through Eketahuna. The dream evaporated but left behind a nice little farming village which is handy, because by now you've been concentrating hard on this tricky road for an hour and a half and more than 90 kilometres. You can have a coffee and contemplate your day, for this is a crossroads and you have a choice.

You might turn off the highway here and head for Akitio, one of those beaches where wool was once loaded onto waiting ships. The river mouth was a safe anchorage if only by the standards of the day, for several ships were lost. Now it's a pleasant beach, and depending on the tide you can see the remains of the jetty. Historical homesteads still stand.

Or you can remain on course for Herbertville.

On 11 August 2014 the *Wairarapa Times-Age* carried this story: Matt Charlton was working on a forest road at Pongaroa when he saw something crawling towards his backpack, so big that he thought it was a baby possum. Then he realised it was a spider, bigger than his hand. In fact, it was a ground-burrowing stanwellia, a tube-web spider, widespread in New Zealand but rarely seen. So you say goodbye to beautiful Pongaroa and leave, hurriedly.

The road beetles up to Weber, named after a German surveyor who was working near Woodville and disappeared in 1886: his body was found three years later. Weber began as a coach stop and grew into a town complete with prison, pub and post office with its own tourist attraction, the Waihi Falls. Most of it, including the falls, is still there.

The highway takes a hairpin bend, the town slightly off it, as if flung away by the sharpness of the turn. The highway meanwhile creeps on through now-familiar tight places to Wimbledon, where farmers still mourn the loss of the agricultural highlight of their year, the annual ewe fair, once the oldest coastal fair in the country. After 107 years, falling sheep numbers saw it move to Dannevirke in 2010.

Time has eroded Wimbledon too. Now it's notable only for its fine old pub built in 1889 and the turn-off to Herbertville. Right on the coast, Herbertville reverses the trend. It's growing. I went surfing there when I was young, drank in a pub which seemed to be half grocery store, half bar, slept in shearers' quarters, fought with local youth, ran away from local youth and generally had a lovely time in a lonely place.

It was probably bigger at the turn of the 20th century, when there was a much grander pub, shops, police station. Schooners would beach on the long sands, load and refloat on the tide. Later Cape Turnagain's jetty was on the steamer route, enjoying its reputation as the fastest-loading in the country, understandably, because it was also said to be the most dangerous. Three Speedy brothers bought three huge stations in 1856 which are still farmed by the family, and the handsome Burnview Station homestead stands proudly along the seafront.

The town went backwards then forwards again, for it's a holiday-home settlement now, with a camping ground that was bought by its campers. But it's quiet, and remote enough to become a refuge for its most famous resident, George Wilder, the 1960s jail-breaker who dodged police for months. Now he dodges reporters and television journalists, and what better place to escape to?

MOMORANGI BAY

LINKWATER

PICTON

QUEEN CHARLOTTE DRIVE

'DEEP, SECRET, EXCITING.'

BEAUTY QUEEN

Like many great beauties, this one begins subtly. The road slants off in a corner of Picton without fuss. Hidden in bush it rises above the clutter of car parks and assembly areas for the Cook Strait ferries and passes the old freezing works where locals tell stories of sharks growing fat as sea monsters on offal. The drive offers a peep of water, then drops into a coastline of logs: cliffs, bays, forelands of stripped pine waiting for a ship.

Kapow! In a few minutes you're in another world, where industry has no part and there's only you, a narrow road made private by its complete lack of space and, always, a bend just ahead. Through the tassels of bush at its edge lies the green Sound.

The water today is still as a bath, dammed by bushy hills. Sounds hills have their own smell, the scent of sea and honeysuckle, and the hills embrace rather than bar.

RIGHT A road of tight bends.

These are the Marlborough Sounds, deep, secret, exciting. On this road between Picton and Havelock you pass two of them, Queen Charlotte and the bigger, wilder Pelorus.

Tight hairpins become the norm, 30 km/h a good speed.

Every now and then the view widens from a glimpse to a vista and then you must stop, for the Sound demands it. This is the Grove Arm.

Down in the bays cottages hide in the bush. The sun lights ponga trees as suggestive as palms. Moored boats look serene in that way they do. The water runs out of sight, around headlands, into bays and bights, all the way to the open sea so many twists and turns away that from here it's just a suggestion.

On the other side of this reach lie some of the Sounds' most popular bays, still accessible only by boat. On this side the road passes Ngakuta Bay, a holiday-home settlement where traces of the old bridle track running through the bay have been uncovered. A new Link Pathway will eventually follow the bridle track all the way from Picton to Havelock.

Then Momorangi, where the Department of Conservation has a campsite and is restoring an ecosystem destroyed by farming in the early 20th century, replanting the great canopy trees which once covered the area.

The road relaxes here, for a while. To the right lies Anakiwa, famous for the Outward Bound school and now the start, or the finish, of the Queen Charlotte Track. Ahead lies Linkwater, five kilometres of flat paddocks lying between the head of Pelorus Sound and the head of Queen Charlotte and once considered for a canal to avoid a 100-kilometre sea trip out into Cook Strait and back the other way. Now it's a straight flat road between bends.

About halfway along it lies the turn-off to what is left of Cullensville, at the end of an old goldminers' trail across the range from the Wairau Valley. Gold put this place on the map in 1888, lasted a bare 10 years before it ran out, and took a whole civilisation with it. Cullensville boasted three hotels, two billiard saloons, a bank, courthouse, shops and a thousand men working on the diggings. Shafts and tunnels ran beneath the ground with great pumps to keep them dry, an aerial tramway to fly quartz down from the hills and a vast stamper battery to pound out the gold.

Nothing remains of it now but a few bits of machinery and shafts leading into the hills from dark holes. The new gold rush in these hills, pine forestry, is not nearly as accommodating: it devastates the landscape and lacks the grace to disappear so completely.

Mudflats announce the arrival of the Mahakipawa Arm, Pelorous Sound, a body of water big enough to include two other sounds, Mahau and Kenepuru. The road into them, and to far-off bays, runs from Linkwater too, for this sparsely populated place is a mighty crossroads.

More bays, more bends, hills cloaked in regrowth. Holiday homes here have the comforting New Zealand look: well-tended, unpretentious, everyone's idea of that endangered species, the Kiwi bach. They reek of sunlight and summers past.

The road climbs Cullen Point and the vast reach of Pelorus Sound etches on your memory a burst of sunlit water. The channels into Havelock wind through mudflats exposed at low tide, hundreds of boats in the marina lying at their end. The Pelorus River runs into the Sound in a plain of tawny-pink marsh grass.

Havelock is more serious, less prosperous, created by gold discoveries in the nearby Wakamarina River. Unlike most gold-rush towns, it simply dug in its toes and stayed. It is remarkable for giving the world the great physicist Ernest Rutherford, who went to primary school here, won a scholarship to Nelson College and went on to world fame. Havelock stayed behind, quietly.

MURUPARA

LAKE WAIKAREMOANA

FRASERTOWN

WAIROA

WAIROA TO MURUPARA

'THE RUBBER DOESN'T JUST HIT THE ROAD. IT BOUNCES, THUDS, BANGS.'

ROAD OF THE MIST

The first inkling you get that this road may be . . . different is the lack of traffic. The second is a sign announcing that the road is unsealed for more than 100 kilometres.

The sign is misleading. Oh, not about the distance or the lack of seal. The road is not just unsealed. It is also bumpy, narrow and in parts like driving over a rockfall, except that these rocks have been in situ for a very long time and show no sign of giving way to rubber tyres.

The rubber, on the other hand, doesn't just hit the road. It bounces, thuds, bangs, shivers and shakes. The scenery is terrific, so they say. For you, in motion, it's a vertical blur.

Admittedly, all of the above might be difficult to fit on a simple road sign. So you give it the benefit of the doubt, possibly even regard it as a commendation: 'Oh well, what do you expect from a road of this reputation?'

RIGHT Still closely related to the old coach road.

Actually, the road fits the country very well. This is the home of the Tuhoe, children of the mist, said to have lived here for longer than anybody can reliably guess. Their lives were so remote, protected by their forests and mountains, that they were the last to feel the impact of Pakeha immigration. In the century and a half since, they have remained mysterious. Mythical. This wisp of a road, the only way through their heartland, fits.

The road up to this point has been no great shakes. You've possibly taken State Highway 2 from Napier, perhaps kidding yourself that the lower the number, the better the road. Number two, in this case, is more a biological description.

It departs the coast a little north of Bay View and immediately rebels. Hills, hairpins, rivers, lakes, gullies and hiccups without a single straight until you're getting close to Wairoa, birthplace of the rugby legend George Nepia and home of New Zealand's only inland river bridge with its own lighthouse. Count yourself lucky on at least two counts: before 1888 traffic used a nearby ferry, and Wairoa is home to a particularly famous pie shop.

Here you make the momentous decision to drive through Te Urewera rather than head north to Gisborne. So you head to Frasertown, ignore the turn-off to the inland route to Gisborne, and press on. Soon you come across the sign. Immediately thereafter you regret your foolish thoughts about State Highway 2. By comparison that was an urban motorway. *This* is the real thing, a state highway only in name, road architecture as true to the original track as you'll find in this country, a bridle path until it grew (only a little) into a coach road in 1897. It still seems little more.

You are driving through living history here. Kokako School was opened in 1897. Its children were starving, for this was the time of the great famine in Urewera: 37 of them died in 1898. Between 1896 and 1901, 23 per cent of all Tuhoe died of starvation, a high proportion of them children. The Kokako school is still there: in summer people swim in its pool, use its barbecue area and sports field.

Tuai, with its little clutter of cottages and stone church on Lake Whakamarino, lies a short run off the main road. It has one of three power stations built in an early hydro-electric scheme using Lake Waikaremoana's water. It runs through the Kaitawa power station (1948), through the Tuai Station into Lake Whakamarino (1929) and on to the third at Piripaua (1943). The truly determined can make a detour at Tuai, heading off on an even narrower and more primitive road through the Ruakituri Valley and on to the Te Reinga falls 57 kilometres away.

Otherwise, stay focused. After Kaitawa the road clings to the side of Lake Waikaremoana, literally. Sometimes it is little more than a cart track carved from the rock of the cliffs dropping to the lake far below.

Now here's a confession. In the several times I've driven this road I've had no more than a glimpse of the lake, just enough to convince me that it does exist. Otherwise, like the children of the mist themselves, it has been hidden in drizzle. This does not diminish the trip one bit. Adds to it. Your imagination can veer off the precarious strip, although the rest of you should stay firmly in place.

You know there are high mountains, deep valleys, thick virgin forest, untracked and impenetrable country all around, a lake as big and many-fingered as an inland sea. You can feel it pressing on you, physically, like a phantom in the night. You ask yourself, 'What's out there?', wondering if you really want to know. You turn up the air conditioning a notch, nestle into the reassurance of soft upholstery. You'd turn on the radio if it wasn't for the supernatural static that clouds every station. All the while you creep forward, trying not to think of the slips and falls which are reasons why, wonderfully, 'they' have no plans to seal the road.

It's almost a shock when the Aniwaniwa visitor centre and museum merge from the mist. Civilisation? Get away! But this was the reason for my first trip to Lake Waikaremoana. Colin McCahon's *Urewera Mural* was on display there, again. It had been stolen by Tuhoe activists, recovered, restored and returned to the little gallery designed by John Scott with grim warnings that security would be 'upgraded'. When I stopped outside, I saw another sign. This said the museum was closed for lunch. It was getting on into the afternoon and seemed rather late for lunch so I rattled the door. A cheery woman appeared and opened it. 'Sorry,' she said, and turned the sign around. Now it said, 'Open'.

I went into a little room of varnished wood. A low rail separated me from the work. It might have stopped a toddler, although none of those I knew. Perhaps there were sophisticated electronic devices guarding the triptych although in truth, given the surroundings, that didn't seem likely. Anyway, I didn't care. The paintings swept all else aside. It was like entering Chartres Cathedral, so overpowering, so complex and gorgeous and colourful I didn't know where to start. During the next hour or so no one came in.

I was lucky. The paintings disappeared again a few years later. This time officials had deemed the building unsafe and the mural was taken to the Auckland City Art Gallery for storage and later exhibitions.

Back in the car the road touched the lake one more time before heading further inland. This time I went to a layby at the water's edge, to check. So much mystery, so many things appearing and disappearing. Perhaps the lake was there. I couldn't see more than 100 metres of it.

Now history was stalking the road. It crinkled through a valley, over a ridge, valley, ridge. At the Taupepe Saddle a logging road ran off to the right. It led to Maungapohatu, the sacred mountain of Tuhoe and site of the religious community founded by Rua

Kenana, self-proclaimed Maori Messiah and successor to Te Kooti. He wanted confiscated land returned and the end of Pakeha rule. Not surprisingly, he so threatened the government that he was arrested in 1916 by a squad of armed police who killed two Maori. Historians have raked through the case ever since, the consensus being that a huge injustice was done. He was released in 1918, reconstructed Maungapohatu, and unsuccessfully predicted both the end of the world in 1927 (the same year a government commission decided that confiscated Tuhoe land would be neither returned nor compensated for) and his resurrection three days after he died. He is now synonymous with issues of justice and Maori sovereignty.

Ahead, the road hairpinned down to Te Waiiti and on to Ruatahuna, where hundreds of Tuhoe died of starvation under siege in the Urewera campaign. Ghosts flickered everywhere.

The most epic pursuit in New Zealand history ranged over the Urewera from 1868 to 1871 and was focused here. The British chased Te Kooti, the allegedly 'rebel' chief, and Kereopa, the Pai Marire chief who had eaten the murdered Reverend Carl Volkner's eyes, a scene so awfully portrayed in the film *Utu*. Volkner was hanged and beheaded by Pai Marire followers.

Te Kooti sought refuge among the Tuhoe people. Under Colonel George Whitmore three columns of soldiers and Maori allies converged on Waikaremoana, destroying villages, pa, crops and food supplies as they went and killing Tuhoe ('a wild hill tribe'). The troops were savage, not least because they spent more time fighting thick bush (one climbed a tree and became the first Pakeha to see Lake Waikareiti) in freezing rain, snow and floods than they did Maori. For three years they rampaged around the Urewera.

In the end Kereopa was given up to the authorities by his protectors, the Tuhoe. Lack of evidence did not deter the court from finding him guilty of murder. He was hanged at Napier prison, despite pleas that the

crime had already been paid for in terms of executions and land confiscation. He received a 12th-hour pardon in 2014. Te Kooti escaped. He later lived in Te Kuiti, was pardoned in 1883 and died in 1893.

The real victims of the long campaign were the Tuhoe. With little fertile land they relied on the forests for their living, which was to become even more precarious. They were stripped of workable land after being wrongly accused as rebels, and sheltering Te Kooti cost them so dearly they shut themselves away in their mountain fortress, refusing to sell land or allow road-building. Some argue that history repeated itself in 2007 when hundreds of armed police raided an alleged paramilitary training camp in Te Urewera. In the end the affair boiled down to a few firearms charges and an apology from the Police Commissioner.

Trampers in the huge Te Urewera National Park now walk the Tuhoe trails. The isolation and comparative poverty of the Tuhoe can be seen along the road in the ragged farms and cottages. You can still sense an uneasy relationship here. West of Ruatahuna I came across a man on horseback driving a herd of horses along the road. I was hesitant but he waved me on: 'Nah mate, it's fine.' The horses didn't think so. As I nosed into them they began to trot, then to gallop. The thin road was full of clamour. Horses pressed against the side of the car, hooves thudded on metal. I went faster. They galloped the more. All parties looked desperate.

Finally one sensed a way off the road. They galloped through a gap in the forest in single file and disappeared. I was alone on the road, except for the figure on horseback. I expected him to shake a fist, at least. He was impassive.

ONGARUE

OHURA

OHURA RD

STRATFORD

MANGATUPOTO TO STRATFORD

'YOU MIGHT AT ANY MOMENT COME ACROSS AN EERIE LITTLE COTTAGE WHENCE ALL HAD FLED.'

The Forgotten World Highway, 155 kilometres long, usually begins in Taumarunui and ends in Stratford, or vice versa. Instead, enticed by signs, this journey took a short cut, turned off State Highway 3 at Eight Mile Junction, took State Highway 4 to Mangatupoto, then plunged into the unknown. A signpost pointed to Ohura, although I liked the second one more: it pictured a petrol pump with a line through it. None for 150 kilometres.

The road immediately narrowed to a strip of tarseal, barely wide enough for the white line down its middle. It set off through hillocks with grit if not dispatch; it was bendy. A train track crossed a stream on an ancient steel bridge. Pine forests almost immediately gave way to native bush. Fenceposts and battens dripped with lichen, looking like pale green bushes all in a row. Lichen hung from totara trees on hillsides. Black goats grazed. Ridges were sculpted as a dinosaur's back. Valleys were chiselled.

The landscape looked mysterious, like a Disney film set, as if at any moment you might come across an eerie little cottage in a clearing whence all had fled.

Instead, there appeared hillsides terraced by sheep tracks. Early wattle gleamed yellow, willow reddened before greening. A railway line shadowed the road, crossing a steam on an ancient iron bridge, our own track hewn from sandstone which rose away from the tarmac in pale sheets.

Matiere arrived, a garage without petrol, another garage, general store, a few others, all closed. A school. The Matiere Cosmopolitan Club, however, looked ready for business.

But we were approaching a major junction and population centre. A large sign welcomed drivers to Ohura with blue sky, sun and, mysteriously for such an inland town, waves. Ohura was not doing well either. Its outstanding feature was a long weatherboard building, a sign announcing

accommodation in the 'Ohura State Prison'.

'Even the prisoners are leaving Ohura,' declared the *NZ Herald* in 2005. 'Ohura was once a bustling little town famous for coal mining. It had a high school, farming stores, markets — even a picture theatre. Now it is famous for its prison and even that will close in November.'

True. This was the most intriguing of ghost towns, one that had become ghostly quite recently, with working parts all intact but no people, as if some calamity had befallen the place and its population had fled. Which was quite true.

Nothing was open. In fact, almost everything looked as if it had been closed for a very long time, although Charlie's Bike Museum contained a few nice old bikes, and Janet's displayed some handsome junk. Except for the Ohura Cosmopolitan Club. Cosmopolitan clubs seemed to thrive in this part of the country.

No one was around. The Bowling Club looked ready for a roll-up, if only there were some bowlers, and I heard voices in the house next door, disembodied. The school was a green oasis and a sign pointed to a golf club but . . . no people.

The town stands on a junction. Here you turn for Stratford. Still 120 kilometres away and no cars on the road yet. A cock pheasant strolled confidently across the tarmac.

Many roads have been given vainglorious titles by hopeful local bodies. The Forgotten World Highway is true to its name. The road was now so slow in places that when a roadworks sign suggested 30 km/h I had to speed up. Smoke from farmhouses slumped on the valley floor.

The seal ended as the road ran into the Tangarakau Gorge, running through what was once seabed 15 million years ago, the rocks of ages rearing above ancient podocarp forest. Coal was mined around here, and water still seeped through seams staining the river a fine shade of chestnut. It is a

PREVIOUS SPREAD
Forgotten World
Highway.

ABOVE Whangamomona,
1915 or 1916.

RIGHT Approaching the
Tangarakau Gorge.

long gorge. A *very* long gorge.

A sign warned of bends. That meant *really* bendy. Cairns made of great slabs of stone stood at its edge. In a grave here lay Joshua Morgan who must have been a fine surveyor, for he died in 1892 at 35 and was still remembered. Surveyors were pioneer settlers' heroes.

The road gave up being shingle and became plain clay. Sometimes it reduced to a single lane, occasionally falling into the river so it was almost no lane at all. A sign announced that the Republic of Whanga was only 22 kilometres away: 'Come and increase our population.' No problem. I certainly wasn't turning around.

The highway vanished into a long, narrow, high tunnel with wooden barn-like beams under its roof. The Moki Tunnel, built in 1936, 180 metres long, fossilised giant crabs embedded in its walls. Now there was a turn-off to Tangarakau Village, once a town of 1200 when the railway was built and now another ghost. A dozen goat skins dried on a fence. A sheep rushed across the road, dragging a train of blackberry.

The long Tahora Saddle was next, almost exactly halfway between the peaks of Tongariro and Taranaki. Crenellated, barren ridges fell to farmland, almost all of it felled and burned in 15 years from 1895 when it was balloted off for little dairy farms which became small sheep and beef farms, then larger ones.

We were getting into *Me and Gus* country. The *Gus* stories were written by Frank Anthony, who bought a small dairy farm on marginal land near Stratford after World War I with a soldiers' rehabilitation grant. He struggled with debt and hard work for five years and wrote in the evenings. The *Gus* stories were billed as comic yarns and I laughed at them as a schoolboy. Read again as an adult, they were tragic tales of unrelenting hardship. Anthony's own story matched. He died of consumption in 1927, his work

only 'discovered' and made popular in the 1950s. His epitaph was written on the land. This was hard country, hard to read, hard to work.

An old hall appeared, stark, little used, like a monument to a past town. But outside it, on the other side of the road, stood a cenotaph, carefully tended except for a single laurel wreath at its base, a relic of Anzac Day months before. The Whangamomona, Kohuratahi and Tahora districts, it recorded, had lost three men in World War II but 41 in World War I. I imagined the loss of all those young men in a such a small place. Its heart must have been ripped out. Lest we forget, said the loneliest cenotaph in the world.

Alice King didn't die in some corner of a foreign field, however. She died in her own, in 1897, of peritonitis. A doctor galloped for hours from Stratford, changing horses along the way. He arrived too late. Her husband John and their two children buried her in the front garden of the land they'd been allocated by the government. They planted trees to mark the spot. The new railway line in 1914 was moved a few metres away to avoid running over her, but railway workers cut down the trees in 1975. Now poor Alice lies here, somewhere.

Whangamomona appeared like a sanctuary in this wild land. No ruins there. A back-country town in aspic, from a time when New Zealand was a land of villages. Even the empty stores were cared for, often converted. The Bank of Australasia, opened 1911. The district nurse's residence, now a bed-and-

ABOVE Clambering over the back country, from Nevin's Saddle.

breakfast. The general store was reduced to a facade. The old Post Office opened in 1912, closed 1988. It survived two world wars but not Rogernomics. The Whangamomona hotel, built in 1911, was said to have been transferred once with a wife as part payment. It served as a hospital in the 1919 influenza epidemic. The bar was lined with stags' heads and old photographs. Two perfect churches and, of course, a sign: we were leaving the Whanga Republic, welcome back to New Zealand.

The Stratford to Okahukura railway line tracking the road was, remarkably, still open (to tourists, at least), the highway crossing and recrossing the line. Work on it started in 1901 but the line opened only in 1932. The war killed the young men who might have built it sooner, and the country's sharp ridges and wedged gullies were hard enough anyway.

The Pohokura Saddle lay on a ridgeline which was a Maori highway from north Taranaki to the Whanganui River, the Strathmore Saddle the last of many. If you were going the other way this would mark the start of the back country. Then Douglas, once a bustling country town with a dairy factory, railway station and the biggest saleyards in Taranaki. The brick kiln, now an historic place, and the old boarding house survived.

In the whole journey I'd passed three cars, four utes and a muddy quad bike towing a trailer-load of dogs with a horse trotting behind. I would remember the forgotten highway for a long time.

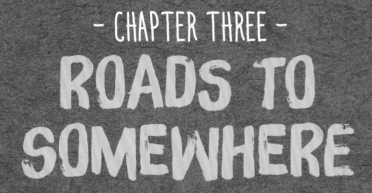

CHAPTER THREE

ROADS TO SOMEWHERE

DRIVING ROUTES

1 WESTPORT TO THE TOWN THAT NEVER WAS

2 COLLINGWOOD TO THE HEAPHY

3 WESTHAVEN

4 COBB VALLEY

5 MT NICHOLAS

6 BARING HEAD

7 RANGITATA RIVER VALLEY

8 MATUKITUKI VALLEY

9 CASTLEPOINT

10 OPITO ROAD

LEFT The road following the Matukituki River to Mount Aspiring National Park.

KOHAIHAI BLUFF

KARAMEA

WESTPORT TO THE TOWN THAT NEVER WAS

'THE TASMAN SEA ROARING ON ONE SIDE, MOUNTAINS REARING ON THE OTHER.'

I once drove to Westport in August just to get warm. After ten days in Rarotonga the Christchurch winter was freezing. A sou'west gale belted across the plains bringing whatever ice and snow it hadn't dumped on the Alps. In a sou'wester the West Coast is sunny while the east shivers. So, to Westport, staying at the cruelly named Cape Foulwind which was bright and cheery.

A micro-climate warms this coast and the balmy road between Westport and Karamea is palmy too, thick with nikau. Not with people. This is a sparsely populated and remote part of the country.

It's an easy road, mostly, best tackled after a thick whitebait pattie from Westport. This West Coast town, unusually, is still a working port, although possibly not for much longer. A cement ship manoeuvres in its cramped basin, towering over the business district.

The coal which has been this coast's mainstay for generations ebbs and flows and currently, ebbs. West Coasters have been through this before.

Commiserations along the road are met with shrugs.

The road heads north in long easy straights to Waimangaroa and here you can turn off on a winding narrow road and climb up to the Denniston plateau. It's an eerie place, full of what was: old houses, halls, the remains of a high-altitude civilisation. Until 1967 this was the country's largest-producing coal mine with a community of 1500. No one would have lived here then by choice: it's windy and wet and bleak.

Ironically enough, people *did* live here later, by choice. Some houses were occupied by the hardiest alternative lifestylers to be found anywhere, although the permanent population now is said to fill only two of them. The remains of the famous Denniston Incline which once dropped coal down 1.8 kilometres of mountain loom at the edge of the plateau. The place is now a ghostly tourist attraction.

The main road rolls on northwards to Granity, Ngakawau and Hector, although it takes a trained eye

or a local to spot the difference between them. The three little towns are jammed between two immense forces, the Tasman Sea roaring on one side and mountains rearing on the other.

The townscapes speak of what was: that old building was once a picture theatre, the mines' building now an op shop, the Post Office an arts and crafts, the grocery store a cafe, the Masonic Lodge now without Masons.

When you arrive at a working mine, you're in Ngakawau. Coal is still an industry here, if a diminishing one. Up on the Stockton plateau huge earthmovers shuffle around sculptured rock mined for the coal which is emptied into lines of railway trucks waiting below for the long journey through the Alps to Lyttelton. The lines of pretty mineworkers' cottages were mined themselves in New Zealand's coastal property boom. They began fetching high prices, some of them bought sight unseen off the internet. That proved to be another West Coast boom and bust.

The road reaches the Mokihinui River a little further north, meets it and swerves off to the bridge upstream. This is the West Coast's third-largest river and, remarkably, it's still pristine. Meridian Energy wanted to dam it, drowning its lovely gorges in a lake, destroying the ancient forests on conservation land. The dam plan died, the river escaped. It's still beloved of whitebaiters, whose utes in season fill whatever

gaps they can find between river and road. A side road runs off to Seddonville and from here you can walk or cycle an old goldminers' road up the river and all the way to Lyell.

The road meanwhile rises and bends around the Karamea Bluff, the only place where it leaves the sea, rejoining the coast at Little Wanganui. It's a flat route from here to Karamea, the West Coast's northernmost settlement. Locals loved the place. One side of the river, Umere, was called the Land of Promise, the other side Arapito, the Promised Land.

This was once a harbour town, until the 1929 Murchison earthquake dried it up, and incidentally cut the road for some two years. Isolation is much more than a word here. The closest attraction is the Oparara Valley, down a logging road running off the highway nine kilometres north. Caves, ravines and arches carved from the limestone trapped more than 50 species of birds over the millennia, many now extinct so that the area is a natural history archive of what once was. Arachnophobes can terrify themselves with the giant spider which preys on cave weta.

Back on the main road, now metalled, you drive to the Kohaihai River, and stop. If you're a driver you have to, for the road ends. West Coast and tourist interests still push for a road through to Golden Bay, so far unsuccessfully. They scowl, environmentalists cheer.

If you're a tramper, you continue on the Heaphy Track. Driver or tramper, you swat hopelessly at ferocious sandflies as you watch the river meeting the sea in a brown curl. This is a wonderful drive.

Moa-hunters' camps have been found on this coast, and between 1898 and 1909 a town was surveyed on the spot where you're standing. Sections, roads, school, a cemetery, an area for 'landless natives'. There were plenty of those, robbed of their land by the scandalous Mackay Arahura purchase, one of the two great Ngai Tahu blocks he bought for a pittance.

The town never happened, of course.

COLLINGWOOD
○ COLLINGWOOD
○ BAINHAM
BROWN HUT,
KAHURANGI NATIONAL PARK ○

COLLINGWOOD TO THE HEAPHY

'THIS WILD ROAD LEADS TO ONE OF THE WORLD'S GREAT WILD WALKS'.

The 1856 gold rush to the Aorere River was not much by the standards of the time, lacking the exuberance of the West Coast or the spoils of Central Otago, but it had two lasting consequences: first, it put Massacre Bay firmly on the map and second, took it off again.

The bay had been grimly named ever since it became the first and only real contact between Abel Tasman and the land he discovered in 1642 which later became New Zealand.

When Tasman sailed into the eastern end of the bay he saw wood smoke from many Maori villages but his view of the place speedily went downhill. His visit ended with four of his sailors dead, along with an unknown number of Maori.

Tasman called it Murderers' Bay, changed by the French explorer D'Urville to Massacre Bay. When coal was discovered in 1842 it became Coal Bay, briefly. After the gold rush it became the happier Golden Bay. For endurance this name has done better than others.

The Maori population then were probably Ngati Tumatakokiri who had only recently settled in the bay and were wiped out in the Musket Wars of 1823. Other names have disappeared entirely, or changed.

The road up the Aorere Valley begins at Collingwood, originally Gibbston. The Nelson provincial government expected a population boom to accompany the gold one and laid out a brand-new town called Collingwood. Previously it was a Maori settlement named Aorere, presided over by Tamati Pirimona Marino who signed the Treaty of Waitangi and is buried at the old Collingwood cemetery along Excellent Street.

A succession of fires destroyed much of its colonial heritage, but it remains a charming town beside a vestigial port where once a busy little steamer brought cargo and passengers to the goldfields. You can drive around it and through it in five minutes then sit on the waterfront and look over the salt flats to Farewell

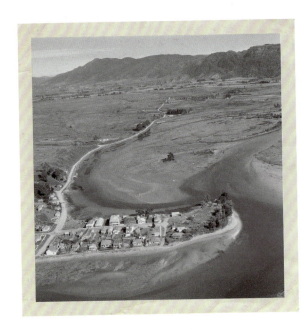

Track. This wild road leads to one of the world's great wild walks.

The valley is now dairy country. Cows graze beneath the steep bushy flanks of the Wakamarama Range on one side and the mountains of the other. A track leading off the road passes a hill named Brown Cow and crosses a pass called Cow Saddle on its way to Boulder Lake, scene of an unsuccessful attempt at sluicing for gold in 1899. The green pastures against the deep mountain forests make an entrancing contrast.

The road runs smoothly along the flats to Rockville, the Aorere's second-biggest settlement. Here there's a choice. You can stop at the Golden Bay Machinery and Settlers' Museum in the old Collingwood cheese factory and look at the ancient tractors, farm machinery and traction engine, and see a way of life here which endured until at least the 1960s. Or you can take the side road which leads to the Aorere goldfields track. Some of this is a 4WD journey: you wouldn't want to risk the family saloon. It passes an old sluicing claim, crosses Druggan's Flat and takes to the hills, following the original miners' track in parts.

Miners have left their mark on this country. The most spectacular is Druggan's Dam, with its tunnel cut through rock and a colossal failure. For me the best is Ballroom Cave, said to have been used by the gold-seekers for dances, possibly best enjoyed if you liked partners with beards. They left their names on rocks.

Back to Rockville and on to Bainham, the road now running close to the northern range. Bainham is best known for Langford's general store, opened by Edward Langford in 1928. A Langford still runs it. It looks like a colonial cottage with a veranda in front and weatherbeaten all over, an intact survivor from a period of post offices and party lines. A trip to town, whether Collingwood or (much more rarely) Takaka was a big trip then. The local store did everything, and

Spit. There's no trace of its early ambition to be New Zealand's capital, instead a kind of loneliness, almost melancholy. Ferntown, on the other side of the valley mouth, was an early boom town. Now it is just a name on the map.

Gold was discovered in this valley by a couple of farmers taking a break from mustering in 1856. Miners rushed in. The settlement grew from two tents in 1857 to seven hotels, 700 Europeans and 200 Maori in 1858. Soon a thousand men were said to be working the diggings. By 1859 it was all over, although people are still searching for gold here. For several years in the 1970s my brother made a precarious living by sucking up shingle from under rocks and crevices and picking out the flecks. I have a photograph of him and his mates in a bush bivvy, all of them bearded and uncouth; it might have been taken 140 years before.

Yet a new kind of gold rush has buoyed this part of the Bay. The road that once carried goldminers now transports busloads of tourists to or from the Heaphy

PREVIOUS SPREAD
One-way bridge over the Aorere River near Collingwood.

LEFT Collingwood, on the Aorere River mouth, 1947.

RIGHT Looking down the Aorere Valley.

it is all preserved inside. Langfords have been here since 1893, and the telephone directory tells you that quite a number are here still. Edward's granddaughter Lorna ran the shop for more than 60 years, until 2008. Her uncle's granddaughter Sukhita then took over. Inside you can find anything from bobbins to books and yes, there's still stuff to buy.

Beyond Bainham the road climbs a crinkly hill and beside it a swing bridge crosses the river. Here are the Salisbury Falls, one of those places you recognise with a start when you're watching *The Lord of the Rings*. The water is jade passing between rocks the palest of greys. Swimming is fun even if the water is cold. You sweep down the river and afterwards lie on rocks warmed by the sun.

As you drive deeper into the ranges the valley walls close in. Ahead lies the Heaphy Track, 78.4 kilometres and none of it by car. That's not for want of trying. Heaphy began searching for a route to the West Coast in 1846. The Track closely follows his path.

In 1909 the Minister for Mines, Roderick McKenzie, making a very rare visit to his constituents in Mangarakau a little further south, received a deputation trying to impress him with the need for a road through to the West Coast. He thought the settlers should do something themselves, and the government might help. Business and regional interests have tried to push a tourist road through the wilderness to Karamea since. The plan has coughed and sputtered and even sometimes been taken seriously. Not by any government however. Confronted with public opposition and, probably more important, the need to spend an awful lot of money, the road plans have always been returned to the dusty file they came from. You could call this wild road a dead end. Except it's so much fun getting to the end of it that you feel very alive.

MANGARAKAU

THE DOWAGER'S HUMP

WESTHAVEN

'SCRUB AND TUSSOCK LEAN OVER AND KISS THE GROUND LIKE DRUNKS NEARING HOME.'

There are two sides to Golden Bay, on two dimensions. Socially the Bay is roughly divided between the hippies and urban escapees who started coming here in the 1970s, starting communes and communities which coexisted surprisingly well with the establishment: farmers and townspeople.

The remoteness that shaped the old guard appealed to the newcomers; in the Christmas holidays people laboured over the Takaka Hill to motor camps in Patons Rock and Pohara but for the remaining 49 weeks a year the place was left to itself.

That divide can still be felt through the overlay of the third age, the holiday-homes suburbs, fainter now because the wild acreages of the communes and the spreads of the ex-hippies, once cheaply bought, are worth quite a lot.

Geographically the bay runs in one direction to the gentle, golden beaches of the southern side, Tata, Wainui Inlet, melting into the regenerating bush of the Abel Tasman National Park; in the other, to the great salt marshes and wild winds of the northern side.

As the tip of the South Island narrows towards Farewell Spit, you can drive to the West Coast in a matter of minutes. Tourists turn off at the old coal port of Puponga, drive to a car park and walk over low hills until the Tasman Sea can be not just heard but felt. This is Wharariki, a beach so huge, so wild, that it swallows them all and still seems deserted.

That path is now well worn. The last time I was there a young German lectured me on seals. He knew rather a lot about them but irrationally I was still a little affronted: my beach, *my* seals.

Instead, you can turn off at Pakawau and cross the low saddle which was once a Maori trail to Whanganui Inlet, or Westhaven, where Golden Bay's European story began. Charles Heaphy and Thomas Brunner came here, and bargained their right of way down the coast with Te Niho, one of Te Rauparaha's chiefs.

The route keeps its mystery. This is not a long road, but it's a drive to another place.

You drive only a few kilometres before the Tasman bashes its way into the car, rattling the air conditioner, drowning the radio. Scrub and tussock lean over and kiss the ground like drunks nearing home. The road to the Kaihoka Lakes sneaks off to the right; you take the left fork, called the Dry Road which seems a little odd because it threads through the 400-hectare Mangarakau Swamp, remarkable for defeating attempts to drain it.

You're still only a loud shout from the Golden Bay foreshore but now you're in another land. Causeway bridges carry the road over the ragged edges of the inlet. Beside you is the grey-green water of Whanganui Inlet, one of the biggest and least-modified in the country and since 1994 a marine reserve with a wildlife management reserve overlaying that.

This part of New Zealand really is magical. Or strange. Dense forest pressing road against water turns blood-red with rata in summer. A peaky little range of hills marks the inlet's entrance, water surging twice a day between Bar Point and South Head Cone, a precarious haven but the only one on the dowager's hump of the South Island.

The road is narrow and unsealed. It's not long, but it seems so. It emerges at Mangarakau, the only place resembling civilisation in this part of the world. Well before gold was discovered in Golden Bay this place boomed. Maori were here when the first Europeans arrived in the 1830s, wading through the mud of the inlet at low tide. They wanted coal. They mined it. The first load was shipped from the port aboard the *Harriet* in 1836. Jump forward to 1866. By then Westhaven was home to coal mining, flax milling, and a thriving trade in milled native timber. When gold was found in the nearby Slaty Creek and the Anatori River a little further south in 1862, well, this place was bustling with a crowded harbour served by tramways, shops, school, town hall, post office, all surrounded by farms.

And all gone now. The gold ran out. Coal mining stopped. The flax mill closed in 1914 when World War I seemed a favourable alternative to its workers. The sawmill operated intermittently until 1968. You can still park and find relics. The town hall remains as a visitor centre and museum, pointing visitors to historic sites. A few fishing boats use the old jetty whose main attraction now is the hulk of the scow *Kohi*. Hundreds of scows, uniquely New Zealand craft, once carried cargos in and out of difficult tidal harbours around the country. Now they're rare, and to find one here is like stumbling across a nugget. Mangarakau Swamp defied progress and remains a symbol of survival, its ecology now being restored.

You can drive past Mangarakau, through the high limestone faces, deeper into the dark ranges of the Kahurangi, the way growing ever stranger. As Dorothy might have said, 'I have a feeling we're not in Kansas any more.' It crawls out to the coast, still following the old Maori trail, to the mouth of the Paturau River, once alive with shops supplying some 500 diggers searching for gold. Here Maori took to the beach. The road, now beautifully desolate, follows slightly higher ground to the Anatoki and stops. A ford crosses the river for the adventurous, aka serious 4WDs. Even that stalls four kilometres south, at the Turimawiwi River and its baches. Nikau, flax and rata surround you. The westerly whips the Tasman into your nostrils. Great pocked cliffs grizzle. Ahead is wilderness.

Sometimes the only thing better than a wild road is no road at all.

PREVIOUS SPREAD Road sign, Cape Farewell and Wharariki Beach.

RIGHT Where the wild West Coast is only a short drive from gentle Golden Bay.

COBB DAM ●

● UPPER TAKAKA

COBB VALLEY

'YOU CAN SEE WHAT NEW ZEALAND WAS MADE OF WHEN THE ONLY CREATURES ROAMING ITS SURFACE WERE VERY LARGE OR VERY SMALL.'

THE TRILOBITE ROAD

The remains of the old Upper Takaka Hotel, aka the Rat Trap, once the relief stop for survivors of the Takaka Hill road but now no more than a slab of concrete, mark the start of the 27-kilometre partly sealed road up the Cobb Valley. This is not a well-known road but it's an exciting one. The valley it traverses, which was named after a prospector called Cobb, runs up the headwaters of the Takaka River and the Cobb itself.

Glaciers once filled these valleys. The adventurous can look down into the perfect U-shaped valley of the Cobb from the cobbly top of Iron Hill at the end of the road. Geologists argue about how far the glaciers reached towards Upper Takaka but a layperson's summary is 'a fair way'. This is a geologist's mecca, in fact. At one cutting beside the road the geological history of New Zealand is presented like a slice of layer cake, from millions of years ago until now.

Beside the Cobb Reservoir the sharp-eyed can

RIGHT Cobb Reservoir.

find fossilised trilobites, tiny bug-like creatures which became extinct around 250 million years ago.

The road was carved out of the rock much more recently and runs up the valley to an early hydro-electric scheme, also the Cobb. Work began in 1937 and was taken over by the government in 1940, the Rat Trap's heyday. It was the local for the 500-odd dam workers who gave the pub its nickname: when men did not turn up for work, they were said to be caught in the rat trap.

The road runs through beech forest and squeezes through a little gorge, a cleft really, where you can look down and see what New Zealand was made of when the only creatures roaming its surface were very large or very small. It's dark in there, and lonely, and you reduce to a crawl.

The road creeps out of the valley, rises, and the splendour of the South Island's north-west corner presses in. Mount Arthur rises on the left. Range after range blocks any sense of distance or space. Here you are running into mountains that don't end until they fall into the Tasman Sea. Snow hangs onto the tops for most of the year, ice greases the road in winter, trees and rocks fall onto it in heavy rain. It is wild country.

The road passes the track to Asbestos Cottage, where Annie and Henry Chaffey composed a love story with a gloriously sad ending. Henry was a successful farm contractor, Annie a Timaru housewife. Both were refugees from disastrous marriages who took to the mountains in 1913, Annie leaving behind her two teenaged sons. Twenty years later, after Annie's husband died, they were married. They became legendary: their monastic life in the mountains made them host to miners, hunters, prospectors, surveyors, drovers, themselves a select band.

They liked dressing for company. Annie wore long dresses, a feather boa and hat, Henry his Sunday best. They'd put out bone china for tea. In a rough shack far away, they were unusual, to say the least. Having found each other, and their place of the heart, they stuck through thick and thin. She never left her home, except once when she was ill.

Henry was the linchpin of this valley's development. He prospected for gold and found the rich asbestos deposits of the Cobb. He told his stories to anyone who'd listen.

Walter Hume, an Australian industrialist, heard of his tales and Hume's prospectors confirmed them: lots of asbestos up that valley. Hume became a great advocate for a dam, and an access road, built at public expense and of course very handy for transporting asbestos out of the valley.

Annie was the home-maker, Henry the provider, a wiry man who would walk to Upper Takaka or even Motueka over the hill and carry in their supplies on his back. He died beside his track in 1951 at the age of 83. It was the end of Annie too. Alone, she was forced to leave. She killed herself in Timaru in 1953.

The road passes by with only a nod in their direction. It passes the powerhouse at the foot of the 2.6-kilometre tunnel drilled through rock from its reservoir, or lake, far above. It's a rather grand building, befitting its special status at the bottom of the longest drop of any New Zealand power station.

The Cobb Reservoir can be imposing or disappointing, depending on how full it is. But its surrounds are always superb. The road ends near the Trilobite Hut on the edge of the Kahurangi National Park. A web of tracks leads to mountains, huts, a sprinkle of alpine lakes. It is an easy walk to the lovely old Mytton's Hut, renovated and maintained by a group of individuals since the Department of Conservation gave it up, a bit of old New Zealand they're taking good care of. Or you can just search for trilobite fossils and, when you're tired, lie down amid the wildflowers.

MT NICHOLAS
TE ANAU
MAVORA

MT NICHOLAS

'THE VALLEY APPEARS TO SWIRL, THE ROCK FORMATIONS CURVE.'

THE KIWI DREAM

If ever there's a road that shows off the beauty of wild New Zealand, it's this one, bush, lakes, mountains, tussock plains and scarcely a building along its length. Its two entrances lead off State Highway 94, the road to Te Anau, in an inverted Y, the two joining at the end of a ridge.

A wide, easy, smooth, gravel country road follows the Mararoa River through a valley of satisfied sheep and settled farms. The road is the Kiwi dream and it only gets better, distant mountains marking the country as something different.

Those mountains quickly grow closer, and bigger, squeezing the valley, bending it this way and that. Green paddocks turn tussock gold. Beech forest begins creeping into their edges, then takes over the slopes. The road branches into the Mavora Lakes. Instant magic. It winds through dusky beech with soft green moss below and ends at two perfect lakes. You park in peace.

Power boating is prohibited and camping is not. People come to be regenerated by nature in an old-fashioned camping ground without spa pools or Sky

RIGHT Broad, flat valley country.

dishes. Instead, there are fishing, kayaking, mountain biking, 4WD driving. You can even walk your dog.

This is the Mavora Lakes Park, part of the Te Wai Pounamu South-West New Zealand World Heritage Area. Treasures. The four-day Mavora-Greenstone walk takes trampers through some of the world's finest country. The two lakes are North and South Mavora, North being much bigger. The road stops in a camping area at the south end of the North lake. It's all far too beautiful to have been overlooked by Peter Jackson: several scenes in *The Lord of the Rings* films were shot here.

Back on the Mt Nicholas Road, the gravel heads towards serious mountains. You wonder, what lies ahead? But you need not. The road drops to the flat floor of a valley. Now you're alongside the Eyre Mountains Conservation Park, created partly by the tenure-review process in which high-country stations have given up the more scenic parts of their pastoral leases to the Crown in exchange for freeholding the balance. It's a huge land swap and you need only drive along this road to appreciate its benefit.

You're driving in a lonely land so huge that you shiver. The landscape seems empty but for a paddock full of calves and three cyclists, passed at a crawl but covered in dust nonetheless.

A river ford, nothing serious at this time of the year, early summer, then a bridge and a fine spot to lie on the grass and contemplate the universe, which in this place seems quite close.

The valley appears to swirl, the rock formations curve. It should, you feel, follow an easy valley to the right. Instead it wriggles across the one you're already on and its character shifts. It narrows, steepens, drops into the Von River valley. A couple of restored shepherds' cottages; a car with only three wheels propped up on stones in the middle of the road.

Lake Wakatipu lies ahead but remains hidden until you're quite near Mount Nicholas Station, whose buildings suddenly spread in front of you . The crook of Lake Wakatipu lies behind them. Mount Nicholas Station is one of New Zealand's biggest and oldest, spanning 40,000 hectares and run by the same family since 1976. It's a long drive in here, or a voyage over the lake to Queenstown, and the station is largely self-sufficient, producing its own power and much of its food.

Walter Peak Station lies some 12 kilometres away, the road creeping along the lake edge and stopping at its gates. Much of this, from Mount Nicholas Station to the Mavora Lakes, was to have been part of a bold new tourist venture. Visitors would have been shipped across Lake Wakatipu to Mount Nicholas, driven to Kiwi Burn near South Mavora Lake, then taken by a 43-kilometre monorail ride pushing 29.5 kilometres through Snowdon Forest, conservation land and World Heritage status notwithstanding, to Te Anau Downs and onto Milford. In 2014 the government rejected the scheme, while leaving the door open to future proposals.

So, watch this space in the Southland mountains. It's perfect, New Zealand in the raw, but it's fragile.

PETONE •
• WAINUIOMATA

BARING HEAD •

BARING HEAD

'THAT HOLLOW FEELING OF STANDING ON THE BRINK.'

TO THE LIGHTHOUSE

The wide Wainuiomata road sweeps up from the Hutt Valley. How smooth it is, and what joy!

They began building a tunnel through the hills here in 1932 but it was never finished and now lurks behind locked gates.

Such good luck, you say, as your car glides over the tarmac, three lanes up and two down, and you think of the town this must lead to: a town developed all at once when 'state' meant either houses or loans, a time warp, a piece of New Zealand history preserved, a gem!

Well, it's Wainuiomata. The road, at least, makes a grand entrance. Certainly you notice a lot of wild cars on this wild road.

This is one of the country's mysterious places, nominally a suburb, in fact a town of almost 17,000, isolated by hills on three sides. For most of New Zealand it is unvisited: it is not on the way to anywhere else. For Wellington it's an enclave with a formidable reputation. (The entire town was once banned from a Palmerston North hotel on the grounds of arrogance. Its manager told newspapers

RIGHT Towards Baring Head from Wainuiomata.

he'd never been to the place but had heard about it.)

For Wainuiomata it's life as usual. Is there any other? The All Blacks Piri Weepu and Tama Umaga lived here. So did Chloe Reeves, the baby-voiced woman with the huge eyes and tiger slippers ('I was losing sleep not having them') who became a national figure after appearing in the *Heartland* television series. The television sitcom *Seven Periods with Mr Gormsby* was filmed in the old Wainuiomata College.

You can see the diversity, although possibly not as you nip through on your way south. Regenerating bush pokes through gorse blooming gold on the Orongorongos, and the Rimutaka Forest Park lies just beyond. The valley flats, once farmed, are slowly covering with regenerating bush; another few centuries and they'll be back to where they were.

The road clings to the Wainuiomata River, the hillsides growing more barren until they are so desolate and beautiful that you know a wild sea must be just around the next bend. On a fine weekend it's quite busy, for this is the road to Baring Head and it's full of people going fishing, shellfish poachers, rock-climbers, walkers thinking of the Orongorongo Valley, families after a breath of fresh air. There's plenty of that. Wainuiomata is warmer than Wellington but when this road flares out towards Baring Head, you know where the capital city stores its surplus wind. It's signalled by the bashed-up bush, the storm-wrack on the beach below.

The area around the lighthouse is now publicly accessible land bought with public money. When the river is right you can cross the bar at its entrance for a three-hour return walk. Or you can leave your car further back along the road, walk across a bridge and up to the Head that way. Both give you that hollow feeling of standing on the brink.

The great ocean spreads before you and its vastness makes you take a step back. The South Island peeks from underneath a rug of cloud. Cook Strait lies to your right. Sometimes the water feathers against Turakirae Head on your left and the milky river flows down to a stern sea which nevertheless treats Baring Head respectfully.

But a calm day is a comparative term only. The wind gathers itself here for a squeeze through the Strait or, if it's blowing the other way, for a blast from confinement to freedom. If it's sunny, an extraordinary feeling of luck and delight creeps through your veins and colours your world.

Beaches, escarpments, terraces, flats were created by earthquakes over centuries, the last big one in 1855. Hillsides here were mined for sheep and the beaches for gravel. Maori knew the place for its seafood, and latter-day poachers did well too.

And what is it about lighthouses? The older ones are always perfect. The newer, stumpy ones are the product of a utilitarian age. The Baring Head lighthouse is relatively modern, finished in 1935 on land donated by a local farmer. This was the age of the public good. It replaced the light at Pencarrow Head and is old enough to be a model of period lighthouse architecture with its balcony, domed top and diamond-shaped lens.

For this is classic shipwreck coast with more than 40 sinkings recorded. The last big one was the 10,000-tonne bulk carrier *Pacific Charger,* which despite the light and modern navigational aids went aground here in 1981. The Wainuiomata Volunteer Fire Brigade attended, having been told that a small fishing boat was on the rocks.

The brigade also saw the demise of the historic Orongorongo Lodge and all its treasures, which lay at the end of the other fork in the road here. This was once the seat of four generations of the Riddiford family and, in the best station tradition, was a village dominated by the big house.

Gone now. But this untamed tip of the island is a monument in itself.

EREWHON STATION

MESOPOTAMIA

MT SOMERS

MAYFIELD

ARUNDEL

THE EREWHON ROADS

RANGITATA RIVER VALLEY

'A DESOLATE PATHWAY OF DESTRUCTION.'

Two roads run up the Rangitata River valley. One, on the south side of the river, ends at Mesopotamia, the high-country station founded by the Victorian novelist Samuel Butler. The other, on the north side, runs to Erewhon, the station named after Butler's most famous novel, which is not quite Nowhere spelled backwards.

Butler first saw the great braided river within this valley in 1860. No roads existed then, on either side of the valley. As he left the plains Butler rode his horse Doctor up the south branch of the Ashburton River, branching off into a side valley which took him to the upper Rangitata. He called the Rangitata valley 'a desolate pathway of destruction'. It was a terrible place then, untracked, a wild river that killed invaders without respect for age, sex or rank. Its first known European victim was Dr Andrew Sinclair, the Colonial Secretary, who drowned in 1861 while accompanying the geologist Julius von Haast across the river. More

than 60 years went by before a road followed Butler all the way up that river.

The 193-kilometre journey from Christchurch to Mesopotamia could take a week in a dray drawn by the six bullocks which Butler bought and hastily taught himself to drive. Even in 1918, on an occasion when a musterer received an urgent call to the bedside of his sick daughter in a nearby town, the ride out from Mesopotamia took two days.

For decades Mesopotamia's wool was loaded onto huge drays which teams of horses pulled across the river to Mount Potts and onto a road on the north side following Butler's path to the wool scour at Mount Somers. The track dodged the mountains through swamps and valleys, a four or five-day round trip when there were no floods, snow or ice.

Charley Dunstan, one of the dray drivers, described his job as 'a hazardous and lonely occupation'. It must have been a great day when the first wagon rolled from Peel Forest along the new route on the south side of the Rangitata, the opposite side to the old one, all the way to Mesopotamia in 1924. Then, in December 1926, the first lorry drove all the way to the station. The days of wagons and epic journeys were over. But the road was still stopped by Forest Creek on the Mesopotamia boundary, not so much a creek as a rampant mountain river with all the bad habits of its ilk: floods, washouts and an eternal ability to misbehave. Forest Creek had to be forded, and that was possible only some of the time.

The local council baulked at a bridge. Malcolm Prouting, founder of a dynasty which still owns Mesopotamia, decided to build one himself. He had no bridge-building experience, and by any standard this was a feat that would now require teams of engineers and a flotilla of heavy equipment. Prouting simply used what he had: farm machinery, a farmer's practical approach to a job, old tramlines from Christchurch's abandoned tramways and timber from the tough native forests in the mountain gullies. He finished the bridge in 1952. For the first time, cars and trucks could drive *all* the way up the river valley to Mesopotamia.

Even now, when 4WD vehicles and utes carry weekend adventurers over the back country, Mesopotamia is a long haul along the dusty road which runs from Peel Forest. Samuel Butler would certainly recognise the landscape, and so would many people worldwide who never set foot nor wheel on the road: it was the location for Edoras in Peter Jackson's *The Lord of the Rings*. Now you can drive from Christchurch to Mesopotamia in three hours, flying above the Rakaia River on New Zealand's longest bridge, zooming over the Ashburton River scarcely knowing it is there, connecting with the inland scenic route around the mountains' feet, slipping over the Rangitata, turning off at Arundel's few houses.

The drive begins at Peel Forest. The forest itself is a carefully preserved remnant of the forest giants which once clothed the valley floors running down to the plains. Further on a thin road branches to the right, leading to the Rangitata Gorge, the gate to the valley, where rafters and kayakers shoot white water rushing between black granite blocks.

The main road, still sealed, takes the easier route, passing by Mount Peel and flowing past Mount Peel Station, with its English country house perfectly transposed halfway round the world and set down amid the wildest mountains of the South Seas. Mount Peel has been owned by the Acland family since 1856. A stone Anglican church settles elegantly beside it despite damage from the Christchurch earthquakes.

To early travellers, civilisation ended on the road past the homestead; now, it is only the end of the sealed road, wheels crunching onto shingle. You climb through gullies on the way up, but what a view of the Canterbury Plains to the sea on the drive back!

Last century the far boundary of Mount Peel Station pressed against the near boundary of Mesopotamia but now several stations fit the space between. So the road rises and falls beyond Mount Peel and on the hard bend at White Rock Station, known to local people as the 'Wow Corner', you know you're in a world apart. Butler's dark and gloomy description is banished by the magnificence of it.

The Rangitata is one of the great braided rivers which are found only in Alaska, Canada, the Himalayas and the South Island. It has carved the land, shaped and sculpted it. Great flats run beside the river. Iron-grey slate shingle shows under purple matagouri, the willows along the river palest green in spring, russet in autumn, ranks of pines angling down.

The road ahead vanishes into nothing, overawed by the ranges. On the left the Ben McLeods loom over the valley, merging into the Two Thumbs Range with the Two Thumbs themselves giving the all-OK to the heavens, surrounding peaks as noble supporting cast.

Behind them the black crags of the Southern Alps step up to the high, white snow which seems to leach the colour from the sky.

Far across the river you can see the place where Samuel Butler once emerged into the valley and felt very much as you do now, awed. It doesn't take much to imagine Jackson's orcs and elves pressing on the golden tussock, nipping through the gullies. Streams of dust tell of other traffic — perhaps, for there isn't much other traffic up here, the rural post, the school bus, stock trucks, farmers, the sparse population of the high country.

Three fords remind you that only the road has changed. They trickle in summer and roar in winter, the water drumming against the bottom of the car. The road runs through the jumble of farm buildings marking Ben McLeod Station. As it crosses Forest Creek it joins a ghostly trail. Maori are believed to have travelled from the Fairlie basin and through the ranges to Forest Creek and the upper Rangitata. Beyond the end of the road lies an old stone structure thought to have once enclosed a Maori garden. Ngai Tahu tell of a pounamu or greenstone trail over a pass at the valley's head, possibly the Denniston.

The road follows their footsteps. On it goes past Scour Stream where a sign announces that you are now on Mesopotamia Station, and rolls up to a junction in a maze of tracks. Go one way and you find yourself at the airport, with probably the smallest terminal building in the country: one room and a veranda. The other way leads to the station's tractor shed, then the woolshed, the cookhouse and shearers' quarters. A driveway loops around a terrace, past several cottages, the remains of Butler's cottage and a school to the big two-storeyed homestead. If you go straight ahead, you pass the tiny graveyard where Sinclair lies buried alongside other pioneers, and cross Bush Stream on another bridge built by Malcolm Prouting's son Laurie.

The river runs on ahead, vanishing under the Cloudy Peaks Range, rising to its source in the Garden of Eden ice plateau with, high above, the Denniston Pass leading over the Alps to the West Coast. The road ends a kilometre or so further on. Well, not so much ends as frays. The intrepid can take tough 4WDs and go further up the river; the fit can leave their cars and follow Te Araroa, the national pathway, between the cliffs of Bush Stream into the vastness which Butler and succeeding generations called The Valley.

Or you can stay where you are, pressed up against the high ranges, just three hours from Christchurch.

There is another way up this valley. You drive back down the valley to State Highway 72 and turn north towards Mayfield. Watch for panthers. A black one

LEFT Rangitata River valley, 1927.

RIGHT The great braided river below its source in the Garden of Eden.

has been seen around roads here often since 1992. The animal is said to be the size of a Labrador, with round head and long tail. It has even been photographed, on the frozen surface of Lake Clearwater. Officially it has been declared to be a large feral cat, but locals know better: try the Panther's Rock bar in Mayfield.

The second road into the upper Rangitata valley leads from Mount Somers, a village with a long history in farming and mining. Coal, sand and limestone were all mined here, each era leaving a legacy of machinery and tracks and rosy old houses; it had a railway of its own until 1968. The road cruises alongside the Ashburton River at first then twists through the Ashburton Gorge. Wildflowers cheer your passage.

Now you are in old Hakatere Station country. This mighty affair once ruled the land between the Rangitata and Ashburton rivers, and the old station buildings are still the capital city of this countryside. It's now hard to believe that a single farm needed so many musterers and shearers that a building the size of a boarding school housed them. It ranges back from the road, bunkrooms and cook shop and long verandas, the old stone cottage built in 1862 for the head shepherds, all of it so lonely that local women were said to walk 20 kilometres for a cup of tea and a chat.

You can turn off here and drive to Lake Heron past the Maori Lakes, a collection of wetlands in a wide, fair basin which in spring is blessed with gold. The road ahead will carry you past Lake Clearwater with its whiffle of baches, across the Potts River and out to the Rangitata through country whose excitement carries through the upholstered steel beneath you. On to Mount Sunday, the site of Jackson's Edoras and a mecca for *Rings* fans still, to Erewhon. And here, where the Clyde River meets the Rangitata in a clash of huge, mountain-fed waters, you stop.

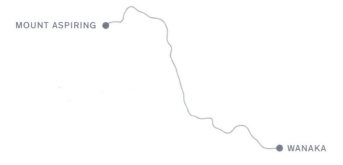

MOUNT ASPIRING

WANAKA

MATUKITUKI VALLEY

'WHERE LUMPS AND HUMPS CARVED BY ANCIENT GLACIERS MAKE A PLANET OF THEIR OWN.'

ASPIRING COUNTRY

Mount Aspiring, Tititea, dominates the peaks at the top of the Matukituki Valley road. It's the symbol of the Mount Aspiring National Park and recognised internationally in the South-West New Zealand World Heritage Area.

You can see from the valley floor that it's something special. People photograph it. They want to get closer. They climb it. They walk over and around it to places like the Scotts Rock Biv, Pearl Flat and, my favourite, the Rock of Ages Biv. To get there they have to drive up the Matukituki Valley road. Some 100,000 people a year do.

The road doesn't look that busy. But it is.

You leave from Wanaka. Drive alongside the lake, past the miraculous Glendhu Bay, past the Treble Cone skifield turn-off where the seal ends and into the Matukituki Valley, with 33 kilometres to go. Suddenly

RIGHT Ford in the valley road, quiet here, a torrent in winter.

INSET Lower Matukituki Valley, 1930.

you're in Aspiring country. The gravel road runs long and straight but you quickly get the idea: whatever the road, it's worth the drive for the unique mountainscape.

Closer to the road bluffs and shadows, lumps and humps carved by ancient glaciers make a planet of their own. The rock seems to have frozen in mid-flow, like ice sculptures melting. Black Peak rears behind. Dust whips off the road in little tornadoes. Sheep are used to traffic. They scarcely move off the road, just stand and watch you drive by. Perhaps they're reversing the old saying and thinking, 'What a country, a few hundred sheep and 100,000 people.'

Now there are glacier cirques high above, great peaks enclosing the world, beech forest, tussock grassland and in the middle of it, you, feeling tiny.

Suddenly there's a gate, and soon after the Mount Aspiring Station homestead and buildings appear beside the road. Now you're in Aspinall country, home to the Aspinall family for four generations. Public enjoyment of this valley and its mountains owes a great deal to this family. The Mount Aspiring National Park was created in 1964 after an earlier generation of Aspinalls relinquished more than 20,000 hectares of their lease. The family's philosophy has always been to give everyone access to the mountains. They've allowed the public into the park through their property, although it's unlikely many of the 20,000, say, who walk over the swing bridge from Raspberry Flat and on to the Rob Roy Glacier each year know they're crossing private land. The late John

Aspinall was a board member of the Walking Access Commission, and an heroic figure in the sometimes contentious issues of high-country access.

The last 10 kilometres of the road get even more interesting. It rounds Camerons Flat, narrows, crawls under a bluff above the river, really just a notch. A clutter of cars marks the swing bridge over the river, carrying the track giving trampers access to the river's East branch. It ends at a place with a most inviting name, Raspberry Flat. It suggests a picnic with wicker baskets spread on a gingham tablecloth. In fact, it lies under the snouts of peaks descending from the mighty Aspiring, Mount Avalanche, Rob Roy Peak.

In summer the road is easy enough. Nine fords, none of them serious. One very long, very cumbersome motor caravan made the journey ahead of me. Sometimes its ends crunched as they beached on opposite sides of the streams, but it made the trip without pause.

Winter is a different story. Gales rip through the valley. Deep snow lies on its floor. The Matukituki River turns nasty. Slips tumble. Waterfalls spring from every crevice. The mountains throw rocks. It gets very, very cold. In heavy rain the streams crossing the road become torrents. Cars can be trapped on the wrong side of them.

Once, the Aspinall family regularly pulled cars and drivers out of trouble, at least one a week. Less so now, despite the constantly rising number of cars using the road.

The latest generation to run the farm, Randall and Allison Aspinall, believe that drivers have become more self-sufficient, carry jumper leads, tow ropes and other useful gear, help each other out of trouble. Still, even new technology can make mistakes. One Israeli party put their faith in their GPS, which led them across the Matukituki. The river is famous for a potent combination of high water, rocks, silt, even quicksand. They got stuck, of course.

TINUI ● ● CASTLEPOINT

MASTERTON ●

CASTLEPOINT

'THE COAST ARRIVES SUDDENLY, TO YOUR GREAT SURPRISE AND DELIGHT.'

THE SUNDAY RUNNER

Looking at a map of eastern Wairarapa with its lumpy little hills and granny-knot of roads you wonder first, how you'd find your way in there then whether you'd ever get out. Lost in a wild tangle of farms and forests on narrow roads which bump and grind and turn all over the place, you might, if you're lucky, merely find yourself back where you started. Otherwise . . .

The Castlepoint road is one of the best-used but that's not to say it's a doddle. It has its share of kinks and the 65 kilometres are going to take you an hour.

It begins as Te Ore Ore Road, leading off to the coast from the northern edge of Masterton. The road starts innocently, leading easily through countryside which always seems to me to be distinctive: I can't say why, but somehow I know I'm in the Wairarapa. The big sky, the nor'wester? Canterbury has those, but not the curly roads, the tufts of bush, the sense that it's a work in progress and there's no one around to ask when it might be finished.

The adage declares that getting there is half the fun and most roads follow it. But this road, really, is more about its destination. So you go to Carswell, an

RIGHT Volkswagen camper with a fine view of Castle Point lighthouse.

FAR RIGHT Castlepoint, 1949.

old name in the Wairarapa but otherwise a fork in the road. If you turn right you can go on to Riversdale, a nice place on the coast which calls itself the biggest beach resort in the Wairarapa.

The title is not hotly contested given the dangerously exposed nature of the coast.

Riversdale is comparatively new, a subdivision dating only from the 1950s. It has a camping ground which became famous in 2006 when, threatened with its subdivision, unhappy campers raised more than a million dollars to buy part of it back.

The left fork leads, circuitously, to Tinui and here you stumble across one of those dots in New Zealand history: this was the first place to have an Anzac Day cross on a hill behind the town, scene of our first commemoration, in 1916, of the Gallipoli landings. The name of Jack Dunn is on the memorial. He was sentenced to death for falling asleep on sentry duty. The sentence was remitted but Dunn died anyway, at Chunuk Bair.

Much later the armed services saw Tinui as an alternative to the long, if fashionable, plod to Gallipoli. In 2009 Judith Collins, then Veterans' Affairs Minister, declared that Tinui was the place to go for people to remember and pay their respects, and Anzac Day has become the town's big day since.

It has a war memorial hall, school, store and pub, and a good café. It's a fine place to stop, because when you leave there's nowhere else. Tinui, incidentally, means many cabbage trees, and there's quite a few of them.

From Tinui you drive through gullies and valleys, beside rivers and streams, under pines and over lumps, and you feel thoroughly shut in. The coast arrives suddenly, to your great surprise and delight. In a moment you're at the old Whakataki Hotel, Castlepoint's social hub although the beach is still a little further on. That's because the Castlepoint port was sometimes isolated by the river running beside

the pub: in a flood you needed to be on the right side of it. And there you are, at the famous white lighthouse rising above the tiny port still used by fishing boats.

Castle Point itself was visited by Kupe, the great Polynesian navigator, and given its Pakeha name by Captain Cook.

Once it was the Waiarapa's main port (until the Wellington to Masterton railway put paid to it in 1880) and remnants of the old town still exist: a cemetery, a school. The Castlepoint Station, long the economic backbone, remains much as it was, blocking further subdivision. Even the baches have that lived-in look that separates them from dreary holiday-home suburbs.

And the Castlepoint horse races are still run along the beach every year the weather and tides will allow them. They started in 1871. Crowds of thousands throng the road that weekend. It's a moment of glory. Then everything goes quiet.

OTAMA

KUAOTUNU

OPITO BAY

MATAPAUA BAY

OPITO ROAD

'A DROP SO STEEP CAR HEADLIGHTS SIMPLY SHONE INTO SPACE.'

THE BLACK JACK

The Coromandel Peninsula always looks jaunty on the map, a happy gesture, finger pointing up, thumb outstretched. Along that thumb lie beaches that many, especially locals, insist are the best in all New Zealand. In the winter, few live here, but in summer roads are packed as the Coromandel's population rises to five times its usual 26,000.

On a good day the drive from Auckland to the Coromandel takes little more than two hours. It's the kind of distance that, for example, Christchurch people used to driving to Nelson or Wanaka for their holidays think nothing of. Yet those two hours remove outsiders to a place of bush and beaches and blue seas full of islands.

Let's say you've taken the road north from Whitianga, or north-east from Coromandel. Either way it looks like a huge hairpin, with a little place called Kuaotunu at the tip.

A little place now, that is. Its surrounding hills are dotted with Maori pa and riddled with mine shafts, for this was once a goldmining town with a population of thousands and even a local School of

RIGHT Opito Bay Road.

FAR RIGHT Kuaotunu Beach, 1965. Black Jack Road in the background, winding over the hill to Otama Beach.

Mining. Some of its character clings still.

The bay here was even to have been a harbour protected by a breakwater. Luckily, the plan sank into the briny and the white sand with the surf peeling off the Black Jack reef has been left to swimmers, nymphs and dolphins.

From Kuaotunu a little road heads more or less west. Even in the 1950s and 60s it was primitive enough to have been a direct descendant of the old miners' tracks. The Kuaotunu Hill road was tough but the Black Jack road was terrifying. One account of it in the 1960s records two lines of gravel with grass in the middle and, at the top where it turned on to the ridge line, a drop so steep that car headlights simply shone into space. It was just as bad by daylight, as one writer noted, 'spiralling up as it fell away on all sides, leaving only sky to be seen.'

The road runs to Otama Beach, still quite undeveloped by Coromandel standards, white sand blinding in the sun. Then to Opito Bay, with its pa looking down from the headland and, in a final burst over a rudimentary road, to Matapaua Bay.

Brenda Sewell, in her book *Opito and Beyond*, recorded the road in the 1960s: steep and rough. At Otama it was essentially sand, with a ford replacing the rocks dumped in the stream and called a causeway. A farm gate blocked the ford so passengers had to wade over and open it. The road shrank to a track by Opito Bay and motorists had to drive across a paddock, along a creek to the beach with two wheels in the water and two on the sand dunes, then along the beach over rocks at low tide.

The road to Matapaua did not exist then. People went there by boat from Whitianga. Now, Otama's fine lines are still largely uninterrupted by the pervasive holiday housing. Impromptu campsites have disappeared from Opito Bay, replaced by some 220 houses, although only about 20 of them are permanent homes. Matapaua, once a dairy farm,

was subdivided into sections so that it keeps an undeveloped if private look.

The Black Jack is now steep but tamed. If you know its genesis you can still see why it was so scary (it was once named one of the three most dangerous roads in the country) but a modern Japanese saloon scarcely registers the climb.

You nip down into Otama, take in the sand, paddle in the clear water and admire a hillside bach which has appeared in architecture magazines. But you don't worry about the road. It gets narrower, and grittier, as it climbs over the point and drops into Opito Bay before turning into the track that takes you to Matapaua. No bother.

Yet all the way along it you are reminded of why people risked their cars and their health to get in here. These bays are beautiful by any standards. Offshore, the scatter of Mercury Islands, the sprinkle of islets off Opito, the archipelagos spreading down the Peninsula, add their magic. The desolation of the mid-20th century is being hidden under regenerating native bush.

The road is smoother but the ride is as exciting as ever.

– CHAPTER FOUR –
BY-ROADS

DRIVING ROUTES

1. INLAND KAIKOURA
2. DARFIELD TO GERALDINE
3. RAWENE TO AHIPARA
4. KOHATU TO MOTUEKA
5. THE MAROKOPA EXPRESSWAY
6. THE PORANGAHAU HIGHWAY
7. KAWATIRI TO RENWICK
8. BEAUMONT TO BALCLUTHA

LEFT Pedestrian traffic on the road between Marokopa and Kawhia.

WAIAU · MT LYFORD · KAIKOURA

INLAND KAIKOURA

'QUITE SUDDENLY THE ROAD LOST ITS TEMPER.'

THE ALPINE BYWAY

Just past the Kaikoura golf course, overlooked by a new subdivision with porticos and wide windows peering at the ocean, the road turned off State Highway 1 and headed inland.

This August the mountains were daubed with snow. They looked high, and difficult. But the road passed them by and they became merely my companions for the next 80 kilometres.

The low hills turned me out into a long flat valley. The road led through its middle towards blue hills, past a little yellow school. The kowhai was bursting in gold slashes and the willow purple and red.

Quite suddenly the road lost its temper. It dropped into the abrupt valley cut by the Kahutara River on its way to boiling drama at the coast. As suddenly, Waiau seemed an awfully long way away.

The road regained its manners and now led through smooth farmland incongruous in the hard

RIGHT The Inland Kaikoura road.

FAR RIGHT Weka Pass, 1952.

country. Then it threw another fit and crossed the Conway River on a sagging one-way bridge, flexing its muscles here in the back blocks.

I was getting used to mood swings, and to one-way bridges, for all of them now were single-lane.

Near the Doone homestead, on the banks of Campbell Creek, a little grave with rounded headstone and ornate railing rested on a terrace above the road. It testified to a lonely past. This road was built in the 1880s, a contractors' camp set up on a unique local feature called the Whales Back. Willie George, the camp cook, lived in a tent with his wife and daughter Alice. A winter drive here would show what hardship was hidden in that sentence. Alice was aged one year and 10 months in 1887 when she fell ill. Before a doctor could reach her from Waiau she died. Did her family have hopes and dreams, or just the need to make a living in hard times?

Yet life wasn't cheap. The doctor rode long and hard to reach her, and the Rev W.R. Campbell, known as the 'Apostle of the North', rode even longer and harder to bury her. The grave site was slowly disappearing when local people tidied and fenced it. Tom Derrett, the first coachman on this road, carted the timber for nothing. The headstone records her full name: Alice Cecelia Sercombe George.

The road rose over the Whales Back Saddle then followed a river valley deep in rusty willows.

The Mount Lyford skifield road led off, a chalet restaurant and bar incongruous in this sparse country. Yet there's no shortage of snow. The year before, the road was blocked by a huge avalanche.

Now the road dropped so low that water lapped the tarmac and I seemed to be driving through ponds. Homesteads became charming, early blossom bright in their gardens. Grander was the Highfield Station woolshed, long and elegant, a sheep mansion. Highfield was one of the early North Canterbury sheep runs and its woolshed, built in 1877, had

24 shearing stands manned by an army of shearers and shedhands.

Waiau appeared. An early account of the town recorded it as picturesque, with hotel, post, telegraph, two stores, two churches, school, library and reading room. It still has most of those things, even the town jail. It was the terminus for a railway line which began at Waipara, 56 kilometres north of Christchurch. The line closed in 1978, but enthusiasts still run trains from Waipara over the Weka Pass to Waikari. It is a relaxed, unpretentious country town and it even has two passing bays on the long, long single-lane bridge over the Waiau River. I passed one car and six motor caravans in the entire 80-kilometre journey.

Rotheram, a few kilometres further on, owes its existence to a 1877 drive to get labourers into the district. But by now I was nipping over the long straights of the Amuri Plains intent on viewing the excellent local scenery through steam rising off the hot pools at Hanmer Springs.

DOUBLE HILL

COLGATE
DARFIELD
GLENTUNNEL
ALFORD FOREST

GERALDINE

DARFIELD TO GERALDINE

'KEEP YOUR WINDOWS UP AND YOUR HEART RATE DOWN.'

UNDER THE NOR'WEST ARCH

Travelling south from Christchurch you can take the high road or the low road. The low is State Highway 1 with its long straights running over the plains to Timaru. Not surprisingly, the high road is more interesting.

The road was born in Amberley and travels to the mountains by way of Oxford, crossing the West Coast Highway at Sheffield. You can get onto it from Darfield too. Both places sit squarely under the nor'west arch created by the hot, fierce wind which bursts across the plains raising suicide and divorce rates in one blow. Keep your windows up and your heart rate down.

Whichever town you leave from, you wind up at Homebush, the seat of one of those distinctively Canterbury families. The Deans brothers, William and John, arrived in Christchurch several years before the revered First Four Ships. They settled first in

RIGHT Rakaia Gorge bridge, completed 1882.

Riccarton then moved to the foothills at Homebush, where the family built their own piece of England, an imposing homestead. Generations of the family lived there for more than a century and a half until 2010 when the huge house was ruined by the first big earthquake and demolished. Now there's a hole in the country idyll. You can see you're marching to the beat of a different drum. High winds and shaky ground. What's next?

Well, it was to have been high water. A huge irrigation scheme has started here, harnessing raw Canterbury: the power of its mountains, the strength of its rivers, big money versus small, agriculture industrials versus clean streams and clean drinking water. Its supporters proposed drowning first one valley then the next behind a dam. They finished with the water but no dam.

Somewhere in the imbroglio Canterbury people lost their right to an elected regional council.

Wrapping all *that* in a single road may be a stretch, yet roads are the capillaries of a nation, and everything the body corporate does finds its way into them.

The road is known as the Inland Scenic Route, but the scenic part of that description may have to be put on hold, as the earthmovers cut and scrape the tunnels and canals and water races for the 'water enhancement scheme'.

To be certain, skip through Glentunnel and Coalgate, two tiny towns which once had their own railway to serve their coalfield. Now the scenic route is earning its stripes. Pass by the intriguing Windwhistle, perhaps a reference to the nor'wester, and zigzag down to the gorge in the Rakaia River, one of Canterbury's three great braided rivers. A narrow bridge joins rock races. Here you're buried in a symphony of rushing water and rock.

If you're adventurous you can drive up the north bank and at the end of the road look across the river and past Lake Coleridge to Mount Algidus Station where Mona Anderson, whose life depended on the river's moods, wrote New Zealand's best-known book on the high country, *A River Rules My Life*.

If you fancy the south bank instead, the strange thing is that while it's only on the other side of the river, it's completely different. This road will take you right to the foot of the Alps, although I prefer to stop halfway and walk up the Redcliffe Stream. It's not listed as one of New Zealand's great walks but when you get deep into its valley with paradise ducks sobbing over the marsh, golden tussock and the huge blue Canterbury sky, it is.

This is skiing country, and Mount Hutt lies between the Redcliffe Stream and the highway. Back you go to the main road and drive south to the turn-off. Skifield roads are not everyone's idea of a great drive, but this one is my pick. It's long, wild, wonderful, creeping up the range, sneaking along ridges and crossing valleys in great loops.

Now the road passes through a string of pretty little towns, Alford Forest, Stavely, Mount Somers, Mayfield. They look settled — of course they are, they've been here for 150 years — but more than that, they're reassuring, at ease with themselves. The roads are so well planted that they often seem more like avenues, adjoining farms like garden parks. Ash, oaks, copper beeches lend a gracious air. Perhaps they are a reaction to the wilderness of the ranges beside them: the kempt alongside the unkempt, the orderly keeping the unruly at bay.

From Mayfield the highway runs in one long straight down to the Rangitata River, brushes by the all but invisible Arundel, arrives quickly at Geraldine and joins State Highway 1 at Winchester. It's a scenic route in the widest sense because it has everything: mountains, lakes, towns, a rich history and a sense of purpose.

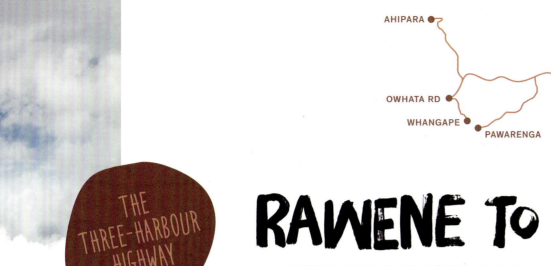

RAWENE TO AHIPARA

'THREE GLORIOUS HARBOURS FULL OF HISTORY AND COLOUR.'

Their descriptions are straightforward. Hokianga, the fourth-biggest harbour in New Zealand, half its 11,500 hectares tidal mudflats. Whangape, a fraction (one 13th) its size, Y-shaped, entered through a narrow channel. Herekino, even smaller, long and thin.

A better picture might run like this: three glorious harbours full of history and colour, each one a spectacle and two of the three reached by narrow roads webbing the thin skin of Northland's west coast. The third, the Hokianga, has a tourist road running through kauri forest to its entrance, yet it still huddles in mystery, quiet water between dark hills.

This harbour is said to have once been home to Kupe, the Polynesian navigator credited with discovering New Zealand. Certainly it spawned the Ngapuhi, once the most powerful and still the most numerous iwi in New Zealand. Many of their network of tracks became roads.

Horeke at the head of the harbour is New Zealand's second-oldest town, the Horeke Hotel the first pub in the country. Governor Hobson came here six days after the Treaty of Waitangi was signed for the treaty's second signing, winning the Ngapuhi to his cause.

Across the harbour looms the dark Marmon's Point. Cannibal Jacky Marmon was a notorious Pakeha-Maori, a runaway convict who arrived in the early 18th century and decided that from that point on he would live (and eat) as the locals did, 'since among the savages I have found more true faithfulness man to man than in the boasted European'.

Rawene is New Zealand's third-oldest town, and this is where the journey starts, by crossing the harbour. It's fitting, because when this town was founded the river was the road, and in its early days had its own road toll: 16 ships were lost on the bar at its entrance, the last a schooner in 1928 when all eight crew died.

The town claims the last shot of the New Zealand wars, in the Dog Tax Rebellion of 1898 when Maori refused to pay dog-registration fees and were fined by a magistrate who was then challenged to fight at Rawene. The town was evacuated and the case seemed certain to make an interesting precedent until a local missionary intercepted the war party and persuaded it to desist. The shot was fired, but only as a signal.

Most of Rawene's best old buildings have been

preserved on the harbour's edge, sometimes like Horeke *over* the edge and hovering above the water on piles.

You drive on to the Rawene ferry and with a minimum of fuss your car takes to the water.

Out on the Hokianga you should get a much better view of the harbour. In fact, you don't. It has so many arms, inlets, bays and branches that you seem to be in a watery maze whose pathways shift as you sail on. But you get the feel, the caress of the harbour. Its history and its secrecy seem to lie around the hills like mist, although locals feel differently about fog: to them, a misty morning means a good day.

To me the Hokianga always seems shadowy, no matter how bright the day. The great kauri forests which brought Europeans here in the first place have gone, and their ghosts join the melancholy of the place. Opo the dolphin might have cheered things up but she was here for only nine months, becoming a national phenomenon and the Hokianga's most famous tourist attraction before she disappeared on 9 March 1957, a day after the government passed a special law protecting her.

The ferry unloads you near the colonial village of Kohukohu, known locally as 'Coke'. It is well preserved too, for this is not just a drive, it is time travel.

Kohukohu's Maori ancestry goes back to Kupe, and its European lineage is illustrious too. The first Roman Catholic mass in New Zealand was celebrated here in 1838, after Bishop Jean Baptiste Pompallier arrived in New Zealand and made it his first job to establish mission stations in the harbour. Kohukohu was a big town then, with a population of 2000 at the end of the 19th century. Milk and butter replaced logs as its main industry. It declined, of course. That's Hokianga's story, although its present is much more mellow.

The word 'picturesque' is the kiss of death for many old towns but in picturesque Kohukohu the rot has stopped. By the end of the 20th century the census recorded 165 people living there, a sharp drop from the previous census. The 2013 census recorded exactly the same figure. But even if most don't want to stay, it's a lovely town to drive through.

The road writhes through Northland country and you keep an eye on the map, or the GPS, for it's a web. You can go to Whangape Harbour two ways from here. You can thread your way west and turn north near Panguru then left again near Runaruna onto Pawarenga Road. The narrow, shingle road, which sheep and cattle regard as their own preserve, takes you to the south side of the harbour at Pawarenga. This tiny place is worth the drive for two reasons:

PREVIOUS SPREAD Sign at Hokianga Harbour.

TOP LEFT Car ferry landing at Rawene, Hokianga, 1954.

TOP RIGHT Rawene, 1951.

the little white church, Saint Gabriel's, and cemetery; and the Golden Stairs walking track, named for its flowering kowhai.

You are just inside the harbour entrance here. It is narrow and canal-like, once a river gorge, widening into the two estuaries of the Awaroa and Rotokakahi rivers, and it has claimed the usual toll of wrecked ships. On the north side of the harbour lies Whangape itself, and it's a long and tricky way round, back the way you came but branching off towards Pukemiro and Broadwood then turning for Awaroa and Herekino.

At Herekino you turn for Whangape, drive through bare green hills once clothed in kauri, and arrive at a spot a kilometre or so away across the harbour from where you left an hour before. Whangape was once a prosperous harbour and milling town but alas, its fortunes fell. It always seemed to me a place of disappointments. Once I spoke to a farmer there, a family from the south. 'They call it the winterless north,' he snorted. 'Huh.' Most recently it was famous for a huge drug bust in 2012. Police discovered seven methamphetamine sites on Ngati Haua's sacred mountain Whakeroro, the same mountain occupied by local people in 1992 in protest at its sale to a Lotto millionaire. The police took $3 million in cash, assets, drugs and drug-making gear and arrested nine people.

The last time I visited Whangape it was a clearly poor but peaceful little settlement under its gem of a church, St Mary's. It is even poorer and smaller now, for six cottages were burned to the ground in the raid's wake.

But you have no need to come here from Herekino. You can make for Herekino Harbour instead, for the road goes as far as Owhata near its entrance. At low tide that is probably the only place you will find any water in the entire harbour.

Herekino, like every other town on the three harbours, is past its prime. Reading a 1887 report by the Commissioner of Crown Lands on the 'special

settlement' here, you wonder whether the place was ever *in* its prime. After inspecting the settlement he noted one common complaint: all provisions had to be fetched from Ahipara, 20 kilometres away, over 'an almost impassable, precipitous track'. The journey took two days and worse, the settlers would often find the storekeeper's cupboard bare and make the long trek back empty-handed. The Commissioner urged the government to subsidise a steamer service to Whangape.

Ironically enough it was a road that did for Herekino in the end. Even in the mid-1960s it was recognisable as a township. When State Highway 1 through the Mangamuka Gorge to its end at Kaitaia was sealed, traffic took the faster route. Herekino went downhill.

But now you can finish this journey by taking the direct route from Herekino to Ahipara. It'll take about 20 minutes instead of a day, and you can count on the shops.

RIGHT Entrance to Ninety Mile Beach at Ahipara.

MOTUEKA RIVER
TYREE PHOTO 1478

PROTECT

MOTUEKA

NGATIMOTI

TAPAWERA

TADMOR KOHATU

KOHATU TO MOTUEKA

'ONCE RANG WITH LAUGHTER AND SONG ALL SUMMER LONG.'

TOBACCO ROAD

The Kohatu Hotel is a signpost. It stands at a fork in the road. Turn one way and you continue on State Highway 6 to Nelson. Take the other and you find yourself in a long, sweet valley, the road following the Motueka River all the way to Motueka.

The hotel is an historical signpost too. When Thomas and Mary Bromell built it around 1876 they expected to capitalise on a brave venture in their new country: the Nelson railway line. For 79 years the line crept south from Nelson, diverted through a tiny place called Tadmor, then Glenhope, lumbered through a hand-cut tunnel at Kawatiri to Gowanbridge and was on its way to Murchison and possibly to Inangahua to connect with Canterbury via the West Coast line when the National government pulled the plug. The line began shrinking, first back to Glenhope then in 1955, finally, right back to Nelson when the entire line was closed down.

Glenhope is not far from Kohatu if you're heading north, and adventurous drivers can get into the Motueka Valley from here. It's not far from the spot where the famous goldminer George Moonlight, whose name is all over the region, was found dead.

At Glenhope a mysterious building, obviously an old station, stands all alone in a paddock. If you leave the highway here the road trails up the Hope River and over the Tadmor Saddle, where stout-hearted labourers forced the railway line up 453 metres and across a lot of unstable ground and tricky creeks, rejoining the highway at Tapawera. That part of the line was finally opened in 1912.

When I first began driving this route decades ago I could still follow the cuttings and benching of the old line. Now they've been largely swallowed by bush and roadworks. The Kawatiri tunnel and line have become a public walkway, popular with tourists.

But now, you're turning at the Kohatu Hotel and heading due north to Motueka. The road bustles along easy terraces to Tapawera, an interesting little town whose infrastructure bears the signs of heavy government investment: this was once a railway town and later a New Zealand Forest Service headquarters, the centre of vast state forests.

The tiny Kiwi railway station is now a museum here. Kiwi in the Tadmor Valley no longer appears on most maps, but in 1955 it was international news.

A group of Nelson women sat on the line for 10 days protesting its closure. The protest ended when nine were arrested, having been branded 'dangerous' and possibly Communist by the Prime Minister of the day, Sid Holland. One of them was the remarkable Sonja Davies, later a human rights champion, Labour MP and holder of the Order of New Zealand.

This lively history can be taken in at Tapawera or you can nip through on the side road to Tadmor, a great drive for two reasons: first, because it takes you through the old goldmining country of the Wangapeka to the famed Wangapeka Track through the Kahurangi National Park; and second, because it leads through jewel-like country of berry farms. Once I commuted nightly in my Ford coupe hotrod from my job in the Motueka tobacco fields to Tadmor, centre for hundreds of berry-pickers, almost all women. Dances at the Tadmor Hall were not to be missed.

Well, it's a quieter place now on all fronts, but just as beautiful.

Back at Tapawera the Motueka Valley road sweeps north, climbing a little saddle and dropping into a valley that obviously was made in heaven, an idyllic place of tended gardens and good houses. This is Stanley Brook, and it has the marks of a once-prosperous settlement in old New Zealand with two churches, school, library, post office. The school and the library are still in good shape, as is a church.

The road becomes more difficult from here, rejoining the river and winding around it. At one wide bend you find McLeans, which is a free camping area and usually has a few house trucks to mark the spot even in the winter. In the summer it's popular, a good swimming hole in the Motueka River. So far the river has survived the plague of dirty rivers and streams sweeping the country but unchecked development still causes much suffering here: deforestation is one cause of the destructive floods which roar down the valley destroying houses and farms and making families homeless.

PREVIOUS SPREAD Ferry on the Motueka River, 1910.

ABOVE Riwaka and the Motueka River with road bridge and surrounding farmland, Motueka, 1956.

RIGHT Idyllic Motueka River valley.

From here the valley takes a different character. Names such as Woodstock and Orinoco feature on signposts. The Baton River running straight from the old Baton goldfields swells the Motueka. This is a popular place for people who want to get away from it all, although the nearest big town is the peaceful Motueka, not one you'd normally want to get away from. The signs along the road, advertising produce, handicrafts, a remote café or two, tell of people content just to support themselves in this fine valley. Ageing hippies, alternative lifestylers from many countries and traditional farmers get along here.

The bendy road carries you on to Ngatimoti, a small place whose name is said to have come from a Maori man, a recent Christian, who carved his new name Timoti into a tree. The nearby school still is a school, and there's a memorial hall and a church and a fire station and a war memorial, the second to be erected in New Zealand (after Kaitaia's). Of the first 14 young men who hurried off to World War I from Ngatimoti, only two survived, both wounded. The news must have struck this little town like a shell from the battlefield itself. Willie Ham from Ngatimoti is said to have been the first New Zealander killed in that war.

Along the road are survivors of an industry much more dangerous than the occasional plots of marijuana discovered here: tobacco. The sunny weather and fertile soil of Motueka and surrounding country was ideal for the crop. The farms died out after the government in the early 1980s no longer forced a New Zealand quota on the tobacco industry. The itinerant force of seasonal tobacco pickers have been replaced by orchard workers, but their traces remain in the decaying tobacco silos and rows of primitive baches in this valley. Once they rang with laughter and song all summer long. They're long gone now but strangely the music seems to linger.

KAWHIA

KIRITEHERE ● MAROKOPA
● MOEATOA

AWAKINO ●

LOST IN
SPACE

THE MAROKOPA EXPRESSWAY

'THE KIND OF VALLEY WHICH IMMEDIATELY MAKES YOU CHECK THE PETROL GAUGE.'

Calling this a road is limiting. It is, in fact several roads, and several more if you get lost, which you're bound to do.

The usual way of getting into Marokopa is by taking the Waitomo Caves turn-off on State Highway 3 and heading west. If, that is, there *is* a usual way, for Marokopa is a tiny, isolated place on the coast.

There's a lot to be said for that Waitomo road. It runs through limestone country formed 35 million years ago as a shallow seabed which slowly rose. The karst landscape it created hides caves and rivers beneath its surface with outlandish forms, arches, towers, pinnacles, gnomes and ghosts on top, and a glaze of fossils. A bridge of limestone crosses Mangapohue Stream about halfway along the route, past a lookout where you can see right down to the trio of volcanic sisters in the south: Ruapehu, Ngauruhoe and Tongariro. Throw in the Piripiri Cave and the

Marokopa Falls and you have a road trip that's hard to beat.

Unless you come from the south. The road is less spectacular but it has a lost atmosphere and it takes you through country which, if you were stranded, say in London, you'd remember as lonely, lovely New Zealand. This road leaves the highway just past Awakino on the coast, heading north. It follows the Manganui River northwards, sheltering in the kind of valley which immediately makes you check the petrol gauge. You have that trailblazing feeling which you keep to yourself, fearing the scorn of locals.

You could be 100 kilometres from the sea but in fact you're quite close, although you only have one chance to take a look at it on this stretch of road between Awakino and Marokopa: Waikawau Beach. You get there through a tunnel built by three men who burrowed through the sandstone cliffs so that cattle

driven along the beach could get up to Nukuhakare Station above.

From here on you are in danger of taking an unexpected tour of the countryside. It is not well signposted and you need to concentrate and forget about instinct. One road looks very much like the next and if you take the wrong one, as I did, you can finish up several kilometres away at a locked gate, wondering where you went wrong.

So you make for Moeatoa, which is not really a place at all. If you take the right-hand fork here you enter a maze of little roads and, if you're lucky enough to find your way out, you might finish up at Piopio. But you're after the wilderness experience, so you crab left through yet another valley and sweep over a ridge where you have another choice.

Straight ahead lies Kiritehere, one of those beaches which surfers tell you about then swear you to silence upon pain of death. It's a nick in a rough coast. If you turn right at Kiritehere you find yourself with a dress-circle view of a wide river valley ending in an estuary. This is Marokopa. It's a magical place although you may not instantly recognise it as such. Maori loved it for its harbour and the kahawai which arrived in great schools in summer and spring: at least one war was

fought over the fish. Pa sites are spread around the area. Te Rauparaha, the great Ngati Toa warrior chief, stayed here with his people on his flight south from Kawhia to Kapiti. An anchor from the ship *Albatross* stands at the river entrance, a relic of passenger and cargo services which once risked the river bar.

At the turn of the 19th century Marokopa was a busy township. The King Country was a dry area and Marokopa's remote harbour made it popular with bootleggers. Now it's a holiday settlement with a tiny permanent population flowering into hundreds in the summer. Ferries take visitors across the river to the Marokopa marae on the far bank. Unpretentious baches squat in the sun; a huge blue couch invites lounging but proves to be concrete. Mobile phones do not work here. The only shop, at the camping ground, closes when the owner needs to do the mail run or drive the school bus.

You drive north, carefully, for little roads run in all directions. If you get it right you arrive on the edge of Kawhia Harbour and, no matter what has happened to you en route, the harbour is worth it. The road sneaks along its edge for a bit, ponga trees on one side and tidal mud on the other. You've scarcely been above 50 km/h in the whole journey but now you look

PREVIOUS SPREAD To Marokopa, the easy way.

TOP LEFT Piopio, 1951.

TOP RIGHT Marokopa township and river, 1958.

back on those speedy roads with nostalgia. The road creeps and so do you. But how beautifully!

A very old river valley, drowned when the sea level rose, formed this harbour, five estuaries poured between limestone cliffs. In the late afternoon the harbour is a world of islands and lakes, hills and estuaries set in a glossy sea, edges ornate as a lace doily.

The road leaves the water but you feel it by your side, and you can sense its best-known son Te Rauparaha stealing through the gloom, escaping the neighbours who had objected to his style.

Without much warning a sealed road announces that you're back in the world. It takes you along to Kawhia, aka 'abundance', spiritual home of the Tainui people. This is where the ancestral Tainui waka made its last landfall. Iwi tradition says it lies buried near Maketu Pa at Kawhia, its bow and stern marked by stones set its length apart, 26 metres.

The government tried to open up the harbour to trade and shipping in the 1880s but was thwarted for a time by local Maori sabotaging navigation aids. Vestiges of subversion have clung to the place ever since. It has its own style, well removed from its more glamorous neighbour, Raglan. That's just up the coast and you can take a short cut that may well become a long cut, full of twists and false starts. But you've heard that before.

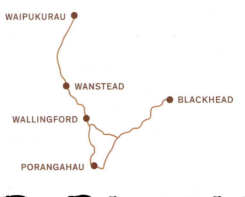

WAIPUKURAU
WANSTEAD
WALLINGFORD
BLACKHEAD
PORANGAHAU

GOING SOUTH

THE PORANGAHAU HIGHWAY

'FROM THE GENTEEL TO THE BLUNT, RULY TO THE UNRULY.'

On the face of it, all that separates Hawke's Bay from Wairarapa is a line on the map invisible to the naked eye. Yet the two provinces are entirely different. If you drive south from Waipukurau you'll get it. You go from the genteel to the blunt, courtly to the brash, ruly to the unruly.

The journey starts in Waipukurau, capital of Central Hawke's Bay and mostly known as Waipuk. It was founded by a runholder, Henry Russell, as a model village. He vetted residents, a tradition which thickened the air for a long time afterwards.

I lived here once and found it plump and rather smug, but never boring. It had a big hospital, its own newspaper, two big pubs and all the accoutrements of a solid town. Banks jostled with stock agents in the main street, car dealers sold big new Holdens and Fords. Economics have knocked it around since. The hospital closed in 1999 and now lies derelict

and subject to investigation by ghost-busters. The newspaper office became a car park. The two pubs, old and new, live on but the ancient Tavistock lost its doughty boss, Ma Bartrum, years ago when she died of a heart attack. She is said to haunt the place.

Once there was a gentlemen's club encompassing everyone who was anyone, as long as they were male. It survives in less exclusive form. Central Hawke's Bay landowners once threaded all the way through government to Cabinet level. That has changed too.

But many of the big names of the district whose families grabbed tracts of land a century and a half ago live on, sometimes in the same places. Their mansions sit in copses of big English trees, and you glimpse a bay here, a turret there, as if you're peeking through a keyhole at a party you haven't been invited to. You can feel their presence as you drive south through farmland which looks tamed, trimmed and properly turned out.

You're heading for Porangahau and your first stop is Wanstead. You know you're there only because of the pub, and it's a good one, very old. Described in its day as 'a commodious two-storeyed wooden building containing eleven bedrooms, two parlours, a clean comfortable dining room, good cuisine, while the liquors are of excellent quality', the Wanstead Hotel was a place that catered for both ends of the trade. It was a stop for the daily mail coach running between Waipukurau and Porangahau along much of the present highway's route. It's the sole survivor of a town nestled among the district's large stations and sits now much as it always has, except for an extended dining room/restaurant.

Down the road a little is one of the reasons for its existence, Wallingford. It looks rather like a little town, buried in its trees and dominated by a vast homestead. In fact, it *was* a township, once; this is the reduced version.

John Davies (J. D.) Ormond stepped off the boat from England in 1847. He and his wife Hannah set up at Wallingford, house *and* village. He took up huge blocks of land here and elsewhere and by the 1870s was running more than 25,000 sheep (which, incidentally, put him only sixth in Hawke's Bay). The village with its two hotels was another stop for the mail coach, which changed its four horses here until service cars replaced them in 1912. The house grew as

PREVIOUS SPREAD
Waipukurau, the start
of Porangahau Highway.

ABOVE New Zealand's
longest place name.

the family did. It had tennis courts and its own golf course, a nursery wing for the extended family and a Rarotongan wing for the Cook Island families who cooked and looked after the gardens.

The third generation of Ormonds were Sir John and Lady Ormond. His various roles included chairman of the meat board and she was a grande dame; I remember the general manager of the small newspaper I worked for in Waipukurau *bowing* as she made her majestic way onto the premises. Ormonds still run the place, now the centre of a much smaller station and available for conferences, weddings and so on.

You have a choice here. You can turn off the highway and take the humpy bumpy road to Blackhead and, if you like, go on to Porangahau from there. Blackhead Reef once sheltered ships landing goods and loading wool from Wallingford and other stations. Now it's a quiet sandy beach with a few baches and a marine reserve, one of those lovely places so far off the beaten track that you feel you've walked into someone's secret life.

Blackhead Point Beach south of Blackhead *was* secret. I used to drive there along the beach from Porangahau to the wreck of the scow *Marororo*, driven ashore while sheltering under Blackhead Reef, ending a previously charmed life in which she'd been posted as missing three times. Otherwise, you needed the farmer's permission to cross his land. But in 2007 he locked his gates, claiming the public was damaging his land and the beach. A three-year stand-off ended when the local council negotiated an access agreement for a new road. It's a rough one, but the beach is worth it.

Back on the highway, you're approaching Porangahau. State Highway 52, the long, windy way to Masterton, angles off just before you reach the town. A short distance down that road you'll find a place with New Zealand's, and by most accounts the world's, longest name: Taumata-whakatangihanga-koauau-o-tamatea(turi-puka-kapi-ki-maunga-horonuku)pokai-whenua-ki-tana-tahu. The short version is that it's the knoll where the great chief Tamatea sat lamenting his twin brother, killed in a nearby battle, on his flute. The place is on a long rocky ridge with tawny flanks running parallel to the road. It looks weatherbeaten and wild.

Porangahau is a short drive from its long, sandy beach (the name means 'mad winds', for the westerly gales here can be fierce). The tiny town looks as if it was once much bigger and, of course, it was.

You pass the handsome Rongomaraera marae on the way in. The rohe, or boundaries, of the people here once reached from Blackhead to Akitio. The Duke of Edinburgh Hotel, locally known as 'The Duke', is imposing. A Saturday at the Duke is a show on its own.

Once there was a coastal steamer service to Napier, post office, Anglican church, shops and a racecourse, where the annual Boxing Day races were a social highlight. Even in the 1960s the school roll topped 200. Well, you can see where they've been. Yet Porangahau still has a cared-for look, the marae tended, the pub popular, the ancient Anglican church nicely restored, an interesting end to a fine drive.

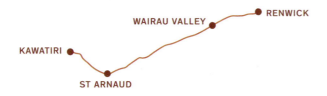

KAWATIRI • ST ARNAUD • WAIRAU VALLEY • RENWICK

KAWATIRI TO RENWICK

THE BACK WAY

'YOU'RE FOLLOWING A FAULT LINE, APPROPRIATELY GIVEN THE VALLEY'S VIOLENT HISTORY.'

This is an uncomplicated road, but it has two superb features. The first are the ranges which rise sheer from the valley. The second is the Wairau River, a wild waterway with a question mark over it: don't put off going there, just in case.

Oh, and perhaps a third: for most of the year, traffic is quite sparse.

You might start at the Kawatiri junction, turning off State Highway 6 as it hooks its way towards Nelson. This was the end of the line for the Nelson railway: a lonely station still stands in a paddock at Glenhope, further towards Nelson, but Kawatiri has only a platform. The station itself was open for just five years and 21 days before the line was abandoned, leaving a tunnel and a public walkway.

The road follows the Buller River to St Arnaud. If Kawatiri is the loneliest station outpost in the

RIGHT On the road to St Arnaud.

country, St Arnaud is the least-known lakeside resort. Lake Rotoiti is a gem. It is set in bush where introduced predators have been so well controlled that bush robins cluster when you stop on a walking track, and the morning chorus is back in business. The lake is lovely. It has a skifield and many great walks. It is on the edge of the Nelson Lakes National Park. But where is the resort impedimenta, the hotels and malls and holiday homes, the throngs? Notably absent. Only some 200 people live here. A lodge, a few motels, a cafe and baches and not far up the road the TopHouse, one of the famous accommodation houses once sited a day's ride apart through the mountains between Nelson and Canterbury.

Otherwise, walk for a few hundred metres and you're gloriously lonely.

Set off east. You drive on the north side of the Wairau River for while, then cross to the south.

You're following a fault line, appropriately, given the valley's violent history. When settlers tried to take the rich valley land in 1843 they were stopped at Tuamarina far downriver by the two great Ngati Toa chiefs Te Rauparaha and Te Rangiheata. Twenty-two Pakeha and four Maori died in the subsequent clash, once called the Wairau Massacre, then the Wairau Incident, and now reborn as the Wairau Affray. The Maori side of the argument was subsequently upheld by Governor Fitzroy but the valley was divided into three huge sheep runs anyway.

Now there's another fight over the valley. This one is a power scheme which sets out to divert most of the river through canals to generate electricity and provide irrigation. Opponents point out that the scheme would criss-cross the fault line, harm wildlife and ruin the river. The plan was approved by the Environment Court then put on hold by the promoter, Trustpower.

For now, the river stays in its natural state, a classic braided river flowing beside the road, while you, the driver, can enjoy the plus side of a fault line: incredible scenery. The Red Hills Range gives way to another, starting at Mount Patriarch, rising up from the valley floor like cliffs. It's a majestic parade and the road, on the other side of the river, gives a view so breathtaking you're held in thrall.

You come to Hillersden, although you have to be sharp to notice it: once, it was the centre of a huge station sweeping over the hills to the south before it was broken up, like its fellows, into smaller farms.

Wairau Valley town is the centre of civilisation here. After driving through this lonely valley you come on it quite suddenly: school, memorial hall, church, fire station, golf course and a pub that has served travellers for a century and a half. The fertile valley is now sprouting vineyards. Unusually for a small rural town, Wairau Valley's prospects for expansion are so bright that the local council is planning for growth.

You're not far from Renwick, where the road rejoins State Highway 6. But you pass one last place that has become part of the New Zealand lexicon: Waihopai. The government built a monitoring station here which is claimed by its detractors to be a foreign spybase on New Zealand soil. In 2008 three protesters broke in, damaged equipment, were charged and acquitted by a jury which agreed with the defendants 'claim of right' that they were protecting human life. The government sued for damages and won, but did not pursue its claim. Waihopai remains the subject of an annual protest camp near the Wairau river mouth. The protesters have succeeded, at least, in making this dot in a huge valley one of the world's worst-kept secrets.

BEAUMONT

TUAPEKA MOUTH

BALCLUTHA

BEAUMONT TO BALCLUTHA

'ONE OF THE MOST BEAUTIFUL GORGE JOURNEYS IN THE COUNTRY.'

THE BLUE MOUNTAIN ROAD

The Blue Mountains road runs south from Beaumont, Central Otago. State Highway 8, the route into Central Otago from Milton, crosses the Clutha River for the first time here. State Highway 8 is much more famous. It passes near Gabriels Gully, where the whole Otago gold rush began, and runs on up the Clutha to the very heart of golden Central.

So turning south at Beaumont is unusual, but worth it for the full Clutha experience. The Clutha is a mighty river, second-longest in New Zealand, dubbed by environmentalists 'one of the most extraordinary rivers on the planet'. Waters coloured turquoise by glaciers and snow-melt flow through high mountains, deep valleys and ancient glacial structures, the Snake, the Devil's Nook.

Its beauty is its undoing. Hydro-electric engineers found it shapely. They built two dams, at Roxburgh and Clyde, and wanted to build more above and

RIGHT The historic Tuapeka Mouth Ferry crossing the Clutha River.

below. Two were planned downstream, at Beaumont and Tuapeka Mouth. Some were horrified at the prospect, for reasons which included losing the town and ruining the river. Some were not, including those looking forward to selling their properties to the electricity company and others who looked enviously at Lake Dunstan behind the Clyde dam, their eyes glazed with dreams of a rich future in tourism. Contact Energy eventually headed off the debate by announcing that it wouldn't be building any more dams on the Clutha.

Which is good news for you as you set off south from Beaumont, for this is one of the most beautiful gorge journeys in the country. The road clings to the Clutha all the way to Tuapeka Mouth and for almost all of that journey runs through the Rongahere Gorge. Above the road rises forest that has stood for 12,000 years, the southernmost stand of red beech mixed with the rarer silver and black of the species mixed with kahikatea and matai. They are a refuge for endangered native birds including kakariki, the yellow-crested parakeet, mohua, the yellowhead and karearea, the New Zealand falcon.

The river's jewel in these lower reaches is Birch Island, otherwise known as a Noah's Ark for invertebrates: beetles, moths, snails, a trove of insects, some of them living fossils surviving unchanged for 570 million years. A kilometre long and an ecological treasure, Birch Island has stayed free of predators and since 2001 has been protected.

Now you feel especially lucky as you drive south, for all of this would have drowned under a hydro lake: biodiversity, farmland, orchards and homes.

And as you leave this wonderful gorge the Blue Mountains rise behind you, a bushy hump in the landscape, sometimes a shadowy blue, home to wild herds of fallow deer. It's a good drive on an easy road, the best kind for admiring this gorge.

You can drive on down to Clydevale and cross the Clutha on a bridge to carry on to Balclutha, and most cars do. But if you do that, you miss one of the world's rarest driving experiences, crossing the river on a punt. At Tuapeka Mouth the Tuapeka River joins the Clutha. Goldminers worked the Tuapeka right down to the mouth and even in 1945 a goldmining company here kept a few men on the job. Paddle steamers plied the river from Balclutha to the port of Tuapeka Mouth until World War II. The Tuapeka Mouth Ferry, or punt, opened on 22 February 1896 and has run ever since without changing much. It is New Zealand's only punt ferry and probably the only one in the southern hemisphere. I think it's the best car ferry crossing in New Zealand, challenged only by the Cook Strait ferry. This one is a whole lot shorter, cheaper and simpler.

The punt has no engines. It has nothing complicated at all. Two boat-like punts support a platform, the whole thing attached to a cable and using only the river's current to propel it sideways. You drive onto the platform and cross the river in eerie silence, sagging downstream in mid-river then miraculously moving upstream again and coming to rest in exactly the right spot to drive off. Astonishing, marvellous, you say, and the ferryman looks gratified although he has made the short voyage thousands of times.

Now you continue along the north bank of the Clutha. You drive through farmland with nothing much around so you're surprised when you come across a tiny place called Pukeawa, with its old church-turned-community hall. I passed through during a working bee. Where did all these people come from? Why do townspeople think the countryside is deserted?

The road ends at the curvaceous Balclutha bridge over the Clutha: its familiar concrete humps are the town's symbol. It is called, musically, a bowstring bridge, designed to resist earthquakes and floods, reassuring given the South Island's most common disasters. But they're another story.

- CHAPTER FIVE -

ODD ROADS

DRIVING ROUTES

1 ACROSS COOK STRAIT

2 CENTENNIAL HIGHWAY AND
TRANSMISSION GULLY

3 COBDEN TO IKAMATUA

4 OLD CHRISTCHURCH ROAD

5 HARPER PASS AND PORT AWANUI

LEFT Road along the
Kapiti Coast.

ACROSS COOK STRAIT

'SOMETIMES FERRIES DISAPPEARED COMPLETELY, AS IF THEY'D FOUND SOME BERMUDA TRIANGLE IN THE LATITUDES OF KARORI ROCK.'

No one ever speeds on the Iron Bridge. This is a slow road.

You arrive on time, an hour before the ferry sails. You wait. And wait.

Someone in a hi-vis jacket gives the signal to move. At last.

Anxiety kicks in. Why is she giving that line of cars the go-ahead? You were here before them. Queue-jumpers. They'll pinch all the good seats for sure. Maybe there won't be room for you. Perhaps the car won't start and you'll be stuck on the wharf. What if . . .?

Wait a minute. You're getting the signal. Your line is shuffled off to another car park. You stop, for so long there's absolutely no doubt about it: you've been abandoned.

Until, oh joy! Someone remembers you. She says sorry, something about trucks.

And off you go, along the wharf and up the ramp where your suspension breaks. The whole car is falling to pieces. That's going to cost. Hold on, it's only the tyres rattling over the steel grips. You're on!

The ship's engines rumble, Wellington starts moving past the windows. You're away, on the so-called 'iron bridge' between the two islands.

Gales and ripping tides make Cook Strait one of the most treacherous stretches of water in the world. Crossing between the islands was always an adventure. When I was a child the ferry left from Lyttelton, and if you were taking a car — only the super-rich ever did — it was driven onto a wooden platform on the wharf. A crane hoisted it into the air, swaying all over the place, the queues for the gangplank shuffling away nervously, for surely someone would forget the handbrake and over she'd go, *squash*. If someone did, I never heard about it.

Two ferries did the overnight service then, the *Hinemoa* and the *Rangatira*. They were household names. The merits of each were nationally debated, but they had a few things in common other than the traditional green hulls and red funnels: you were jammed into cabins with narrow bunks whose occupants were either drunk or sick or both, and you were woken at six by a stern steward who demanded you drink his tea and eat his two wine biscuits, for the

Union Steamship Company didn't trust you to get up on your own.

The *Wahine* tragedy in 1968 effectively ended the overnight ferry service. The company commissioned a new *Rangatira,* billed as a bigger and better *Wahine,* but it didn't take. We'd found other ways of crossing the Strait, and one of them was a new Picton-to-Wellington service on the *Aramoana.* The *Rangatira* sailed on until 1976 when the service ended, became a floating barracks during the Falklands war, and was eventually broken up in Turkey.

I once wrote that the new Picton ferry seemed to make the country a lot smaller, like taking the bends out of State Highway 1. Certainly it was easier, just a matter of driving on at one end and three and a half hours later driving off at the other. But these were the days of New Zealand Railways, who put their own stamp on the new service. Their food seemed to consist solely of mince on toast, although you only had their word for it: the grey mass assembled on your plate resembled neither, and you almost cheered the cooks and stewards when they went on strike. As they seemed to do whenever you wanted to cross the Strait.

Crossing Cook Strait then became even more interesting. Determined entrepreneurs had always

seen Cook Strait not so much as a vicious stretch of water as a monopoly in need of a challenge.

A parade of vessels followed. We saw ferries that went too fast, or too slow, or turned in circles when the rule of the sea suggested they'd best go straight ahead. Sometimes they disappeared off the run completely and were never heard of again, as if they'd found some Bermuda Triangle in the latitudes of Karori Rock.

The fast ferries didn't take either, and we went back to the good, solid, roll-on, roll-off, real, hefty ships. But at least there was a choice now, between New Zealand Railways' successor KiwiRail and Bluebridge. No mince on toast on either.

Some things don't change much. KiwiRail's pride and joy the *Aratere*, given a new bow and an extra funnel, lengthened and flashed-up, then broke down, was detained by Maritime New Zealand and finally, in November 2013, snapped a shaft and lost a propeller.

Today we're taking Bluebridge's *Straitsman.* We slip out of Wellington making scarcely a wave, around the corner where jailbirds in Mount Crawford once pined for a ride, past Eastbourne twinkling in the afternoon sun, the ship-eater Barrett Reef toothy on the other side, under the landing lights of an aircraft approaching the runway in Lyall Bay, leaving Karori

Rock on the right-hand side and setting off across the Strait.

Today, it's calm. The ship scarcely rolls. The café and the bar do good business. Once the done thing was to stake out a table in the bar and get in as many beers and pies as the human body could stand in three hours. Sometimes when the sea was rough, waves would break right over the superstructure and everyone in the bar would yahoo. For a little while anyway.

We've outgrown that. Haven't we? Perhaps. The Interislander website reports that 'Each year 96,578 pies and 63,210 litres of beer are consumed on board the *Kaitaki*.'

Backpackers stake out rows of seats and go to sleep.

We go through the sharks' teeth of the Tory Channel entrance. Captain James Cook wrote of the incredible stillness inside the Marlborough Sounds after the storm without. Past the new industries of the Sounds, salmon and mussel farming. Past pine forests. Past places where pine forests have been, hillsides stripped bare as a Tegel chicken. Whoever thought it a good idea to allow forestry in this fragile landscape?

Baches snuggle in green bays. A hard right turn then a sharp left around Dieffenbach Point. Then a straight run down to Picton, which seems to have cheered up after the government ditched the idea of moving the ferry terminal to Clifford Bay near Lake Grassmere.

Please go to your cars, says the loudspeaker, like the start of a Grand Prix. Across the deck, down the rumbly ramp. The best drive you can have without driving.

ABOVE Queuing for the ferry.

PAEKAKARIKI

TRANSMISSION GULLY

PAUATAHANUI

LINDEN

WELLINGTON

DREAM ROAD

CENTENNIAL HIGHWAY AND TRANSMISSION GULLY

'THE NEW MILLENNIUM WAS GOING BADLY. CARS WERE PLOUGHING INTO EACH OTHER AT AN AWFUL RATE.'

No one would have thought in 1940, the good old days of the Centennial Highway, that their creation would become an accident black spot, subject of countless inquiries. The 1940 Centennial was a rah-rah event designed by the Labour government to revive the pioneer spirit with a spot of progress. In a rush of rebranding, the section of State Highway 1 between the Ngauranga Gorge and Paekakariki became the Centennial Highway.

The Pukerua to Paekakariki coastal strip, opened in 1939, lay right beside the original foot track of the 1840s. If you stand at Pukerua Bay it's not hard to see why. There's nowhere else it could go. The Paekakariki hills become one long, spectacular precipice here, dropping to the sea. When you've squeezed in a

railway line as well as a state highway there's nowhere to fit anything more. As the number of cars and trucks on the road increased, it became a dangerous bottleneck.

The highway begins on the edge of Wellington Harbour, soaring up the Ngauranga Gorge in several lanes before levelling out. It always seems rather cold and dark, although when the first European settlers arrived they were welcomed by the Te Atiawa chief Te Wharepouri who had his kainga here.

Then comes the most claustrophobic section of motorway in the country by my count. Traffic is hemmed in by high walls and barriers. They seem to press against the sides of the car. Noise ricochets. Anxiety amps up. Suburbs whip by — Newlands,

ABOVE Travelling up Ngauranga Gorge, Wellington, c. 1939.

Johnsonville, Tawa — but this is no time for admiring the Wellington townscape. Your nose sticks over the edge of the steering wheel like Kilroy's. Your knuckles gleam white in the gloom, for it's drizzling.

Porirua is not usually seen as one of our more beautiful cities except when viewed from north-bound motorway lanes. Then it becomes the symbol of hope and, more important, the progress which that Labour government intended. Yippee, you think, the worst lies behind. You're wrong.

Certainly, as it roars downhill the silvery Porirua Harbour appears ahead alluring as a lagoon, if short on palms. Intriguing Paremata is off to one side with a nice array of boatsheds and moored boats down on the water. The road sweeps easily up towards Pukerua Bay. Oh marvellous, you say, especially as you pass the top of the hill and the full joy of the Kapiti coast opens below. Then, oh yes! The road follows the coast. Well, perhaps not so much follows as trespasses on it, the sea breaking against the seawall and the rocks beside you.

You can't see the Paekakariki Hill Road from here, for it sneaks through the Horokiwi Valley. To get onto it you drive to Pauatahanui and branch off from there. For almost a century from 1849 this was the main road north to Paekakariki following first a Maori track then a military road built during the conflict between Ngati Toa and the colonial government. It was the way north until the new coastal road opened properly on Christmas Eve 1939.

Back on the Centennial Highway, the coastal road, the new millennium was going badly. Cars were ploughing into each other along the coastal road at an awful rate: in one year seven people died in four head-on crashes. This was the famous war chief Te Rauparaha's rohe and if he had been around a century or so later he would not have bothered killing his enemies, he would just have bought them a car and sent them north on the expressway.

Road authorities settled on a solution: a wire

barrier built along 3.5 kilometres of highway. The idea now was to get as close to the car in front and to 100 km/h at the same time. The death rate fell, but the journey north remained messy and slow.

New Zealanders' ingenuity with wire is legendary, but it was not the long-term answer here. That came in the form of a road famously known as the Transmission Gully highway.

Debated for decades, the road is at last ready for the off. The plan is for the new expressway to branch off the present highway at Linden, just before Porirua. It will poke through Wellington's short steep hills returning close to its origins as it passes Pauatahanui, and rejoin the present route at a new interchange just north of Paekakariki at McKays Crossing.

The US Second Marine Corps camped here in 1942-43, training for their war in the Pacific. The war over the new motorway lasted much longer. The new road was expected to cost $3.1 billion and could be a toll road. Eventually it will roll on to Otaki.

The coastal road will become a secondary route, part of the good old days.

Map locations: IKAMATUA, BLACKBALL, COBDEN, TAYLORVILLE

GHOST ROAD

COBDEN TO IKAMATUA

'YOU CAN STILL SEE WHERE THEY'VE BEEN AS YOU DRIVE, SOLEMNLY, THROUGH THIS PLACE.'

The main road from Greymouth to Reefton follows the south bank of the Grey River but there's another, more moving and much more intriguing way of covering part of that journey. A drive into the past. From Greymouth you go north of the bridge but instead of driving on to Rununga turn off the road at the sign pointing to Taylorville. Very soon you are back on the Grey, but on its north side.

I last drove along here when the valley was filled with drizzle and mist, cursing my luck.

As it happened, my luck was in. Thick West Coast bush seemed to press against the side of the car, felt rather than seen. Spectral shapes rose from the fog. The old mining town of Taylorville suddenly appeared, the ghost of the metropolis it once was, the West Coast palette of brown-rusted corrugated iron and rotting wood generously sprinkled through it. A pub right on the road, an old general store, an ancient lodge which

must have held hundreds, a bright bus shelter with a painted nikau palm and a mauve bus behind shining through the murk. Oxford and Cambridge Streets spoke of grander days. Waterloo, Nile, Wellington and Trafalgar pretty much concluded the streetscape. The school here was once the second biggest in the whole Grey Education Board's area, capable of taking up to 400 students in its lofty classrooms.

The town's prosperity went back to 1848 when Maori, who knew the site well, took the explorer Thomas Brunner up the Grey River by canoe. He discovered a rich coal seam on the north bank at the place first called Brunnerton, now Brunner. Ngai Tahu worked the seam first, and Pakeha followed in the mid-1860s. By the 1880s the mine produced more coal than any other in the land.

The Grey River ran through the middle of Brunnerton borough, which included Stillwater on

ABOVE Brunner bridge and township, c. 1880.

the other side of the river, and Taylorville, and Dobson, and other places vanished from maps. It was miners' heaven. But mining waxes and wanes and often leaves destruction in its wake. Relics lie all over the West Coast. At the edge of Taylorville you get the first signpost to disaster: a memorial statue. On 26 March 1896, headlines in the *Nelson Evening Mail* proclaimed a tragedy at Brunnerton. An explosion had ripped through the mine. 'Sixty men entombed with no hope of rescue. Two men already dead. Heart-rending scenes at the pit mouth. Wives of entombed men weeping piteously.'

The final death toll was 65 men and boys. Brunnerton died more slowly. The last coal was taken from the mine in 1942. Surrounding mines on the coalfield decayed and disappeared. Dobson across the river, which had its own explosion in 1926 killing nine miners, was the last to go, lingering until 1968. A district where 90 per cent of men were employed in the industry couldn't absorb the blows. It shrank as the mines died.

You can still see where they've been as you drive, solemnly, through this place. Beehive-shaped coke ovens, brickworks, tunnels, remains of old mine buildings and machinery, graves. The suspension bridge across the Grey linking Buller and Stillwater has been restored. But you stay on your side of the river and drive on to Blackball, the town which just won't die. Blackball mined coal too, but here eating a meat pie had consequences lasting right up to now.

In 1908, Pat Hickey, a miner's union leader, refused to go back to work when his 15-minute lunch break ended because he had not finished his pie. He was fired. The Miners' Union went on a strike which they won so resoundingly that a national Federation of Labour was founded. The Labour Party was born in this town and it was once the headquarters of the Communist Party.

The mine closed in 1964 and two years later a flood

RIGHT The townships of Taylorville (foreground), and Wallsend (over the Grey River), 1951.

carried away the bridge over the Grey and the railway line to Blackball was closed. The town was expected to vanish into the bush, although so many books (notably Bill Pearson's *Coal Flat*), plays, songs and poems have been written about the place that it would still live on forever. Instead, reports of its death were exaggerated.

The town is burgeoning. Even on a dull day it still seems vibrant. The hotel, called 'Formerly the Blackball Hilton' after a dispute over names with the international hotel chain, is the de facto town centre, its weekends thronged with events.

In the 1970s you could buy an old miner's cottage here for a few dollars. Many did, and kept alive the basics of a town, the stores and ambulance, swimming pool and tennis courts. Now many of those cottages have been restored and all of them come at a price. Blackball salami is as famous as the miner's pie. Locals now boast of a population of 370 and rising, a thriving school and playcentre, a community. The road runs on up this gloomy, beautiful valley to Ikamatua, which claims to be the driest town on the West Coast but not in the usual sense: it gets less rain.

HOKITIKA • • • OLD CHRISTCHURCH ROAD

THE LITERARY ROUTE

OLD CHRISTCHURCH ROAD

'IT ENDS IN A TWIST.'

The Old Christchurch Road has become New Zealand's most literary road. It is signposted off State Highway 73, the West Coast highway, about halfway between Aickens where the road leaves the Otira River and turns west, and Kumara Junction, where it ends. The road didn't always run down the Taramakau River as it does now. Instead, the main road ran from Christchurch, over Arthur's Pass and on to the centre of West Coast civilisation, Hokitika.

The West Coast gold rush gave wings to the work and the first Cobb & Co coach rattled over the road in 1866. It remained the only route between Canterbury and the West Coast until 1923. This was the road made famous by Eleanor Catton in her huge novel, *The Luminaries*, which won the 2013 Man Booker Prize.

The road lies at the centre of Catton's plot. On 14 January 1866, the hermit Crosbie Wells is found dead in his home on the Arahura River. The timber box, drenched in 'the smell of loneliness', lies some kilometres up the river, 'plainly visible from the Christchurch road'. That night, Anna Wetherell, a whore, is found unconscious on the Christchurch road, and Emery Staines, a local magnate, goes missing. The plot revolves around these three events and the Christchurch road runs between them.

Well, most of the old road has been buried beneath the new, or bypassed. Unusually, rail superseded road here, for a while at least. A railway line was driven inland from both coasts and finally, in one last massive effort, through the Main Divide itself. The Otira Tunnel, burrowed under the mountains, opened

ABOVE Taramakau, West Coast, sometime between 1900 and 1930.

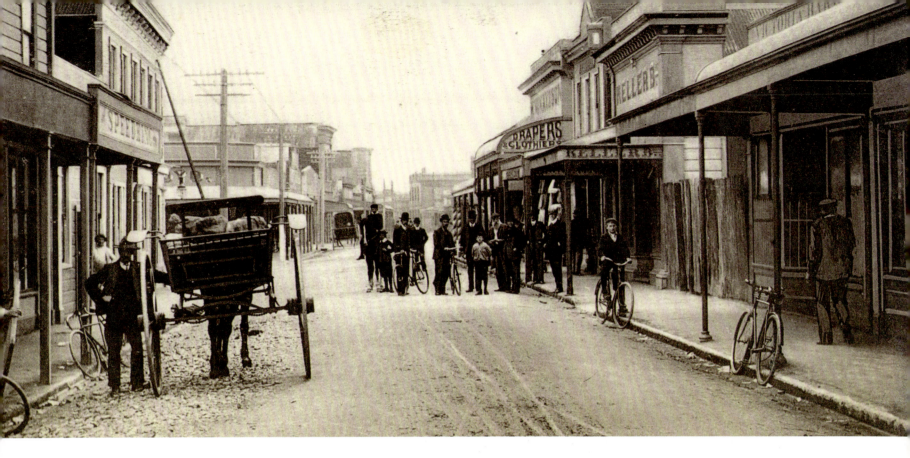

in 1923, and that year the last Cobb & Co coach made the journey.

The road languished, although it had never been popular. Even in the gold rush merchants and bankers preferred sea routes. Always dreadful, often closed, usually dangerous, it was so unattractive that for quite some time the preferred method of taking cars between coasts was loading them onto railway wagons.

The road has constantly been rebuilt and realigned, so that it now carries traffic to the coast before turning south for Hokitika. But a short segment branching off the main road into the Arahura Valley and making for Hokitika, the Old Christchurch Road central to Catton's plot remains intact.

Travelling from Hokitika it runs off the coastal road on the north side of the Arahura River, one small sign indicating the Old Christchurch Road. It's a sealed road at first, too narrow for a centre line, neatly edged but rather strange, for it is raised up high so you feel as if you're driving along an old embankment. Immediately it passes the new Arahura marae, which must be smartest in the country. It is marked as a school bus route, far from poor Crosbie Wells, and would be unremarkable but for the sense that you're driving through both history and literature.

This is the West Coast, and seal soon turns to gravel. Soon you're among the familiar mixture of scraggy paddocks and bush, then quickly, just bush. The Arahura Valley sweeping up to the mountains is sometimes visible below.

It is a short drive. It ends in a twist, circling through the pass separating the two valleys in a tight 'S'. I emerged on the smooth wide tarmac of the West Coast highway confused, not knowing which way to turn. A bit like the plot of *The Luminaries*.

PORT AWANUI

LAKE TAYLOR

HAWARDEN

WAIKARI

RUATORIA

VANISHED ROADS

HARPER PASS AND PORT AWANUI

'THE LANDSCAPE FEELS EMPTY, AND YOU HAVE THAT OTHER-WORLDLY FEELING.'

Once, all of Canterbury wanted to rush to the West Coast. The reason was gold. They'd found plenty of it on the Coast. Cantabrians envied Coasters. They were desperate to get together but something came between them: very high mountains. The Main Divide, the Southern Alps. Even now there are only three passes. In 1865 there were none.

Canterbury folk were impatient. Arthur Dobson had discovered Arthur's Pass. J.S. Browning found Browning Pass. But they needed a road.

Leonard Harper came from a different direction. He persuaded Tainui, from Kaiapoi near Christchurch, to show him a well-known Maori route. They went up the headwaters of the Hurunui River in North Canterbury and crossed the Main Divide over a pass which became known as Harper's. On the other side they travelled down to the Taramakau River past the bend now called Aickens on the West Coast Highway.

Heading west, the highway turns sharply at Aickens and follows the Otira River up to the Main Divide. If you're driving that way you see the Harper Pass far up the Taramakau looking attractively, but deceptively, low and gentle.

The government thought it tempting too. It decided to cut a road over the pass although it was not the preferred choice. For one thing, it was the long way round: traffic had to head more than 70 kilometres north of Christchurch before turning left for the mountains.

But by February 1865, gold fever was running high. Cobb's coaches were full of miners making their way to the Hurunui and over Harper Pass: in one week, more than a thousand men. Gangs began working on the new road.

Still, the Canterbury provincial government felt there had to be a better way to the Coast. George Dobson was rushed off to his brother Arthur's pass to see whether a road could run that way instead.

The rest, obviously, is history.

Work on the Harper Pass road, being pushed through from both the Canterbury and West Coast ends, stopped. The route was largely abandoned until the 1930s, when it was reopened with several huts in an effort to copy the famed Milford Track. It's now a popular route — for trampers.

The present-day road runs through Waikari and Hawarden, turns into a winding shingle track and pushes into the mountains at Jacks Saddle. This route is still well used. It leads on to lakes and keeps close company with the Hurunui River, running deep and green alongside. It is popular with anglers and whitewater enthusiasts.

Nor does it forget its history. It follows the original track and at several places along the route you can stop and admire the careful stone-work of those early road-builders, so well done it has lasted a century and a half.

The road nods at its origins in Maori Gully, recognising the Ngai Tahu who used the route as one of their pounamu trails between Canterbury and the West Coast, using flax ladders to cross gullies. The name now encompasses the whole gorge, the river turning to white water as it rushes through the bush.

A grog shop for thirsty miners once stood where the south branch of the Hurunui joins the river. But this is the road that never was. It stops at Lake Taylor, the first of three lakes on the way to the Divide. The smaller Loch Katrine is next, followed by the more expansive Lake Sumner. Little lakes lie all around.

Signs warn that the road from Lake Taylor onwards is for four-wheel-drive traffic only. It struggles on for a while and then becomes the track familiar to both Harper and Ngai Tahu.

In the meantime, the signs are right. The last time I drove over it my small Japanese saloon laboured through deep furrows, over hills of mud and through potholes full of water and, like the Harper Pass road itself, expired.

PORT AWANUI was one of the three vanished ports of the East Coast, along with Waipiro Bay and Tuparoa. It is on the map still. You turn off State Highway 35, the East Coast highway, at Ruatoria and follow the Waiapu River, slipping through gullies and around stumpy hills. The road is deserted, the landscape feels empty, and you have that other-worldly feeling you get often on the East Coast.

On the most direct road you arrive at a farm gate. If you went on, you'd drop down a valley and over a bluff directly into the old port. But you cannot, for the gate is locked.

So you go back to the road you came from and drive on to a beach where a sign announces that you are at Te Horo. Without the sign, you might not have known. Surf pounds on shingle, foam flies high in the air. The East Cape's blunt snout sniffs the wind to the north, its little knob of an island at its end.

But we're not at the vanished port of Awanui, yet. It lies to the south. A kind of track sets off along the foreshore to where it once was. Port Awanui was a busy place. Manuel Jose, a rather mysterious Spaniard, arrived here in the 1830s. He set up a trading store. The port flourished, two hotels (one can still be seen, moved to the East Coast town of Tikitiki), post office, police station, a whaling station, all the trappings of a big town. Ships anchored offshore and sent their boats to the port through the surf. A precarious anchorage and a perilous journey. Sailors must have cheered when improved roads made the place redundant.

All that's left is an olive tree planted by Manuel Jose, a whalers' trypot and a Spanish fiesta, both in the East Cape town of Te Araroa, and a remarkable number of Ngati Porou with the name 'Manuel' in their whakapapa. Other than the tree the port town has disappeared. The road to such a town must have been substantial, once. It has gone, too. The road that was.

PREVIOUS SPREAD Lake Sumner Road, Hawarden, Hurunui District.

ABOVE Port Awanui, c. 1910.

RIGHT Ruatoria Hotel, on the road to Port Awanui.

- CHAPTER SIX -

FERAL ROADS

DRIVING ROUTES

1 HAAST

2 KUROW TO BURKES PASS

3 THE OLD DUNSTAN ROAD

4 THE NEVIS VALLEY

5 SKIPPERS CANYON

6 TOPHOUSE ROAD

LEFT Nevis road.

BRUCE BAY

HAAST PASS

WANAKA

THE LOWEST PASS

HAAST

'A RUFFIAN EVEN AMONG THE ROUGH.'

On the evening of 10 September 2014 two young Canadian tourists were driving south over the Haast Pass. A fierce storm slashed the dark. They didn't know it, but the road was being closed behind them.

No one knows exactly what happened to them. The best guess, from the police, was that they found the road blocked by a rockfall at a notoriously unstable stream called Pipson Creek, near the equally infamous Diana Falls. They'd turned back only to find their retreat blocked by another slip at a feature ironically called The Trickle. They'd turned around again, parked, and were swept off the road into the flooded Haast River by yet another fall.

The Canadian couple were not missed for six days. Then the woman, Joanna Lam, who was a sonographer, did not turn up to her new job at Nelson Hospital. The alarm was raised. Next day the police found what was left of their rented campervan squashed like a bug on a rock in the river. Three days later Lam's body was washed into a South Westland beach north of the Haast river mouth. Her partner, Connor Hayes, disappeared forever.

All West Coast highways are precarious. The region clings to the coast, jammed between high mountains and the Tasman Sea. But the Haast Pass is a ruffian even among the rough. For all of 2014 and most of 2013 it seldom missed a mention in the NZ Transport Authority's monthly road warnings.

Slips at Diana Falls closed the road to night-time traffic for 14 months. On 5 November 2014 it was officially reopened to 24-hour traffic and the day before Christmas Eve to two-lane traffic.

Above the road the most complex slip-prevention system in Australasia held back the rocks. Below it, the Haast River ran the spectrum between roaring and rage.

Whole industries and especially tourism, the West Coast's main employer, depend on the Haast Pass. Holiday-park owners, car-rental agencies, hotels and motels, tour businesses, cafés and restaurants all count on the road for a living. The local economy stumbles when it is blocked. When the pass is closed they might as well be too. A lot more than cars rides on this road.

The NZ Transport Authority announcement of its full-time reopening 'in time for the busy tourist summer season' was gratefully received, with

reservations: locals knew their unruly country well. Even before the year was out, the road had been closed several more times.

The Haast was always a tough route. Maori used it for the same reason the colonists did: for access between the West Coast and Otago. The Ngati Tama chief Te Puoho led a raiding party over the route in 1836 to attack the Ngai Tahu. (The raid proved fatal for Te Puoho and most of his party.)

The Haast is the lowest of the three mountain passes between east and west, not counting the Homer Tunnel, which goes under rather than over. Julius von Haast, explorer and geologist, claimed to have been the first European over it although a prospector named Charles Cameron reckoned *he* was the first. Cameron was vindicated a few years later when his powder flask was discovered on Mount Cameron directly to the west of the pass.

Richard Seddon, West Coaster and New Zealand Premier from the late 19th century, promised Coasters a road from South Westland to Otago. In the meantime people had to make do with the packhorse track which since 1880 had carried goldminers, drovers and settlers over the pass.

The track remained the main route until 1929. Then, hundreds of men displaced by the Great Depression were put to work pushing a road north from Hawea. They had reached the Gates of Haast when war broke out. The road work stopped as men swapped picks for rifles. It did not start again until 1956. In fact it was some seven decades after Seddon made his promise before the new road was completely opened in 1965, and another three decades before it was sealed in 1995.

The highway quickly became famous. With the lovely Lake Wanaka at one end and the primeval South Westland at the other, it was a round trip that tourists from New Zealand and abroad just had to do.

Five years after it opened, it was the most discussed road in the country. The body of Jennifer Mary Beard, a Welsh hitch-hiker, travelling through the Haast to meet her fiancé in Milford, was found under the Haast River Bridge on 19 January 1970. She had been sexually assaulted and strangled.

Beard had been seen last in the company of a middle-aged man driving a greeny-blue Vauxhall. There were some 33,000 of the cars in New Zealand then and the police checked all of them. They came up with a prime suspect, a Timaru man. He was

PREVIOUS SPREAD Going over the Haast after a storm, dark and alien.

ABOVE Cars on the (then) new Haast Pass road, 1966.

not charged and died in 2003. The killing was never solved. The nation took her murder as a personal affront. People talked of little else. Even now individuals are still coming up with new leads, all of them followed up by police, none of them leading anywhere.

As for the Haast, its reputation went from wild to savage.

When I drove over the Haast for the first time I stopped at the bridge and walked around underneath it wondering what the rocks knew. The sun was shining but this place seemed dark, and cold, and I hurried away.

In the 21st century something more lethal than middle-aged men in Vauxhalls has menaced Haast traffic. The glacial pedigree of the valley and its surrounding mountains has haunted the roadmakers since the beginning. The trouble with mountains, an engineer once remarked to me, is that they want to become plains. The trouble with the mountains beside the Haast Pass Road is that they do not so much

'want' as have an overwhelming desire to fall down.

Despite the optimism of the November 2014 announcement, no one really believes that the road's troubles are over. The Diana Falls slips are more than mere humans can contain. The road engineers have done their best, but the rockfalls continue.

So when I set out to drive over the pass in early December 2014, I was not surprised to find a sign at Lake Hawea advising that the road was closed and it would not reopen until 11pm that night. The pass was up to its old tricks.

It was then 6.30 pm, a fine time for the beautiful drive along the lakeside and over the low saddle separating Hawea from its neighbour. The late afternoon sun played on Lake Wanaka and etched dark folds into the hills. A barrier stopped traffic at the Makarora pub the last oasis before Haast township on the other side. Only mountains and beech forest lie between.

The woman responsible for shifting the barrier was behind the bar. She reckoned it would be more like midnight before the road reopened. Another woman said, 'We've lost two.' I realised she was talking about the two tourists, the community talking responsibility for them, and us too.

Meanwhile, it was happy hour at the bar. Locals and travellers mingled.

The mountains grew grim in the way they do at night. The fading sun caught a waterfall, a trickle of light on the mountainside. A tough little wind tore at the trees. It was shaping up for a good Haast night. The drive is always an adventure.

I drove around the barrier and stopped at the pass. It is quite gentle, not high, set in bush without the drama of other passes. If it wasn't for a plaque you'd scarcely know you were there. The plaque says that this was an old Maori route used by Charles Cameron and Julius von Haast. Several other cars were parked and I went to sleep. Around 11 pm I heard a vehicle come past the other way, reasoned that the road must be open (it was), and decided to try my luck.

The Diana Falls area lay a little to the north, unmistakable. A maze of road cones was arranged on a bare surface to direct traffic, or possibly did in daylight. This night they were just a maze. The place was deserted. I seemed to be in the only car in the world.

I thought of the billions of tonnes of rock in the blackness above, cradled in a web of high-tensile steel, and prayed it would hold for just a bit longer. I thought of the Haast River below. I thought of the Canadian couple and felt their terror as they sat trapped in their van in the dark alien world crashing around them.

All the stories came back that night. I wished I'd stayed on the pass at least until morning. But I was on a tight schedule. A few days later the *Greymouth Star,* under a picture of great slabs of bald rock, reported that the road was closed again. Boulders 'the size of houses' were getting in the way of its reopening, 'adding to nervousness among South Westland business owners.'

I inched down that road with everything crossed, and over the Gates of Haast Bridge. What an ominous name. I could sense the hounds of hell.

Over the Haast bridge without a thought for Jennifer Beard, thinking only of getting away.

Yet I did not. Oh yes, I reached South Westland, and threaded my way around Lakes Moeraki and Paringa. Somewhere past Bruce Bay I rounded a bend and sensed something different in the darkness ahead. Then it moved, resolved into two black cattle standing in the middle of the road.

For a split second we regarded each other in horror. I aimed the car between them, hopelessly. I'd once seen what could happen when a car hit a cow; it had gone over the bonnet, through the windscreen, and killed the driver.

Both sides of the car were struck at once. The headlights went out. I was in total darkness. I stopped a little further around the bend. Climbed out. One headlight was missing. I slapped the other and miraculously it came on. Drove back, wondering how to clear two huge corpses off the road.

The animals were gone. They were off the road, both standing, looking at me reproachfully. No houses, no lights, no gates, no fences. No mobile phone reception either.

I drove on very slowly, until I got a signal, telephoned the local constable, left a message, parked for the rest of the night. Within five minutes my phone rang. 'Police HQ,' said a woman's voice. Stock on the road? Where? South of the Jacobs River? Had I talked to someone? No one to speak to? This was dangerous. Police would have to track down the owner forthwith.

I wished her luck. I felt she hadn't quite got the hang of the country down there. Slept until first light, then inspected the damage. It was bad. This was a rugged, rented 4WD. Cows 1, 4WD nil.

That's the pass. If it doesn't get you one way, it finds another.

RIGHT Clearing another rockfall from the Haast Pass Road – a constant task.

KUROW TO BURKES PASS

THE HAKA HIGHWAY

'DON'T BE DISTRACTED BY THE BEST VIEW IN NEW ZEALAND, THE SOUTH PACIFIC, POSSIBLY THE WHOLE WORLD.'

Most people heading north from the lakes take the smooth road through the Mackenzie Country from Omarama. But, if you're adventurous, have the time, and want the best view in all New Zealand, you could take the Haka Highway.

You set off from Kurow, whose favourite son Richie McCaw, the great All Black captain, left the building quite some time ago but lives forever in its heart. The other big news in Kurow has been how to get out of town. From 1881 two one-way wooden bridges carried road and rail traffic across the mighty Waitaki River to Hakataramea on the north bank. At 662 metres long they were among the longest wooden structures of the age.

Locals fretted: 132 in wooden-bridge years made them ancient structures. What if they fell down? They were the main link between Kurow and the north by way of Waimate. If the main bridge over the Waitaki at Glenavy was closed, there'd be no detour through Kurow for State Highway 1 traffic. As for the Hakataramea Valley, why, it would be isolated or, rather, *more* isolated.

So now you cross the Waitaki from Kurow on two fine new concrete bridges. If, like me, you rather liked the old wooden ones, you're in luck: the plan was to preserve sections of them for display on what is called Kurow Island, lying in the middle of the Waitaki between the two bridges.

You cross the river nicely insulated from the torrent below and find yourself immediately in Hakataramea. This town was once ambitious. A railway line ran to it, over the bridge from Kurow. It was to have been extended up the Hakataramea Valley through a new town of 10,000 people. Neither the town nor the railway line ever happened. Hakataramea remained the terminus until 1930, when the line stopped instead at Kurow. Now it's a tiny town where traffic going north over the bridge usually turns right and heads off to join State Highway 1 at Studholme.

Instead, today, we're heading north through the Hakataramea Valley where there's absolutely no trace of a town, imaginary or otherwise.

The *New Zealand Railways Magazine* noted in 1938 that:

Between the last ramparts of the Mackenzie Country in the south-west corner of Canterbury and the Waihao basin of fertile downlands south-eastwards, lies the broad valley of the Hakataramea, 25 miles in length. Today this is practically a closed valley. But when the other 20 miles of road across the Hakataramea Pass is made, it will [. . .] be a direct route for tourist traffic between Lake Tekapo and the scenic area round the new Lake Waitaki.

Well, it's direct all right, but not much tourist traffic is using it today. The road sets out over a saddle then drops into the broad river valley flats. A nice, lonely country road minding its own business with no traffic other than the odd farm ute, straights so long you welcome a bend or a bridge; one-way, for there is no other kind.

The valley is separated from the Mackenzie Country by tough-looking ranges, although it is a whole geological shift away. In this valley enormous baleen whale fossils, 23 million years old, have been found, for this was once part of a shallow inland sea. Scientists working on their recovery regard the area as one of the planet's last fossil frontiers and it is certainly true, as you look around, that this is rural New Zealand in aspic. The road goes by farms, and more farms, and just to make sure, past Farm Road. It's as green on this side of the ranges as the Mackenzie Country is gold on the other.

No cafés, burger stops, gas stations, picnic areas, big houses or welcome signs.

Wait! Here's a place: Cattle Creek! An old hall. An old school. This was the Cattle Creek School, which, by September 2004, had run out of pupils. Completely. The next month it closed. School, hall, swimming pool, tennis courts, all that work and community effort, were put up for sale.

This is the end of civilisation as we knew it. The seal stops. Still 72 kilometres to Tekapo. Ahead, several dust trails. Hang on, there is only one, divided into little puffs hanging in the still air like smoke signals. Pale blue sky, brown hills to the left, brown mountains to the right. The car's rear window itself takes on the look of a clay hillside, now and then collapsing in little avalanches of dirt.

Even farmhouses become scarce. Car, don't break down. Help seems a very long way away.

Hawks glide and swoop. A few sheep run beside the road then, in that way sheep have, in front of the

car. Who says they're dumb?

A sign. 'Caution. Narrow roads. Steep grades. Fords. Snow. Ice. Drive carefully.' The sign-writer had a sense of humour.

We roll through a farmyard. You don't see that often. 'Close the gates', says a sign.

The dust road narrows. A man on a quad bike in a paddock, dogs on the carrier, stares, waves. The puffs of dust ahead dissolve into a ute parked in a farm gate. This time the dogs stare.

Now we are alone in a tawny world. A sign points to a pass in the hills ahead. The road gives up going straight and turns crooked, shimmying around hills, through creeks, following a valley somewhere in the headwaters of the Hakataramea.

A tail twitches. We just miss a cow's backside, sticking out of a matagouri bush. No room to swerve. The cow looks as if it might wave, too, but goes back to eating instead.

We go through a ford. I think I hear the tyres hiss but it may be my passenger. A rock scree leads away up the mountainside. Then another ford. Impossibly, the road narrows even more. Forty-five kilometres to Tekapo now. That's reassuring. Only another two hours at the present average speed.

The mountains on either side grow closer. They squeeze. We pop out, onto a smooth saddle between the ranges. The Hakataramea Pass at last!

And a gate: 'Keep shut at all times'. In other words, close the bloody gate and don't be distracted by the most spectacular view in New Zealand, the South Pacific, possibly at that moment the whole world! It is so sharp, so huge, it seems to penetrate your eyes.

The Mackenzie Country spreads itself far in front of us. Mount Cook rises into the pale sky with its acolytes ranged attentively on either side. Shadowed white and silver, still, secret, impervious. So much New Zealand in just one view, so impressive.

This is James McKenzie's country, the wide, empty

basin where he and his dog Friday drove thousands of sheep stolen from Canterbury farmers. He used passes then unknown to Europeans, for McKenzie was an explorer as well as a sheep-stealer. One of those secret routes became the McKenzie Pass, and that's where McKenzie was caught. He had stolen a thousand sheep from the Two Levels Station owned by the Rhodes brothers and this time he was tracked and captured. He was tried and imprisoned in Lyttelton jail, escaped twice then was pardoned within a year, so flawed was his trial.

For all the thousands of words written about McKenzie, little is known about him, not even how he spelled his name: it is 'McKenzie' in the records, 'Mackenzie' in the place names he left over this region. The legend simply grew, and the romance bloomed in the fine, free air of the Mackenzie Country.

The Mackenzie Pass lies only 20 kilometres in a direct line from the Hakataramea. The road is tight and the ranges so uniform that as you scan them you understand why McKenzie's route remained his secret. Why this peak rather than that? This gap more than the next?

Back at the Hakataramea road the surface improves a little. Now it is merely rough. Another ford, deeper, bigger rocks. The faithful car seems to brace itself, grunts, dives in, climbs the rockface. Cattle stops, more fords. A magpie attacks a hawk.

Twenty-five kilometres to go. Another dust plume. I wouldn't be surprised if McKenzie himself came riding out of the hills. Now other dust trails appear. Perhaps there is still life on earth? Certainly there is plenty of earth on life. The car looks like an Afghan refugee.

An intersection at last: Haldon Road. The station lies at the other end. We turn away and the god of roads blesses us for suddenly there's tarmac. Fences, distant homesteads, power lines.

The road through the Mackenzie Pass turns off to the right. It wriggles between the Dalgety and Rollesby ranges then sneaks through hills until it emerges near Fairlie in South Canterbury. The Haka Highway goes on to Burkes Pass and Dog Kennel corner, where some lonely hound was once based to keep stock within the boundary. Civilisation. Isn't life wonderful?

It's hard to believe on a fine day but Burkes Pass is a mountain pass with all the wintry character of the breed: snow, ice and a sharp gradient to slip on. Michael Burke may not have been the first European through the pass in 1855, but he was the one who left his name on it. The road was first a dray track into the Mackenzie Country, then a road. So Burkes Pass became a stop for teamsters and travellers and was called Cabbage Tree Creek before it grew into a town. My family often stayed at the Burkes Pass Hotel, largely built of sod and the first licensed hotel in Canterbury: it burned down in 1994. Now several cob cottages made of clay, straw, earth and water have been restored along with other buildings including the little white weatherboard church, St Patrick's. A modern pioneer, Sir William Hamilton, inventor of the jet boat, is buried in the cemetery.

The village has an air of care and attention and the excitement of a pass, that feeling of adventure. There's wild country beyond, and you're on the brink of it.

RIGHT A fine display of lupins brightens the Mackenzie Country.

OLD DUNSTAN RD
LOGANBURN RESERVOIR
CLARKS JUNCTION
OUTRAM

THE OLD DUNSTAN ROAD

'THE MOST DIRECT, THE COLDEST, THE ROUGHEST AND DEFINITELY THE MOST INTERESTING ROUTE BETWEEN DUNEDIN AND CENTRAL OTAGO.'

GOLD FEVER

Passing through the lovely old village of Outram early in the morning is not the last near-mystical experience travellers can expect from the Old Dunstan Road, but it is a promising start. Early-morning mist steals through the town, sneaking up the hills, covering the horizon like a show about to start, then parting with a flourish. Introducing: the Rock and Pillars.

A sign warns that distracted drivers are dangerous. But are there any other kind on this spectacular road?

The Old Dunstan Road is the most direct, the coldest, the roughest, and definitely the most

RIGHT The Old Dunstan Road still behaving itself as it approaches the Rock and Pillars.

INSET Rock formation, 'Old Woman on Leaning Rock', on the summit of the Dunstan Range.

interesting route between Dunedin and Central Otago. The miners who built the road were only interested in the first. In the summer of 1862–63 they wanted to get into the Dunstan gold rush just as soon as they possibly could. The road got them there, but not quickly. It crossed no fewer than four mountain ranges. The route was both high altitude and exposed. Even now it is closed in winter, from the beginning of June to the end of September. Snow, rain and ice make it impassable, but if you were a miner driven by gold fever you had no option: you took your chances, and a miserable journey it must have been.

From the air this country is like a brain, the skull cut away to reveal the grey matter smooth and bare and lumpy and criss-crossed with capillaries.

I drove over it one bright December day, when winter was just a memory, travelling from Outram on the Middlemarch road to Clarks Junction, where the Old Dunstan Road begins. The Clarks Junction Hotel, pink and worn, marks the spot. The road was started even before the gold rush, as a way between the huge runs here. It is sealed at first, growing narrow, and the country goes from farmland to that distinctive Central Otago character quite quickly. On the second day of summer the outside temperature is zero, and stays that way until mid-morning.

The track drops off the Maungatua Range to Rocklands Station at Deep Stream, braces itself and tackles the Rock and Pillars. It is bumpy, but not too bad, and I stay in two-wheel drive for the whole journey. At the top the rocks stand jagged and alone like rotting teeth. Ahead, though, the hills lie in pleasing sweeps, Dunstan brown.

Now there is a glimpse of water, blue, incongruous: the Loganburn Reservoir which was once the 'Great Moss Swamp'.

Everything looks so faraway, forever in the distance. And deserted, not a house, nor even a hut, but somehow not abandoned. All around rise rocks that *look* like houses and huts, and villages, and people, and dinosaurs. My, you think, that looks like a festival up ahead, people and wagons and buildings. But of course, they're rocks. A couple of months later they *might* have been a cavalcade of horses and wagons and people, for a procession is now an annual event celebrating the road's mining ancestry.

Here you can scale mountain-tops, or so they look in this remarkable landscape. When you reach them, they're perfect miniature peaks. It is hard to believe, now, that a power company wanted to dot this landscape with so many wind turbines it would have become the biggest wind farm in the southern hemisphere. In some landscapes they are sculptural. In this one, they would have been barbaric. Locals and others who loved the land rebelled. In 2012 the scheme was scrapped.

Now the road tops a hill and you look down on a wide, green valley and it is such a surprise. The road drops sharply into it, and at the bottom a cluster of stone buildings stands amid willows behind a gate. The old Styx Hotel was built in 1861, an overnight coach stop. Beside it stands the jail which accommodated both gold bullion and prisoners. Stables lie near the hotel.

The Upper Taieri–Paerau Road is shingle but it feels like a highway. Old stone farmhouses still stand along the way. My brother lived in one of them once, farming in the valley and using the Old Dunstan Road as his most convenient route to Dunedin, summer *and* winter. I thought his house was like living in a refrigerator.

The remains of an old gold dredge are displayed beside the road but this valley is now preternaturally green. Irrigation has fluffed up its pastures. New, barren cottages are scattered around, the mark of corporate dairy farming. Dairy is the new gold here.

Soon enough you find your way to the other side of the valley, past the park-like Linnburn Station and through a knobbled landscape to the beginning of the Old Dunstan Road's second section. I went a little further, trying to find the entrance to the old Serpentine road. My plan was to drive up through the old Serpentine mining settlement and rejoin the Dunstan Road at the top of the range. I asked a farmer for directions. He leaned out of his white ute and took a long slow look at my truck in that way farmers have. 'Whoo,' he said. 'In that? I don't think you're going to make it. Maybe by going straight up.' He looked at my truck again. 'I dunno. Why don't you go up the Dunstan Road and turn off at the ridge, come down from the top?' Although, he added, it was a long way and the road wasn't too good.

I took his advice. Obviously he'd had some experience of digging city 4WDs out of trouble. So I went back to the Dunstan Road's iron gate, surrounded by stone fenceposts, and took off up the range known, properly, as Rough Ridge. It was rough. Rockier, more bumpy and gut-thrashing than the first section. It was cobbled with the same sharp rocks sprouting from the landscape, hard on the car but light on the upholstery for I spent a good deal of time in the air.

Tawny tussock and gold-green Spaniard daubed the blunt landscape. The car started a dark hare big enough for its mother to have wooed a wallaby.

At the top the Long Valley Ridge Road led off towards Serpentine. It wasn't so much a ridge as a sawn-off range which would be flat, or at least sweeping, if rocks weren't scattered about like giant sandpaper. Not a trace of the old Black Ball Hotel which once stood here.

The farmer was right. The road was long, and not too good. I didn't so much drive as bound. Ahead

lay sites rich in gold-mining history, mine shafts, stamping battery, water wheel, ruins. I saw none of them. Ten kilometres was enough. I stopped at a point where the old Serpentine church, once the focal point of its village, rose in the far distance. It is the highest church in New Zealand or, if you prefer, the closest to God. It wasn't used much even in its heyday but in that cold, lonely place I could see why miners wanted it. For me a more spiritual sight was the far-off range, still mottled with snow, jagging into a clear blue sky.

I turned back to what was now the main road. The rockscape became grander, taking its cue from the mountains. Not a tree anywhere, not even tree-shaped rocks. Below, the many arms of the amoeba-like Poolburn Reservoir appeared behind the dam built by Depression labour in the early 1930s to irrigate the Ida Valley. An archipelago of islands. There were cars. Cottages, some of them used for Rohan village in *The Lord of the Rings*. A corrugated-iron paradise. Even people. More fun than the Serpentine and no churches. A found civilisation after the lost one in the hills.

Through the badlands. Out to Moa Creek. From here the road went on over the Raggedy Range to the goldfields. The journey took miners five or six days from beginning to end. They used it for only a few years before the Pigroot, from Palmerston through the Maniototo, became the main road. It was longer, but easier. Now the drive over the Old Dunstan Road takes a few hours. In one of those strange turns of history it has become famous, much more used now than in the 1860s. Even stranger, the country it passes over remains substantially unchanged.

The road is a registered historic place, Heritage New Zealand says, 'by virtue of its historic importance and association with the very early days of Central Otago gold mining, its rarity as one of the country's oldest extant roads, and its length, which is far in excess of any other recognised heritage road in the country'.

RIGHT End of the road as it nears the Loganburn Reservoir.

BANNOCKBURN

NEVIS

GARSTON

RUBICON ROAD

THE NEVIS VALLEY

'HISTORY HAS BEEN QUARANTINED IN AN ISOLATION WARD.'

Bannockburn is another boom town, although now the rush isn't for gold or dairy cows, but grapes. Vineyard signs are everywhere. So are new houses. A few old buildings in the town centre remain, outposts of a former age, but the message is clear: the gold rush was never this good.

Still, the town is proud of its legacy. The sluicings have left a sculptured landscape. Water races, ruins, the rough miners' shelters in caves, the remains of their rock shelters, the rock spikes marking out their claims.

A rough 4WD track takes adventurous traffic from Bannockburn through Carricktown, a short-lived place where miners lost their dreams in hard rock, leaving the usual intriguing ruins, stamper battery, stone dams. An old wagon track runs through the remains and heads into the Nevis Valley. Its prize feature now is the restored Young Australian water wheel, first hauled up the valley in 1874.

The safer way, if that is the right term, of getting into the Nevis Valley follows what is thought to be an old Maori track between Bannockburn and Garston. Moa-hunters left traces of a summer hunting camp with ovens.

According to Heritage New Zealand Maori used it as a path between Murihiku in Southland to Central Otago, and told early European settlers of the route. Until the gold rush in 1862 few would have lingered. Winters have been known to throw up three weeks of daily frosts.

Even fewer stayed in the Nevis. The miners have long gone. Except for the stout-hearted handful who take their holidays in the old cottages up here, the population centre is the Ben Nevis Station.

At first the road is beguiling. The valley is green. The rosehips are red and the thyme purple. The houses are pretty. Some move the hearts of the dourest do-uppers. The mountains hide their teeth behind smiles. True, a sign warns that the road has been damaged by floods and recommends you not use it, but who can believe it on such an excellent day?

Mysteriously, it is closed from the second Tuesday in June to September 30. Inclusive. It seems so little used that sheep run away from the car and gather again in front, just in case you've changed your mind.

Then, enough of Mr Nice Road. Another notice: Steep grade for the next nine kilometres, and the

The bridge at the old town site of Nevis Crossing is small and perfect, over clear water running deep between rocks. I hope it is counted as one of the many river crossings along this road: officially 27, although I lost count.

You get very used to two things on the Nevis: water crossings and gates. Farmers here rank tourists who leave gates open as one of the three leading nuisances, the others being keas and rabbits.

The road officially passes through a gorge between the Lower and Upper Nevis, but to the layman the whole thing is essentially a gorge, the Hector mountains on one side, the Garvie Range on the other, and the Nevis River rushing between the walls in a single thread. Nearby on Schoolhouse Flat lie the remains of the last gold dredge.

The old village on the Lower Nevis, the second settlement, tells its own story of survival in a harsh, isolated environment. At the peak of the gold boom 600 people lived in the Nevis. Chinese miners, perhaps 500 of them, toiled over old workings until the late 19th century.

Miners and farmers made do with what they had, mainly lots and lots of rock. They built their houses, stables, shops, hotels and everything else from it, and what wasn't rock was corrugated iron. Iron couldn't be made on the spot. It was a scarce commodity, recycled to its end.

Mining went right through to the 1950s, yet the lack of pressure from anything else has left the archaeological record intact. History has been quarantined in an isolation ward. The old village here boasts the ruins of its hotel, closed only in 1952 and effectively ending the community. The bakery, store, telephone exchange, library, houses, schools and cemetery with some 40 graves can still be traced. The very first school dating from 1874 survives near the mouth of Coal Creek for yes, coal was found here too, conveniently in this icy place. An old homestead

sign-writers were not kidding. A sign announces that Mount Cook is 198 kilometres to the north, and there it is, peeking over the far ranges. The road chugs up to Duffers Saddle, at 1300 metres claimed to be the highest public road in the land. It isn't. Island Saddle on the Tophouse or Rainbow Road, is higher. The Desert Road, a lowly 1074 metres, is the highest state highway, the Crown Range road, at 1076 metres, the highest sealed road. Duffers Saddle is definitely unsealed. It may not be the highest but it could be the loneliest of them all.

Dropping into the Nevis Valley is, frankly, scary, a fall into nothingness. With warning signs, of course, 'affected by adverse weather' etc.

A car passes in the opposite direction. We stop and talk. The comfort of strangers, or the herding instinct. The driver says he thinks the road ahead isn't too bad, although they stopped at the bridge over the Nevis just below, and how would he know? Still, I treat him with the respect due to fortune tellers, and press on.

built by one of the first settlers is still lived in by a family whose 1899 homestead also remains, along with the bakery. A sign announces the town's current, permanent population: three. As a legacy of the gold rush it is, well, as good as gold.

But piles of tailings, stripped hillsides, rusting machinery lie about from an age when the country's environmental resources seemed limitless. Miners pulled the place apart and it has taken nature more than a century even to start putting it back together again. I'd like to think those old miners would never get resource consents today, but who knows?

The first goldfields warden described his territory as a 'cold, sequestered and ice-bound region'. A farmer on the Lake Wakatipu side of the range, whose property ran into the valley, once told me the same.

At a boundary gate a sign announced there would be no hunting in the Nevis for a coming weekend because 'hundreds of people' would throng the place. This seemed so unlikely I looked it up and found that the Nevis would be the venue for a 'Highland Events Rogaine'. Rogaining is long-distance cross-country navigation for people on foot. The miners' successors roam the valley for fun.

The flats are now spiked with orange-green Spaniard, the mountains tussocky and gold. The road rises over the Hector Mountains before dropping into Garston in another, different valley far below: green paddocks, no tussock, no Spaniard, no mines. The shingle road, by now looking quite innocent, ends at our old friend, State Highway 6.

No distance at all in a straight line; geographically, another planet.

DANGER ROAD

SKIPPERS CANYON

'THE COUNTRY LOOKS AS IF IT HAS BEEN DROPPED FROM HIGH. THE LAND IS CRACKED, SHATTERED.'

Well, you were warned.

Perhaps you were lulled as you drove up the road to Coronet Peak. A very nice road it is, fitting into the cultivated landscape of New Zealand's premier ski resort. You can sweep on up to nicely groomed snow, your only thought for the mountainscape being how well your new ski gear will fit.

The turn-off to Skippers Canyon is a different story. It starts with three short chapters inscribed on signs. The first, quite decorative, says, 'Road Warning. Historic Skippers Road Is Narrow And Prone To Slips. Caravans and Trailers Are Not Suitable. In Winter Snow Can Close the Road. Some Vehicles Are Not Insured Past This Point. No Turnaround For 6 Km.' And, as an afterthought, 'No Exit.'

The second is sterner: 'Narrow Winding Road With Steep Drop-offs. NO SAFETY BARRIER.'

The third is downright abrupt. 'Back Country Road. Vehicle Damage Possible.' Just in case you thought of pitching a tent: 'Strictly No Camping.'

They might have added 'slippery as a crook' and 'lumpy as King Kong'.

Perhaps you'd done some research already. You'd have discovered that the Skippers Canyon Road is in the world's top 22 most dangerous roads with an overall fear factor of seven out of 10. Most of it is one-way, narrow or steep, usually all three, with sheer drops of several hundred metres. Or you may have searched the internet and found such warnings as 'I am not kidding. Do not take your car here. *Extreme danger!*'

Well, yes. Yet some have driven it and lived to tell the tale. I am one of them.

It was a superb day, the kind that appears on posters all over Queenstown and hardly ever when you're there for the weekend. Mountain flanks glowed amber and copper coated the low hills, the afternoon sun striping shadows across the land.

Oh yes, the signs, but they were for tourists weren't they? Besides, this was late summer, well before the time when skiers fall on their knees and give thanks for snow. So, over the cattle stop and down to the rock cutting at the entrance to the road. That was the easy part.

This country looks as if it has been dropped

from high. The land is cracked, shattered. Pieces lie everywhere. It is both very high and very low. One moment you have that heady feeling of being close to the sky, the next you're in the depths.

The road was built in the 1880s. Early goldminers did not have a road to worry about. They just clambered over the mountains, down the stone walls and into the Shotover River, 'the richest river in the world', far below. The only way of getting supplies in and out was by packhorse, over dangerous trails whose traces can still be seen on the hillsides. If the road is frightening now, the pack tracks were worse, and they were the miners' only lifelines: by the time the road was built, the gold rush was over. In the first winter of the rush, in 1863, lack of fruit and vegetables brought scurvy to miners, who lived in tents wherever they could find space. The canyon is so steep that many were drowned that first winter, when the river rose suddenly.

Now it is an all-year-round road: dusty in summer, slippery in the rain and icy in the cold. Starting at Hells Gate you get the picture immediately. The road slices through the rock, leaving blunt instruments pointing at the sky. It gets into character, clinging to the cliff. You get into character too, anxious. Oh all right, scared. It's like bracing yourself for something by thinking, it can't be as bad as it seems. It is.

The road gets bad, then it gets worse. Will the car even fit? Well, yes. But you hope there isn't another coming the other way. Going ahead is bad enough. Going backwards . . . don't think about it. Don't change your mind, either. You're going onwards, for there is no other way.

The road goes down to the river by way of Big Bend and Castle Rock. McCarrons Beach. Can it be? No sign of sand or deckchairs.

Along to Pinchers Bluff and the Devils Elbow. Now you're getting the drift.

These three kilometres are 180 metres above the Shotover River, blasted, hand-drilled by workers hanging from ropes. Those roadmen would recognise their road today. It has stayed substantially the same ever since: a notch in a sheer rock wall.

When a slip took away a five-metre section of it, the Queenstown Lakes District Council thought about modern options such as bridges and realigning the road but in the end went back 130 years and rebuilt it much as it was, for more or less the same reasons: cheaper, easier, faster.

The Shotover got its rich reputation when Raniera Erihana aka Dan Ellison, and Hakaria Meroa, deep in Skippers Canyon, lost a dog in the torrent. Ellison went in after it, rescued the dog and got rich in a single swim. Grounded on a little beach he found gold.

They collected 300 ounces of it that day, 8.5 kilograms, worth at 2014 prices around $450,000. Kindness can be more than its own reward, although Ellison did not hold on to his just desserts for long. Maori were not allowed to bank and he trusted his fortune to an assay clerk who promptly vanished.

PREVIOUS SPREAD
The start of the Skippers Road viewed from its safest part: the car park.

LEFT Horse-drawn cart on Skippers Canyon Road, sometime between 1891 and 1910.

RIGHT Julien Bordeau's warning to travellers.

That place became known as Maori Point, a flat-topped, arrow-like rock pointing to the river, which soon accommodated a boom town, Charlestown. Hotels sprang up, shops, post office, bank, police station, a court. A thousand people moved in and as quickly moved on. By 1884 the population was 400 and dropping. Now there's scarcely a trace of the town, or any of the thousands who once thronged this canyon. They probably didn't admire the scenery, much. Theirs was simply a harsh life in the mountains. Now, high on a sheer cliff with a vertical drop to the river far below, the scenery starts at your nose. Superlatives aren't enough. Start with magnificent and work up.

The road zigzags through Gooseberry Gully, then Horse Gully, then Wong Gong Creek. Chinese miners picked over the workings along the canyon and laboured on the road too. Wong Gong supplied them from a store here. According to the Department of Conservation only one Chinese miner is left: A.H. Quay died of starvation and was buried at Skippers.

Now you reach a fork in the road. The Branches Road continues on up the Shotover and ends at the Branches Station. The other fork leads to the Skippers suspension bridge which, for vertigo, matches the canyon perfectly. It was finished in 1901, 96 metres long, 90 metres high, and is still the country's best.

You leave the car here, gratefully, and head across the bridge to what was in the late 19th century the centre of civilisation: Skippers Township, named for Malcolm 'Skipper' Duncan, once a sailor, then a goldminer. The stone Skippers Point school still stands amid mining artefacts, and the Mount Aurum homestead has been restored. The station here farmed sheep even before the gold rush. Tracks take you to the gold mines dotting the landscape.

Julien Bourdeau's store once stood here. For 50 years the French-Canadian made two trips a week into Queenstown carrying passengers and supplies,

each trip taking two days, which must have left him little time for his other occupations, storekeeper, farmer and publican.

Nothing remains of the Otago Hotel except a few strawberries and raspberries around the site. By the 1940s the town was deserted. Now tourists populate the canyon. Bungy jumpers were diving off the bridge the last time I drove over the road. I went a short distance up the Branches Road and found a vantage point to watch. The jump-master signalled me to wave encouragement and I did. There's something heady about exhorting people to do something you'd never do yourself, such as hurtling into space on the end of a rubber band.

No amount of encouragement would persuade the last jumper to leap. She would shuffle to the edge of the platform, adopt the position, and sensibly stay where she was. Eventually she shuffled a bit too far and over she went, feet first. We saw her later, her legs streaked red with rope burns, looking very proud of herself. After braving the Skippers road, I knew how she felt.

RAINBOW

LAKE TENNYSON

ST JAMES RANGE

HANMER SPRINGS

TOPHOUSE ROAD

'THE ROAD CRABS ACROSS SHINGLE SLIDES WHILE THE WIND COMBS THE TUSSOCK INTO PERFECT TRESSES.'

OVER THE RAINBOW

The Clarence Valley Road is the open sesame to wilderness known as Hanmer's back country. It runs through Jacks Pass and ends at an intersection. Turn left for Rainbow Road, right for Molesworth. Yes, it is a heck of a choice.

Today it's the Rainbow. Settle back for around 110 kilometres and three hours if you're scared of the country, more if you're fascinated by it, and much more if you're both. 'Adventure awaits you in this amazing landscape of wetlands, drylands and high mountain ranges,' you're told, which seems to cover just about everything.

The first thing you need to know about the Rainbow Road, or the Tophouse Road, is that you really need a 4WD vehicle. The second is that for most of the year you need a key, otherwise you'll find your way blocked by Hells Gate. Seriously.

The road runs through Rainbow Station, and driving over it is a courtesy granted by the runholder. It's open to the public from Boxing Day until Easter, upon payment of a toll at the Rainbow cob homestead, which is worth the money on its own.

Outside these dates gates are locked at both Hells Gate and at a point near the Rainbow skifield turn-off at the St Arnaud end.

Part of the route was used by Maori travelling overland, then by early drovers moving stock between Nelson and Canterbury. Most of the road is more modern. It was built in the 1950s to service the power pylons running alongside.

Just up the road from the junction is what's left of the St James Station farm buildings. St James was once several smaller stations whose area had grown to 78,196 hectares when the government bought it in 2008. Now it's the St James conservation area, home to the famous walkway, full of glacial valleys, lakes, tarns, rivers and wetlands, a gem of a place.

The St James homestead burned down in 1947 but all over this huge property lie other old homesteads, stables, woolsheds, men's quarters, woolsheds.

The road to the Hanmer Springs Ski Area branches off here. It skirts the conservation area and runs along the Clarence River to Lake Tennyson. The lake is quiet water, its bed carved by glaciers, a little off the

road, wedged under the mountains of Nelson Lakes National Park at its top end, easing out on to the flats then relaxing onto a small beach. Forest and scree and red tussock frame the still water.

Beside it the Clarence Valley runs north, golden in the early summer, morning mist fading into a blue sky, impossible to imagine its ferocity in mid-winter.

The road treads so gently through this lovely landscape that you're on the Island Saddle before you know it. The saddle claims one of those records which seem so common to South Island passes: this one is said to accommodate the highest 'publicly accessible' road in the country. It doesn't feel so high, no struggling engine or hairpin bends, but here you're on the boundary between Canterbury and Marlborough and the whole wild best of both opens before you, a magnificent broad valley rising to mountains whose snow has all but melted, revealing shingly flanks, hills below, a patch of trees, a gap in the far distance filled with bright cloud and looking religiously significant, if you're so inclined.

You ford the Rag and Famish Creek and arrive at the Sedgemere Lakes where the mountains take on personalities: Turk Ridge, Mount Balaclava and the

Crimea Range have the stern gaze of their Crimean War ancestry. Cross the Wairau River on a bridge.

Across No Mans Creek near the boundary of Rainbow Station, everything changes. Abruptly, the road takes you into the mountains. No bush around you, just lumpy, craggy mountain faces. You seem quite alone. From here it is 16 kilometres to the Rainbow homestead, 54 to St Arnaud. Well, you think, that was quick, and not so bad either, but the road is not going to let you away so easily. It comes with a warning:

The formed roads and tracks have not been engineered, nor are they maintained to meet the standards for public access. Parts of it are hazardous. The hazards are not individually signposted or marked. Sudden weather changes can cause additional adverse conditions and/or additional hazards.

Almost straight away you discover the truth of it. The road crabs across shingle slides reduced to little more than tyre marks on the stones while the wind combs the tussock into perfect trusses beside. You cross the bridge over Coldwater Creek, think about joining the family camped beside the creek below. It looks nice. The grass is green, the sun shining. Why go anywhere else, you wonder.

Especially when you reach the gate at Hells Gate. Your memory files it under black iron, clang-bang shut.

This is not Hells Gate, in fact.

Hells Gate is the gap carved through the rock by the river rushing far below. It may be the most intriguing river in the world. But you are determined to stay on the road rather than view it more closely, so you grip the wheel and drive on.

The Wairau meets the Rainbow River. The country eases onto flats. The road crosses the Rainbow, travels under the sharp features of Spaniard Face and arrives at the Rainbow homestead. White and

PREVIOUS SPREAD
A cyclist tackles the Rainbow, power pylons marching behind.

LEFT Jollies Pass, 1974.

cob, fitting perfectly into its country, comfortable as a sock, and you wonder how far New Zealand architecture has come since then. The house once stood in a public reserve set aside for one of the string of accommodation houses that ran from the Tophouse to the Hurunui from the 1860s. It burned down and the one standing today replaced it. The Rainbow run rises behind it.

Not far now. The ubiquitous power pylons which have accompanied you all the way march stolidly north. The Rainbow skifield road takes off to the left where the St Arnaud range separates the road from Lake Rotoiti. To the right lie beech forest and broad valleys, a tramper's paradise. The main road to St Arnaud crosses ahead.

This was once a very long journey. A letter concerning the road from a Mr W.T.L. Travers appeared in the *Nelson Examiner* of 6 June 1865. The road then followed a slightly different route, running over Jollies Pass from Hanmer, along what is now the Acheron Road through Molesworth until it reached the Alma River, then cutting northwards past the Tarndale accommodation house (now part of Molesworth) and rejoining the present route at the Sedgemere Lakes.

Travers was not impressed with it. Over Jollies Pass, the track was in 'a most abominable condition', tilting at a frightening angle, 'impossible to ride over and dangerous even to walk upon'. The track along the Clarence River was 'atrociously bad', rivers could only be crossed by swimming, he and his horse were saved only by lucky accident from being dashed to pieces on the rocks, the track through the swamps around Sedgmere only a foot wide: 'one single false step would bury your horse in a swamp'. The rest of the journey involved a good deal of swimming, crossing dangerous fords and narrow escapes from certain death. It took several days.

Today the drive takes three hours, maybe six. Perhaps longer, as in the case of a hypothermic tourist who had spent the night in his car trapped by a snowstorm, encouraging calls for yet more signs. For this road's history is not all in the past.

CHAPTER SEVEN

SLOW ROADS

DRIVING ROUTES

1 RAETIHI TO WHANGANUI

2 MOLESWORTH

3 THE CATLINS HIGHWAY

4 LE BONS TO PURAU

5 RAHU SADDLE TO REEFTON

6 COROMANDEL COAST

LEFT The coastal road
to Cape Colville,
Coromandel Peninsula.

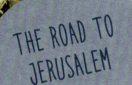

THE ROAD TO JERUSALEM

RAETIHI TO WHANGANUI

'IN THE EYES OF THE LAW THE WHANGANUI RIVER WAS A PERSON. WHEN YOU DRIVE THROUGH THIS STRANGE LAND YOU KNOW THAT'S JUST AS IT SHOULD BE.'

It's raining, hard, the water smashing against the windscreen. Raetihi seems diminished by the rivulets, although history is running against it too. It was once the biggest town in the King Country, but is now a quarter of its prime size.

The town site first stood in forest so dense people avoided it. Maori camped there: they didn't stay until much later, for the Ratana Church is sited nearby.

In 1887 the government bought the Waimarino block from Maori and opened the ancient forest to sawmilling. For almost half a century the town prospered as forest giants — totara, rimu, kahikatea, matai — were cut down and sawn into building timber in dozens of sawmills. Then the timber ran out and took much of the population with it.

The town still has style. Old buildings appear through the rain as memorials: the town's railway station, now a museum; the Bank of New Zealand; the Theatre Royal, oldest theatre in New Zealand. The theatre came alive again in 2005, housing the crew of

Vincent Ward's film *River Queen*.

Skiing reversed the fortunes of nearby Ohakune and tourists have given this town a bounce too.

Raetihi was always a staging post for the journey to Whanganui and still is today.

State Highway 4 will take you there. But the river road is much more interesting. It runs alongside another kind of highway: the Whanganui River, New Zealand's second-longest river, the longest navigable river in the country and once the only way from the coast to the central North Island.

The river was both road and source of food for Maori, a vital part of their lives. It was critical for early European settlers too. Soon steamboats ran its course and a trip up the Whanganui became one of New Zealand's great tourist attractions. Pipiriki was as high up the river as most went, although some services ran all the way to Taumaranui and still do.

Alexander Hatrick ran the first steamboat service starting in 1892, from Whanganui to Taumaranui

and not for nervous passengers. The service ran until 1958. Two of his boats have been restored and one, the paddle-steamer *Waimarie*, still runs up the river.

Jetboats carry tourists higher, through the gorges and thick bush to the Bridge to Nowhere.

The country here was once settled by soldiers returning from World War I. It was so hard and steep that it defeated men who'd survived the most brutal battlefields the world has ever known.

The concrete Bridge to Nowhere replaced a shaky wooden structure carrying those settlers into 'the valley of abandoned dreams'. Too late. By the time it was finished the settlers had lost and left, the bridge their lonely memorial.

Pipiriki is a camping ground and a couple of cabins now, the rain beating down so heavily I can scarcely see it as I turn the car downstream. Perhaps not being able to see clearly is a blessing. The road is not good, and little slides of rock and mud are making it even narrower.

Far below, the Whanganui slides by, grim and powerful. The road may be bad but the alternative is much, much worse.

A woman is walking through the mud. I offer a lift, and she climbs in gratefully. She's living in Jerusalem, or Hiruharama, she says, in the old convent revived in 1883 by Suzanne Aubert and the Sisters of Compassion. It is an oasis of calm in a turbulent world, the order says, and few visitors will end up there by chance. Both true.

Now people go there to find peace. My passenger did. In fact, she might have found a little too much of it, for she seems lonely. She's the only resident, and I echo through its rooms and dormitories.

Aubert was a woman who waded against the tide, helping the poor and desperate, running the gauntlet of public odium by taking in the children of unmarried mothers. For my money her most courageous act was sharing a cell with Kereopa, wrongfully convicted for the murder of the Reverend Carl Volkner, the night before his execution in Napier. The convent seems quiet as a tomb, more silent than she'd like: a picture of her and her children, happy, laughing, noisy, hangs on a wall.

Jerusalem's second-best-known resident was the poet James K. Baxter, who came here to explore Maori spirituality and live in a world without money. He formed a commune in 1969. He didn't survive the experience and died three years later, history gilding his life rather more than his fellow citizens did at the

PREVIOUS SPREAD The Bridge to Nowhere.

TOP LEFT The Dress Circle on Pipiriki Road, c. 1910.

TOP RIGHT Sheep on the Parapara Road, c. 1950s.

time. The commune died with him. A picture of its young members hangs in the convent, and I wonder what happened to all that life and hope.

The rain turns to mist. The country looks as if it has beaten off all comers at last, and stands battered and bruised but recovering. It is patchy and green in the dull light. The slender spire of the elegant St Joseph's church rises in benediction. Patiarero marae, much older, huddles in the drizzle.

The road is slippery. It greases past Moutoa Island where Maori from downriver fought the insurgent Pai Marire in 1864 and won. Grateful European settlers erected New Zealand's first war memorial in Whanganui's Moutoa Gardens: 'To the memory of those brave men who fell at Moutoa 14 May 1864 in defence of law and order against fanaticism and barbarism.' History declares that to have been disingenuous: Maori were fighting over the sovereignty of iwi versus pan-tribalism. Defending law and order, in fact, didn't do Maori much good. Land claims up and down the Whanganui River have been fought for a century and a half, for the last several decades occupying a great deal of the Waitangi Tribunal's attention. Those claims have sometimes flared into national affairs, the occupation of Moutoa Gardens for 79 days in 1995 becoming a symbol of past grievances.

Maori kainga or villages once lined the river, a great attraction for early 20th-century tourists. Many survive. The settlement here at Moutoa Island is Ranana, home to a very old Catholic church and otherwise remarkable for its name. It's the Maori version of London. The name was given to Maori by the missionary Richard Taylor in the 1840s along with several others along the river, including Hiruharama (Jerusalem). Koroniti (Corinth) has two excellent restored meeting houses and, high on a bluff before the settlement, the venerable fighting pa Operika. A little downriver is the modern kaitiaki, or guardian: The Flying Fox, an eco-lodge.

Of Atene there's no sign other than a spectacular skyline walking track high above a sharp kink in the river, and a small meeting house.

But first you go past Matahiwi, with its restored Kawana flour mill given to it by Governor George Grey. Nearby is the wreck of an old sternwheeler. The marae has a long history but is right into the 21st century: it's available for conferences and meetings.

Then Parikino, Pungarehu and Kaiwhaiki, all with carved houses, Pungarehu's by the famous carver Hori Pukehika, Kaiwhaiki with its twin-gabled house. The Whanganui River is sparsely populated but before the river road ends I meet one of its residents, driving truculently along the middle of the carriageway, which leaves little room. I skid sideways and she passes a side-mirror's distance away without a glance.

Well, it's another country and I'm the interloper.

In 2012 the Whanganui River became a unique legal identity. It always had its own personality. Now, in the eyes of the law, it was a person. When you drive through this strange land you know that's just as it should be.

DASHWOOD

MOLESWORTH

HANMER SPRINGS

MOLESWORTH

'TURN OFF THE AIR CONDITIONING, SNIFF THE AIR, SENSE THE MAJESTY, SHRIVEL IN ITS VASTNESS.'

Unless you count the hot water (and everyone does) all the adventurous parts of Hanmer Springs start at the Clarence Valley Road: the Hanmer Springs Ski Area, the Rainbow Road, the whole wide bald brown intrigue of Marlborough high country — and Molesworth Station.

You can get to them all by a short trip from Hanmer Springs up the Clarence Valley Road and over Jacks Pass. It's a kind of Yellow Brick Road, taking you far away from the crowds soaking in the hot springs.

The Molesworth road is probably the best known and least travelled in the country. Molesworth is the nation's biggest high-country station, as big as some small countries. A little larger than Stewart Island. Celebrated in song, film and print. Best of all, still in public ownership, saved from the asset-sellers by fast footwork in the new millennium. Yet the run is remarkably little visited. Molesworth Station was opened to its public owners, officially, only in 1987.

The public road, the Acheron Road, runs the length of it, open Labour Weekend until Easter. At last count, fewer than 10,000 people a year had made

the journey in the open season, perhaps a few less than a Super 14 rugby crowd.

Here the players are mountains and streams and gullies, without a beach and scarcely a patch of bush anywhere. Yet it's country that lights your soul.

It begins in a gout of yellow broom and it's not long before you come to the first outlier, the Acheron Accommodation House. This was built of cob in 1862–63 and used until 1932 by the travellers and stockmen for whom it was also the social centre of the universe. The house was one of a chain reaching through the harsh country between Nelson and Christchurch, the Tophouse, Rainbow, Tarndale, Acheron, Jollies Pass, Waiau Ferry and Hurunui, each of them a day's journey apart.

Sleeping here, and eating, would cost a drover and his horse three shillings and sixpence, a fair whack of his five bob daily pay. Its small rooms must have been crowded, often, but its thick walls kept the grinding country at bay and to a cold stockman it must have been a palace. These were beautiful, graceful whitewashed buildings grown from the soil, truly organic and suited to their environment.

The Acheron Road follows the Acheron River, and although many other roads were formed through Molesworth, this is the one used by the public. It crosses Wards Pass and follows the Awatere Valley to Dashwood, and it takes drivers through the tamer parts of Molesworth Station. If you stop anywhere beside it, turn off the air conditioning, sniff the air, sense the majesty, shrivel in its vastness. You can only wonder about the rest, what lies beyond the range. The country it traverses is burned and hot in the summer but in winter, when it's closed to the public, it could freeze the horns off a bullock.

Usually, some towering figure founded each giant station. Molesworth rather trundled into being, an amalgam of people and places, only *thought* to have been named by Frederick Weld, a former Premier. Its beginnings were rakish: one early owner, John Caton, later went to jail then drowned; another, John Murphy, claimed to be the first to live there in winter. It changed hands often, and the first time it joined the high-country establishment, the old boys' club of the time, seems to have been in 1890. Then, it was bought by William Acton-Adams, who already owned the neighbouring Rainbow and Tarndale Stations. Molesworth slowly became an amalgam of surrounding stations, Tarndale, St Helens, Dillon and the original Molesworth.

Maori are thought to have traversed this country for six centuries or so before. When Te Rauparaha and his allies attacked Ngai Tahu in their Kaiapoi pa in 1831, part of his force travelled south through Tophouse and Hanmer using what later became the drovers' route. Early settlers found a way into this vast valley from the north but at first couldn't find a proper route out until Edward Jollie, a runholder, in 1852 discovered a path through what is now Jollies Pass into the Hanmer plains. The stock route was open for business, and was used until the 1930s.

The Acheron Road originally ran through St Helens Station, leading to what is called the 'Battle of the Acheron' although in truth it wasn't much of a fight. Henry Low, who then owned St Helens, grew sick of paying for a road which others regarded as public. After all, the stock route had been commissioned by the Nelson provincial government and was widely used. One day Low simply blocked it. An entire wool clip from Molesworth had to be left beside the road and was ruined. Molesworth sued, won and was awarded compensation. Other runholders settled out of court.

That lethal cocktail of high-country poisons, high stocking rates, erosion, rabbits, vile weather and stock losses eventually forced Low out, as it did so many others.

The modern Molesworth also sprang from this toxic mixture. Mismanagement dealt the final blow to the station and in 1938 it was bought by the Crown. Slowly the government managers rebuilt the ruined farm.

Now the road follows Low's embattled route past the lower Acheron suspension bridge, a replacement for the original used to move St Helens sheep across the Acheron. The brown hills of Molesworth explode, the peaks opening up to mountains, the mountains to ranges, the ranges to hills. They're a composition in sepia shadowed in purple, with here and there just a suggestion of green.

At the junction of the Acheron and Severn rivers the road crosses a place called Isolated Saddle, although why one place in this huge land should be called isolated rather than another is known only to early stockmen who used a finer comparative scale. This is the Red Gate where Mt Augarde looms rather ominously, given its history. Women were scarce here in the hills, and Ivanhoe Augarde must have congratulated himself when, as a worker on Mt Helens, he found Kate Gee, in the Upper Wairau. He wrote her a letter in 1868 and asked German Charlie to deliver it. Charlie did so. He also read the letter to men

PREVIOUS SPREAD
Cattle like roads
too: Molesworth.

RIGHT Sunburned
Molesworth
expecting rain.

LEFT The Acheron River, from Pudding Hill.

ABOVE Molesworth cob homestead.

he met on the way. They were much entertained.

Augarde found out. He was not at all entertained. He promptly shot the messenger, Charlie, who later died. Then he shot himself, at the spot you're at now.

The track to Tarndale Station branches off here. The cob Tarndale homestead, built in 1874, is still used. The road crosses Isolated Flat, a flowering meadow in late summer and autumn, crosses Wards Pass at 1145 metres and drops to the flats beyond.

Not far from here lies the Molesworth homestead settlement. When I first drove this road it took traffic through the settlement, more a village, but it now detours around the place. Instead, a walking track takes passers-by to a hill from which they can see the homestead, ancient woolshed, workers' accommodation and, among the outbuildings, the working blacksmiths' shop. When the Lewis Pass road opened in 1938 it spelled the end of the packhorse era, but Molesworth is still heavily dependent on horses and the smithy's forge is in constant use.

One outcome of the detour is that in this whole 60-kilometre, two-hour drive you pass close to only two buildings, the Acheron accommodation house at one end and the equally venerable original Molesworth homestead, also built of cob, at the other. This homestead is spartan, and small, but a haven after a hard day on the run.

By now the inland Kaikouras are closing in. Tapuae-o-Uenuku, the giant at their northern end, towers over the Awatere. It is another 100 kilometres from here to Dashwood, a long drive, and completely different. The country is dramatic, but on a tidy scale. It even becomes pretty.

The road runs through as fine a gorge as you'd find anywhere, a chasm far below, Skippers-like without all the fuss. At some point the road becomes paved for a short distance, gives up, tries again, then again, until eventually the seal takes.

Then there's a white line, and vineyards. Taylor Pass runs off to the north, so we're on the old main road to Blenheim. Then Dashwood on State Highway 1, which shouldn't feel strange, but does.

KAKA POINT

OWAKA · · NUGGET POINT LIGHTHOUSE

FORTROSE · · PAPATOWAI

WAIKAWA

CURIOSITY ROAD

THE CATLINS HiGHWAY

'ITS BENDS AND TWISTS KEEP IT PRIVATE, SO YOU CAN IMAGINE YOURSELF ALONE ON THE ROAD.'

Fortrose is a good place to start the journey north through the Catlins, for it sets the tone.

On 29 April 1881, Fortrose was the first settlement to hear of New Zealand's worst-ever civilian sea tragedy. The steamship *Tararua* struck the Otara reef at Waipapa Point, some 16 kilometres away from Fortrose, in the early hours of that morning. She was on her way from Port Chalmers to Melbourne with 151 people on board. All were well, at first. The sea was calm. A young man swam ashore to find help. Word reached Fortrose, then Wyndham. When rescuers arrived, the reef was in a different mood. The wind and sea had got up. The ship was breaking up. People on shore watched helplessly as 131 passengers and crew died.

Even on a quiet day now, the tragedy darkens the coast. Fortrose is a few houses where the road touches the sea before ducking inland through the Catlins. A lighthouse, built three years after the tragedy, stands at Waipapa Point.

The Tararua Acre, where some of the dead are buried near a memorial from children of the Fortrose school, lies nearby. Graves of victims are dotted throughout the South Island. Captain Francis Garrard is buried in Christchurch.

Slope Point, at the southernmost tip of the South Island, lies a little to the east of the reef. Everything looks low-slung, and windswept. As an introduction it is entirely appropriate, for no part of the Catlins is the same as any other. The Catlins highway, the route through this country, is interesting enough but the treasures lie in the web of roads beside it.

Now that you're at Waipapa Point, best you stay on this little road, which takes you around the South Island's bottom to the startling Curio Bay where at low tide you can see a 170-million-year-old petrified forest, trunks and stumps black as rock. If you stand quietly, it is quite likely you will see hoiho, or yellow-eyed penguins, coming ashore to their burrows in the cliffs here.

They jet out of the water, look around them and shriek — as well they might, for their numbers are dropping and they're facing extinction. The world's rarest penguin at one of the world's few

petrified forests. The name Curio Bay is a complete understatement. This is a unique place.

Roads were quite a recent innovation here. Until they were built, the sea was the coast's highway.

Waikawa Harbour nearby was a major port, loading timber from the Catlins forests. Timber was both its business and its downfall; as the forests fell, the harbour silted. It became a busy little fishing port, but the fishing fleet has dwindled too. Now it's a pleasant place with a few holiday homes around the water. An old church, the store and the museum are the only trace of the bustling town.

A new industry has replaced the old along this coast: tourism. A couple of decades ago the Catlins was scarcely known outside Otago and Southland. Now the roads in summer are full of motorhomes and visitors. Farm houses and holiday cottages have been pressed into service as tourist accommodation. It has become a film set: the location for *Two Little Boys* made by Dunedin's Robert Sarkies, based on his brother Duncan's novel.

The road now stays in bush for much of the journey, its bends and twists keeping it private, so that you can easily imagine yourself alone on the road. Just past a spot on the map marked as Chaslands a track takes you down to the Cathedral Caves. They're deep tunnels leading into the rock, accessible only at low tide. At nearby Chaslands Mistake the steamship *Otago* met her end on 4 December 1876, also en route from Port Chalmers to Melbourne. The 120 crew and passengers all survived.

It is worth abandoning your car when you reach the Tautuku estuary to go ahead on foot. The path becomes a wooden boardwalk taking you above a tawny sea of grass to the sea itself, rare fernbirds clicking beside you.

Surfers make the trek to Papatowai further down the road where the big waves curl. Maori settled there for eight centuries. This whole coast was well known to the Ngai Tahu, Ngati Mamoe and Waitaha, who left artefacts, traces of their campsites and urupa or burials at beaches and river mouths. Signs ask visitors not to disturb them.

Past Tahakopa the road curls inland, and again most will take to the side roads. The lacy Purakaunui Falls, once the best-known feature of this road but now one of many, lie down there.

Just before Catlins Lake, a road branches off to Jacks Bay, and Jack's Blowhole. Both are named for the famed Ngai Tahu chief Tuhawaiki, known as Bloody Jack, who was once trapped here by one of Te Rauparaha's parties and escaped by leaping off a cliff and swimming eight kilometres to Tuhawaiki Island.

The blowhole is deep, noisy and popular, and the Clutha District Council has declared the Hina Hina Bridge over the Catlins River and on to the bay safe. Locals had complained that it was falling apart. 'Most family vehicles' would be safe on the bridge, according to the council. Somehow, the story seems to fit the country.

PREVIOUS SPREAD The road to Nugget Point.

LEFT The end of the road at Nugget Point.

The main road though continues to Owaka, the Catlins capital. It sits near Pounawea, once a busy port; now the only shipping in sight is the old scow *Portland*, built in 1910 and moored in the river here for years after a hard life hauling goods between difficult ports and rivers around New Zealand. Nearby is Surat Bay, named after the ship *Surat* which, carrying a full load of immigrants, hit a reef at Chaslands Mistake and struggled north until it was beached and wrecked on the beach here.

Shipwreck stories along this coast seem to follow the same plot and you're tempted to add 'etc etc'. No one died in this one.

There's still more to the Catlins but you have to drive almost to their end, then turn back along the coast. First you reach Port Molyneux, although you'll have a hard time knowing you're there: it's nothing more than an old building and a swamp. Port Molyneux was the unluckiest town in the country. It

stood at the mouth of the Clutha River, a flourishing port town full of hope. But one day in 1878 a huge flood swept down the Clutha River. It shifted the mouth north, permanently. Overnight, Port Molyneux lost its reason for being. It simply died.

Kaka Point next door stayed on. It looks nice. It was home to the poet Hone Tuwhare, who died in 2008. Its New Zealand character endures. But you drive on until the road ends, for the best lies ahead.

The glorious lighthouse at Nugget Point looks over the offshore rocks known as 'nuggets', some 20 of them, individually named by Maori. A track, so narrow that people need to sidle past each other, takes you along and across a razor-backed ridge to the lighthouse. You stand there at the end of the world, looking over the steel-blue sea and southwards past the cliffs and bays of the Catlins. It's not a long road, really, even with all its side trips and detours. It just takes a long time, but the ride is worth it.

PURAU ● ● PORT LEVY
LITTLE AKALOA
PIGEON BAY ●
● OKAINS BAY
● LE BONS BAY
AKAROA ●

LE BONS TO PURAU

'THE ROAD IS LIKE A RODEO STEER, BUCKING, SWERVING, TRICKING ITS RIDER.'

Banks Peninsula started life as a volcanic eruption and has remained unusual since. It settled down into two huge craters, now Lyttelton and Akaroa, both busy ports after cruise ships deserted one for the other following the Christchurch earthquakes. The peninsula, famously, was charted by Captain Cook in 1769 as an island.

Akaroa, sheltered from Christchurch's cutting easterly wind, is a popular resort whose European beginnings transcended the early 19th century whalers. In 1838 the French whaler Captain Jean Langlois thought he had bought the entire peninsula from Maori and organised a French colony. The British feared a French attempt to claim the whole country as their own, so the first boatload of French settlers arrived to find British sailors waiting for them. A British cannon still stands guard at the town wharf.

All of this means the drive over the hills to Akaroa ends in French street names, a telephone directory which still has a touch of ooh-la-la and an awful lot of Franglais. Much French-tinted colonial architecture survives all over the Peninsula whose most surprising

feature, for somewhere so close to a city, is that it is remote.

This route is not for anyone prone to carsickness. It goes up and down and round and round . . . all of it. Roads are a comparatively recent development around the Banks Peninsula bays, which were served by steamers until well into the 20th century. For some, the only access for many years was by boat. Roads simply developed from the farm or sawmillers' tracks which webbed the peninsula bays until quite late in the 19th century. They have an improvised nature to them, kinking off in all directions, often narrow, always twisting. You don't cover a great distance, in a straight line. But when you finish, you've had a day's drive.

The results of all this are bays full of perfect settlements, all self-contained with churches, halls, schools, shops, and even after a century and a half very well preserved. It's a journey through early New Zealand history, layers of settlement still clearly visible.

For me it begins in Takamatua in Akaroa Harbour. The road branches off the main Akaroa highway, rises over the crater rim and curls into Le Bons Bay, although you look hard for a French name among early settlers here. Enough of those settlers' houses remain to give the bay the timeless look shared by all of these peninsula bays. The church was built in 1869, the Memorial Library in 1919, for these good people obviously believed the fallen were best remembered by something useful. The school closed in 2012, the principal declaring it had simply run out of kids: these communities are quite distinct, all once self-sufficient, but now gently declining. Now Le Bons is a pretty, well-preserved little settlement.

The road climbs out of the bay, humps over a couple of ridges and drops into Okains Bay. It's a sandy bay, biggest on the Peninsula, apparently named after the author of a book being read by a passing sea-captain. It's a peaceful place, and like most of these bays, once inhabited by Maori until successive wars in the early 19th century. Murray Thacker, a descendant of the bay's first European settlers, bought the old cheese factory here and converted it to a museum, housing many of the artefacts he excavated from pa, for this bay was also a pounamu-working site. The museum's collection grew to reflect a composite picture of the area's Maori and European past, some of it still standing: the store, the old school built in 1871, the first public library on the peninsula to give local workers an alternative to their favourite occupation, drinking, and the stone church, damaged in the earthquakes. It's a pretty bay to drive into, an easy one to spend a lot of time in.

On the way to the next big bay, Little Akaloa, you drive past all that's left of another sawmilling settlement, Chorlton. It's the old hall, which once roared to the noise of local dances. Now its owners reckon that four passing cars make a busy day.

Little Akaloa once had a pub, the Pig and Whistle, which was burned down three times before finally being abandoned. The road passes a hidden gem, Saint Luke's church, whose interior is covered with what at first sight appear to be kowhaiwhai, or Maori patterns, but a little off-key. They were designed by a local farmer, John Menzies, the church builder, decorator and furniture-carver. One person who attended its consecration in 1906 quoted the Queen of Sheba: 'The half was not told me.'

The road climbs up the valley, dallies with the summit road without quite joining it, and hares off downhill again to Pigeon Bay. Along the route the stumps of totara forest stand like ghosts, with a few corpses still lying on the ground. The bush growing in these bays was dense, and without roads it could take days to beat through it and get anywhere else at all. Quite often, travellers didn't; early accounts are full of people getting lost, and sometimes never seen again. Fires could smoulder for weeks. The forest survived the first two waves of settlement, Maori then whalers. Then the sawmillers arrived. They hacked down the bush with amazing efficiency, ran it through sawmills whose rackety remains can still be found in many of the valleys, and shipped it off to the towns and cities springing up all over New Zealand. Then the farmers took over, growing cocksfoot seed, grazing dairy cows then sheep and cattle. By the turn of the 20th century photographs showed a barren landscape, all but ruined. But farms are now long established and several local initiatives are restoring the forest. In Pigeon Bay, the early homesteads grow grander. These were men and women of substance, pre-dating Canterbury's 'first four ships'.

The road skirts the foreshore, passes the now defunct Pigeon Bay store, church and school, climbs around Holmes Bay and tackles Wild Cattle Hill. This road really does live up to its name. No stray cattle roam, but the wildness remains. It's rather like a rodeo steer, bucking, swerving, tricking its rider while you do all you can to keep your seat. Many do not. This road is famous for accidents, ranging from mishaps such as merely running off the road, to collisions (it is narrow),

PREVIOUS SPREAD Cattle grids and sign, Little Akaloa.

RIGHT Banks Peninsula road, winding through low cloud.

to truly innovative adventures: I once towed out a driver who had managed to go off the road backwards.

Then, I lived in Port Levy, where you now arrive: a wonderfully self-contained community with a rich history: they run their own affairs, maintain their own fire engine, and dig their own graves. Nothing of that is visible from the outside. It just looks like another tiny place with a marae. But the secret life of New Zealand is another story. For now, you're only a high pass away from civilisation, and it is sometimes blocked by snow in winter. Purau, the next bay, leads to Diamond Harbour on the road which runs around Lyttelton Harbour en route to Christchurch. You're back in the real world, perhaps with a little regret.

REEFTON
BLACKS POINT
RAHU SADDLE
SPRINGS JUNCTION

RAHU SADDLE TO REEFTON

'YOU CAN STILL HEAR THE FAINT THUD OF MINERS' BOOTS.'

The Rahu Saddle carries State Highway 7 through the Victoria Range and on towards Reefton. Coming off the long straights leading into Springs Junction it's a gnarly little pass, still hinting at its past as a serious grind. This is trampers' heaven and old gold-mining country. Tracks lead into bush both thick and mysterious here, in the Victoria Forest Park.

The road drops from the saddle into the Inangahua River valley, which slowly widens. Now you're in a park within a park, the road carrying you through a wild, beautiful landscape where trees, river and mountains seem perfectly placed. It exudes peace; not much happens, but once did. Nineteenth-century prospectors and miners covered every inch of the country in search of gold. The mountains teemed with them. They left their mark everywhere. Your map will show you the crossed picks of old workings all along the route, reached by tracks where you can still hear

RIGHT Rolling along the Inangahua.

FAR RIGHT Blacks Point on the Inangahua River, c. 1910s.

THE TURF OF HEROES

the faint thud of miners' boots.

Soon you come to the town of Crushington, where quartz was crushed on massive mining machinery. It is the birthplace of Jack Lovelock, the Rhodes Scholar and doctor who won a gold medal at the 1936 Berlin Olympics in such compelling circumstances he became one of New Zealand's greatest sporting heroes.

Not much remains of Crushington now and nothing resembling a town. But this is the turf of heroes, for just down the road at Black's Point lives the cinematographer Alun Bollinger, most famous for his work on *The Lord of the Rings,* who is to film what Lovelock was to athletics.

Black's Point is everyone's idea of what an old mining town should be, a place of miners' cottages on tight streets, a main street where pubs and post office and churches and shops once jostled, all jammed into a tight bend in the river. The Murray brothers discovered gold in the Black's Point hills in the 1860s and the town sprang up; unlike many, it remains.

The Black's Point Museum records its history and contains the stamper battery which crushed the quartz from the Golden Fleece mine. Fifty-nine mines once pitted the hills around Black's Point and Reefton. The hills ring with the names of old mines: Energetic, Inglewood, Ajax. You can leave your car, take the Murray Creek walk from here and realise you're in country not much changed since the brothers prospected there a century and a half before.

Reefton is only a few kilometres further on, one of those West Coast mining towns whose fortunes have depended on gold and coal and sometimes timber, hopping up and down according to fresh surges in mining, forestry, tourism. Like most of them Reefton has ebbed, flowed, ebbed again. Named for the quartz reefs in ancient settlements you can still walk to, it was once a metropolis, populated by thousands, the first town in the southern hemisphere to have electricity.

Coal trains still rumble through Reefton, but

like most traffic they're coming and going from somewhere else. Reefton is mainly what was. Conjectures on what lies ahead fill Rotarians' speeches: the OceanaGold mine opened in 2006, rapidly stripped heavily forested country to rock, and closed in 2013. 'Temporarily,' locals said.

To me, this is one of the most beautiful of West Coast towns, its history as tangible as its present. From here the roads go north to Inangahua or south to Greymouth, swift, easy roads with no hint of where they came from.

CAPE COLVILLE

COROMANDEL

THAMES

COROMANDEL COAST

'AN ANCIENT AVENUE, GRAND AND GRACIOUS.'

Every story has two sides and the Coromandel has at least that number. The east side has the bays and beaches, the baches and bars. The top has the mystery and the isolation. The middle has the bush and the ranges.

The west-side story is out on its own. A skinny road is glued to the Firth of Thames between Thames and Coromandel, where it goes through a personality change. It becomes positively anorexic as well as tricky, dodging here and there until it gives up the ghost just past Cape Colville.

The town of Thames is fascinating. It's quite big, for a New Zealand town, but it always gives the impression that you're coming into something much bigger. That's because it *was* much bigger. This was once New Zealand's second-biggest city, after Dunedin. Both owed their rise to gold. The gold ran out, but Thames remained the biggest town on the Coromandel. It did not so much shrink as stand still.

Getting to the place is faster now a new Kopu bridge has been built over the Waihou River. Gold was discovered in the rivers here 1867, lifting Thames into the national spotlight and saving Auckland from Depression. Thames was three towns then: Shortland, Tookeys Flat and Grahamstown.

Now you can drive through Thames and know you're in the presence of history. There is something to be said for gentle growth: heritage buildings are left as they are rather than bowled over for new development. Fish and chips at the old port, beside boats nesting in the mangroves, is a peculiarly Thames attraction.

You drive north, through pohutukawa, penned between the Coromandel Range on one side and the sea on the other, only a few flat areas at the mouths of streams. The road slips past Tararu's old cemetery then Ngarimu, which must be one of the few places in the country to be rechristened by European settlers with a Maori name. It was Otohi up to World War II. When Lieutenant Te Moananui-a-Kiwa Ngarimu was killed in Tunisia and awarded a Victoria Cross posthumously, it was renamed Ngarimu.

Tapu was the first European township along this coast as hundreds of goldminers moved into the valley in the the late 1860s. If you want that middle Coromandel driving experience you can turn off here

logging and the sanctuary was established. Some 400 kauri were saved, best of all Tanenui, sixth-biggest in the country and 2500 years old. You stand before it in awe. What must an entire Coromandel of forest giants have been like?

You don't need to go back very far to find out. The British naval ship *Coromandel* stopped here in 1820 to buy kauri spars and give the place its name and after that it was all downhill for kauri, literally. Nearby Driving Creek tells the story: it got its name from the practice of damming a stream, banking up kauri logs behind, then collapsing the dam, the kauri logs swept down in the flood.

Coromandel town did very well out of kauri and gold, for a time. But the trouble with timber and gold is that when they run out, they are gone and nothing is left.

Not quite true of Coromandel town, however. Many nice old buildings are left, and tourists like them enough to arrive in ferries and cars and keep it afloat.

Keeping things afloat is the harbour's problem. It is shallow and tidal, so boats cannot float for long, which ended its tenure as a commercial port.

But now, Whanganui Island at the harbour entrance heralds the chain of islands reaching up the coast. The road dodges along the coast but never leaves it. You pass the old and the new. The old is Koputauaki, which Ngati Porou trading ships once used as a haven, a place where war between the Maori owners and encroaching miners was averted only by Governor Grey. The new is Papa Aroha. Or perhaps not so new. For me this is a holiday village and campsite of the nostalgic kind, of homely cottages and caravans reeking of summers past.

The pohutukawa are thick, and the closer you get to the cape, the more they crowd in, salute, embrace, never ornament. They're a sculpture park on their own, an ancient avenue, grand and gracious, truly New Zealand monuments which, even when knocked

and take the road to Coroglen on the other side of the peninsula. The shingle road winds through the bush and up and over the range so thoroughly that several times along its quite short length you wonder where you are.

Northwards the road breaks its grip on the coast and squeaks past Deadman's Point over a hill to Manaia at the head of Manaia Harbour. For sailors it's not as good a sanctuary as the harbour next door, Te Kouma, but Manaia has special significance for Maori. Ngati Maru gave the land to Ngati Pukenga in gratitude for the Bay of Plenty iwi's help in the musket wars of the early 19th century, when muskets changed inter-tribal fighting from battles into massacres. It remains one of the largest Maori-owned areas in the region.

It is one of the last kauri bastions too: the Manaia Forest Sanctuary gives visitors an idea of what the great kauri forests were like before the millers moved in and all but wiped them out. In 1972, when the nation was becoming alarmed by the decline of its forests, rivers and lakes and a new conservation movement was rising, locals here protested kauri

PREVIOUS SPREAD
Coromandel coastal road nearing Port Jackson.

LEFT Oamaru Bay on the Coast road, 1956.

ABOVE Final approach
to Port Jackson.

down by age or storms, rise again.

The pohutukawa along this road rank with
mountains and lakes among the nation's most
spectacular assets. Every one of them has a character
of its own, each a work of art. They lead to and away
from Paritu, where granite jetties and chiselled rocks
tell of a past. This was the granite quarry which
supplied stone for such buildings as the Auckland
Museum, the old Auckland Chief Post Office, the
Auckland Railway Station, Parliament House, the
Hall of Memorials below the carillon of the National
War Memorial, the Seddon and Massey memorials. It
reopened as recently as 1996 to supply granite for the
Parliament Buildings refurbishing. The jetties were
used by the scows which carted the granite blocks
across the gulf, the *Lena Gladys*, the *Jane Gifford* and
the *Rahere*. It's a quiet place now but the thing about
granite is that it lasts. It lies all around the old quarry,

blocks with finger-like marks where they were split,
squared-off faces, geometrical shapes.

A short distance away lies Cape Colville, one of
New Zealand's more peaceable capes. It was named
by Captain Cook after a naval commander. Twenty
kilometres away across the Colville Channel the
humps of Great Barrier Island are clear. Like many
capes it seems an anticlimax, in fair weather at
least, the land simply running down to the sea and
ending in a clutter of rocks. The road passes inland,
runs on for a short distance and stops at Jackson
Bay. A walkway joins it to the road running up the
other side of the peninsula, through Port Charles.
Moehau looms above. Its peak shelters the grave of
Tamatekapua, captain of the Arawa waka.

The walkway saves the road from becoming a loop.
That would be much, much less magical.

- CHAPTER EIGHT -

LOW ROADS

DRIVING ROUTES

1 BULLER GORGE

2 MANAWATU GORGE

3 NEW PLYMOUTH TO HAWERA

4 KARANGAHAPE ROAD

5 RIVERTON TO PORT CRAIG

6 THE BLUFF HIGHWAY

LEFT Manawatu Gorge.

THE ROLLER-COASTER

BULLER GORGE

'AT BEST, A PASSAGEWAY MISSING A SIDE. WITH THE RIVER RUMBLING AND GRUMBLING A SHEER DROP BELOW.'

Travelling the Buller has always been tumultuous. Turn up the car radio and, with that sense of sheltering from the storm, remember the first European who tried it.

In 1847 Thomas Brunner tackled the Buller River with two Maori, Kehu and Pikewate and their wives, who knew the river as the Kawatiri, a Maori pathway. Brunner renamed it Buller after an English politician and director of the New Zealand Company.

The river runs from Lake Rotoiti more than 170 kilometres to the Tasman Sea at Westport.

Brunner's objective was to find good land and acquire it. For three months they battled down the river. They began to starve. They resorted to eating fern roots and eventually had Brunner's loyal dog Rover for dinner.

They reached the coast, spent a cold, frugal winter there, discovered coal up the Grey River and went home, remarkably, back up the Buller.

By now Brunner had injured an ankle, lost one guide and a wife, had a stroke losing the use of one side of his body, was kept alive only by the faithful Kehu, and returned home after 18 months of starvation, a ferocious river and truly awful weather.

He wrote an enduring description of the Buller:

The immense, gigantic rocks that belt the river rendered it impossible for us to keep to the bank, and the mountains were too high to ascend, so our day's walking was one continual ascending the spurs and descending the water courses, which only brought us on a short distance by nightfall.

And later:

Rain and thunder continuing. This was truly a wretched day to spend on a cliff in a black birch [beech] forest. The rain poured down in torrents and loosened the stones of which the hill is formed, and these rolled by us and plunged into the river with a fearful noise. The wind tore up the trees on every side, and the crash which ensued caused a simultaneous shudder by all hands.

Not surprisingly, perhaps, Brunner died at 52. The Buller endured and today remains very much the same. You might start this journey where State Highway 6 leaves Murchison and passes the junction with the Shenandoah highway. The road, on the map, looks very much like a piece of cooked spaghetti that has been dropped on the floor. It wriggles and squiggles. In three dimensions, it writhes.

It crosses Sullivans Bridge at the junction and four kilometres on bypasses New Zealand's longest swing bridge, 110 metres of it swaying over the rocks and rushing green water below. You drive by Newton Livery, once a Victorian hotel with stables and a blacksmith and a refuge for the coaches which travelled through the gorge to Westport when the roadmakers slowly followed Brunner down the river.

A sign announces that you are now at Lyell. The sign is all that remains. Yet Lyell was once a big town. Yes, another gold rush. Gold was discovered here in 1862 by Maori, who came to appreciate its value, at least to Pakeha, very quickly. They found a nugget weighing more than half a kilogram, which rapidly captured miners' attention.

Five Irishmen claimed to have found 1.4 kilograms in five days. In the resulting rush Lyell grew to a town of more than a thousand people, and there was no way of getting there except by river until a rough road was built in the late 1860s. The town was called Lyell after a British geologist, said to have died without ever hearing of the place.

Yet it had a newspaper, school, banks, hotels, police station, courthouse, even a brewery. As the gold ran out, so did the town. Fires destroyed many buildings. The very last, the Post Office Hotel, burned down in 1963. Now Lyell is just a bend in the road. A big grassed campsite marks the spot where the town once was. A track leads to the old town cemetery; others to ancient mines and batteries, including the place where Maori made the first strike.

But some are benefiting from the miners' efforts still. A goldminers' road is being reborn as the Old Ghost Road, an 80-kilometre tramping and biking trail through magnificent country leaving Lyell and running to the Mokihinui River, passing through five ghost towns on the way.

The main road creeps along the Buller to Inangahua Junction, which narrowly escaped being a latter-day ghost town itself: the Inangahua earthquake, magnitude 6.1, struck the town just before dawn on 24 May 1968, year of the *Wahine* tragedy. It wrecked houses and triggered huge landslips in the surrounding mountains but for townspeople, the worst was a massive slide which blocked the Buller and raised it 30 metres above its normal level. If the dammed water were to burst through, both Inangahua and Westport would be in its path. Many were evacuated.

A day later water broke over the top of the dam and the West Coast held its breath. They were spared the deluge. The water lapped over the dam and chewed it away gradually enough for disaster to be avoided. Inangahua and Inangahua Junction beside it never fully recovered. The gold rush had long gone. Its

PREVIOUS SPREAD
A landslip on the Buller Gorge road.

LEFT Hawks Crag, 1930.

RIGHT Through the gorge, just.

population had dwindled to around 300. With 70 per cent of the town's houses made uninhabitable many people moved away and did not return.

Now the place has a peaceful air: when you've survived a catastrophe like that, not much can hurt you. Between trains, it's quiet. People work in their gardens, stroll, talk. It's different, with that West Coast air of an unconnected universe.

The Gorge road was wrecked, blocked and broken in more than 50 places, sometimes by immense falls, sometimes collapsing into the river. 'Many years of difficult and costly work on improving and sealing the state highway system in the Inangahua and Buller Gorge areas was virtually ruined in a few seconds by the earthquake,' groaned the Ministry of Works.

No sign of that now. The scars can still be seen on the mountainsides above it, but the highway and bridges have been restored and over the years improved so much that a newcomer approaching the Gorge itself is in for a shock. First you pass the old Berlin's Hotel, a landmark for a century and a half, known fondly to generations of travellers. John Berlin was born in Gothenburg, Sweden and when he built his hotel and post office in the 1870s he called it 'The Old Diggings'. Everyone else called it Berlin's, and the name stuck. Once there was a settlement here, of sorts: the post-mining population of the Gorge road numbered 62 souls, supported by the gold dredges in the Buller River and the district's timber.

New Zealand's most unlikely rush started in the Berlin's bar.

In the mid-1950s uranium was the wonder-mineral. The Cold War was chilling and nuclear weapons were sprouting. Nuclear energy was going to save the world. New Zealand joined the uranium hunt in its own Kiwi way. The Geological Survey produced a booklet, *Prospecting for Radioactive Minerals in New Zealand*, a do-it-yourself guide for the person in the street, who was then urged to make a Geiger counter following the

instructions within and go forth unto the mountains.

Frederick Cassin and Charles Jacobsen, prospectors and seventy-somethings, were having a beer in Berlin's one November night in 1955. Driving home, they were caught short. They stopped to relieve themselves at Batty Creek and, ever diligent, Jacobsen put the Geiger counter on the rock face, where it went right off.

That comfort stop started a fevered hunt, Cassin claiming they'd stumbled over, or peed upon, one of the most highly radioactive deposits in the world. Prospectors rushed in. The West Coast greeted its new saviour wildly, as always. Hotels gave guests radioactive rock fragments, someone produced uranium ice cream, shop windows blared, and Berlin's did very well.

Alas, it all came to nothing. But Cassin and Jacobsen were immortalised. Two new peaks appeared in the gorge, Mt Cassin and Mt Jacobsen. They were each awarded £100 under the Atomic Energy Act and later, another £400.

Before tourism the West Coast economy was based on two simple rules: you dig it up, or you cut it down. Outsiders are still viewed warily, especially those with

a tint of green in their make-up. So conspiracy theory also did very well. Many Coasters believe in a hush-up, that there's lots of uranium glowing in them thar hills at secret locations kept under lock and key by the government. Try any public bar, although possibly not Berlin's, which has been reborn as a café.

You leave Berlin's and almost immediately arrive at Hawks Crag. Now you know you're somewhere . . . different. Surely, you say, you're not expected to go *there*? It's just a nick in the rock. At best, a passageway missing a side. With the river rumbling and grumbling a sheer drop below . . . and much, much closer in a flood. This road was built in 1869, but how? With West Coast determination, or the lure of gold, or both.

A 1939 Railways poster shows the road very much as it is now, one-way, cars creeping along nervously. Above you is the rocky roof, and you know there's a lot more of that rock above. It's exciting, spectacular and scary. The spot where the two old boys found uranium is about a kilometre further on and you probably won't notice. You're too busy concentrating on the gorge, and there's still a way to go. The railway line is sneaking along the other side of the river, now and then vanishing into tunnels, the kind with walls on *both* sides.

You probably won't notice Sinclairs Castle rearing up either, but if you do, you're just about out of the gorge. A kink or two later, and you're on the long straights running into Westport. You feel as you do when you're climbing off a roller-coaster, still shaking. Let's go back and do it again.

ASHHURST
MANAWATU GORGE
WOODVILLE
PALMERSTON NORTH

MANAWATU GORGE

'PASSENGERS CLOSED THEIR EYES AND PRAYED AS THEY WOBBLED ON THE EDGE OF THE ABYSS.'

SLIP ROAD

On 18 August 2011, an ancient landslide high above the Manawatu Gorge spawned another. The slip had lain dormant since the Manawatu River scoured a gorge through hills and rock thousands of years ago and created a worldwide rarity: a river gushing *between* ranges, from one side of the mountains to the other, instead of *from* them. Now a new landslide gathered at the toe of the old and crashed onto State Highway 3, the gorge road, below.

The hillside slipped again, and again, the scar growing higher and wider each time. On the night of 17 October 2011 heavy rain brought another fall. Rock, mud and bush crashed onto the road. A huge brown scar disfigured the hillside. The gorge highway was immediately closed to traffic. Disaster had struck before, most recently in 2004 when rockfalls and

RIGHT Manawatu Gorge road, and slips.

landslides closed the gorge for 70 days. But this was much, much worse. This was the biggest road slip in New Zealand history. The main link from one side of the North Island to the other was in serious trouble.

East–west travel through the gorge was always tenuous but critical to both the Maori and Pakeha way of life. When the first European settlers arrived, the Manawatu was navigable from the Manawatu right through to Hawke's Bay. Maori knew the gorge as Te Apiti ('narrow passage') and would haul their waka through the rapids.

Maori have a richer story for the gorge: it was gouged by a restless totara tree.

On the Woodville (eastern) side of the gorge the bush was the densest podocarp forest not just in New Zealand, but the world. It was called 70 Mile Bush, thick with birds. Huia flocked here, sighted by workmen in the gorge 30 years after they had been declared extinct. The 70 Mile Bush was so dense no one could get through it. It blocked the way between the Wairarapa and Hawke's Bay. Scandinavian immigrants, accustomed to the cold, were brought in to cut a road on the promise of land, hence the Hawke's Bay towns of Dannevirke and Norsewood.

Settlers also had to find a new way through the Manawatu Gorge. A surveyors' line grew into a road of sorts. Coaches picked their way through. Passengers closed their eyes and prayed as they wobbled along the edge of the abyss, wondering what was worse: rocks from the sheer hillsides above, or the drop to the river. Punts and wire cableways carried them across the river.

Why would they take the risk? Because they had to. The gorge joined west to east. Industry, commerce and communications depended on the route, as they still do.

Like other critical passes and passageways such as the Desert Road, the Haast, the Otira, the march of progress often slowed to a crawl against the elements.

Sometimes it stopped altogether. Technology would push through but at the crunch it was a no-contest.

All through last century the Manawatu Gorge road was improved, widened, stabilised and shored up but never taken for granted. Road warnings, speed limits and repair gangs were drivers' constant companions. Even when the road seemed clear only fools rushed in. Once, in the 1970s, quite late at night and travelling from Wellington through Palmerston North to my home in Hawke's Bay, then the fastest route, I rounded a corner to find a lethal-sized boulder on the road. I wasn't going fast for there's always a dangerous air about the gorge, and had time to stop.

You know that despite the advances in road technology and all the anti-lock braking, anti-skid, all-wheel drive, stability control features you bought the car for in the first place, there are still elements well beyond the car's or your control. You get the same feeling on a high alpine pass, except that here you're deep in a rock cleft, clenched between the Tararua Range and the Ruahines. Below you the gorge walls are vertical, and they seem almost as sheer above. It's gloomy down here, and dark. On the other side of the gorge the railway line creeps along its own edge.

The project to mend the fractured state highway through the gorge was huge. The slips had made the steep hillside above it even steeper. It was fragile, unstable. From the air it looked as if a whole mountainside not only *could* fall onto the road, but *would*.

A track was cut to get machinery above the slip, a task in itself, for the gorge is nothing if not inaccessible. A giant bulldozer known as 'The Bandit', used to recover everything from swamp kauri to derailed trains, was half-buried and used as an anchor for earth-moving machinery. Contractors cut benches into the rock above the slip, so that huge steps seemed to drop down from the top. Each one of them was bigger than a rugby field. Workers and machinery

tottered 155 metres above the road.

When the hillside was stabilised the gorge highway was cleared and damage to the road and its bridges repaired at a speed previously thought impossible. Deadlines came and went but on 31 May 2012 the road was reopened to one-way traffic only six and a half months after the first slip. I was one of those who drove through it then, creeping past machinery and safety fences and the huge slip itself, fingers crossed that nothing would go wrong. A few weeks later, it did. On 6 July flooding severely damaged the temporary road and it was closed again for almost eight weeks. Yet the following September both lanes were re-opened, and in mid-November the NZ Transport Agency proudly announced that work was finished. New Zealand's worst-ever road slip had been repaired in just over a year. The cost was horrendous.

Detours had been opened. The Saddle Road between Ashhurst and Woodville was widened and improved. This road has its own charm, running past the windmills of Meridian Energy's wind farm, with great views to both sides of the ranges. The little-used Pahiatua Track over the Tararuas from Palmerston North also became well worn. The detours added about 20 minutes to the journey. Even so, quite early in the disaster timeline the region's economic development agency Vision Manawatu estimated the cost to gorge users at $62,000 a day. Plus the cost of motorists avoiding travel through the Manawatu and Tararua.

Poor Woodville at the Hawke's Bay end of the gorge found business suffering as drivers used bypasses. Real estate agents reported that the town's property market was dead and would stay down until the road was reopened. Ashhurst, at the other end of the gorge, was doing quite well as the Saddle Road detour routed drivers through the town.

Now you drive through the gorge quite comfortably on a smooth, two-lane asphalt road with all the proper markings of a New Zealand highway. Certainly there are more than the usual numbers of safety fences and gabion baskets. If it wasn't for the river, and the sheer rock walls, and the tight gloom of the place, and the huge slip properly tamed, you might think it rather like any other highway.

But here's what the Manawatu Gorge story tells you: don't be fooled.

ABOVE Manawatu Gorge.

RIGHT Manawatu Gorge, 1949.

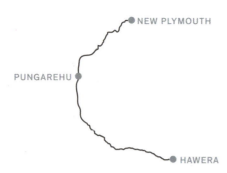

NEW PLYMOUTH

PUNGAREHU

HAWERA

NEW PLYMOUTH TO HAWERA

'A RIDE THROUGH SOME OF THE WILDEST TIMES IN NEW ZEALAND.'

SURF HIGHWAY

Once, pa stood on almost every headland from New Plymouth around Cape Egmont to Hawera. Calling the road the surf highway is not a misnomer, exactly, for there are probably as many surf beaches as there were pa. But the real story of this road lies in its history, not its surf.

The road itself is so smooth you need not drop below 100 km/h for its whole length; you don't get excited by it, unless you're a surfer. It glides easily between Taranaki and the sea, perfect cone on one side, blue over green on the other.

This is a surfer's paradise. The egg-like curve of coast means the wind is always offshore at some point, hollowing the swell, smoothing it into perfect

RIGHT With Taranaki always beside you.

INSET Coach on New Plymouth–Opunake Road, c. 1900s.

breaks. Kumera Patch, Bog Works, Graveyards, Pines, Secrets, The Legend, Fences and a dozen others offer lefts and rights and point breaks but nothing to match a ride through some of the most chaotic times in New Zealand history.

So you pass by Oakura's long wave and at Okato a sign announces you are leaving South Taranaki. Nothing changes, not the landscape, nor the abandoned dairy factories which lie all along this route and well to the south, their settlements often dying with them. What must these places have been like? Busy, tight. Each with its own hall providing entertainment, social centre, meeting place.

Down at the coast from Pungarehu lie the cape's two perfect lighthouses. Every lighthouse can post a catalogue of adventures but a better story lies in the other direction, not signposted, its only hint a road name. A little above the main highway, Parihaka remains a monument to right and wrong. Te Whiti was right. He led non-violent resistance to Pakeha confiscation of Maori land. The colonial government of the day was wrong.

On 5 November 1881, 1600 soldiers and settlers led by two cabinet ministers invaded Parihaka, by then the biggest Maori village in the land. Its 2000 inhabitants sat quietly while the leaders, Te Whiti and Tohu, and a third prophet, Titkawaru, were led away and later imprisoned along with hundreds of their supporters, many in the South Island. Parihaka was sacked, women raped, the rest of the town turned out into the countryside, the press censored.

Their story still resonates, but the pa remnant is a quiet place now, a monument to Te Whiti without condemnation. You can do nothing but bow your head in shame.

A little further along the highway, at Rahotu, an old anchor lies across the road from the shop. It marks one of the great stories of colonial New Zealand. The anchor came from the barque *Harriet*, wrecked on the coast here in 1834. All on board survived, until several of the crew were killed by Maori. The Guard family — Betty, Jacky and their two children — were captured. Jacky Guard negotiated a deal: he'd go back to Sydney and return with gunpowder in exchange for his wife and children. Instead, he returned with the man-o'-war *Alligator*, which rescued the family and killed many Maori in the process, the action subsequently condemned by a British House of Commons inquiry.

At Opunake a little way on you can still see the evidence. The town is famous for several reasons: it is the place which gave us the runner Peter Snell, All Black captain Graham Mourie and prop Carl Hayman, former Prime Minister Jim Bolger, the novelist Graeme Lay — and its problematic artificial surf reef.

But if you go around the fringe of town to the coast, you'll find what's left of Te Namu pa. The *Alligator* pounded Te Namu to pieces to 'rescue' Betty Guard (evidence suggests she was reluctant to be saved) and her daughter Louisa, and later did the same at Waimate pa further along the coast at Manaia to rescue the other child, John.

The pa is a rocky bastion defended by sea and deep gullies. It is famous also for a siege in 1833, when 800 Waikato warriors camped outside. They stormed the pa five times unsuccessfully, and on the sixth attempt were beaten back by rocks and a single musket. Worse, they were then routed by the 150 defenders. A sign outside the pa says, modestly, that 'here in 1833 the Taranaki tribe defeated the Waikatos . . . The defensive works and the village were destroyed in 1834 by a landing party from *HMS Alligator*.'

The new breed of warriors haunting Opunake in surf shorts, moko tattooed on hefty thighs and shoulders, now hang five.

PONSONBY ROAD GRAFTON BRIDGE

THE OLD JADE

KARANGAHAPE ROAD

'ITS REPUTATION WRAPS IT LIKE A WIZARD'S CLOAK.'

Almost every popular image of Karangahape Road, known as K Road, is wrong. Auckland's most famous street is constantly changing. Currently, like a respectable middle-class gent who fell upon hard times and kept a bawdy-house, the road has done its time, paid its debt to society and has emerged as a reformed character.

Its reputation wraps it like a wizard's cloak. People all over the country see it as the image of Auckland: bright lights, noise, excitement and a lot of people making money. Slightly subversive and more than a little anarchic. They've seen the movies *1Nite* and *Sione's 2: Unfinished Business*, read the magazines, and you can spot them wandering along K Road with their travel bags, slightly apprehensive, wondering what's behind that mysterious door, what lies at the top of those dark stairs.

Well, could be anything. This is one of Auckland's two best-known drives. The other is the Harbour Bridge, but that one is short on mysterious doors and dark stairs. The bridge and its approaches are longer, but the K Road mile will take you a lot more time.

In heavy traffic which, these days, is more likely at 5 pm than midnight, you move at the same speed as a dedicated kerb-crawler. Certainly you can nip through in a moment sometimes and see scarcely more than that old jade, the Las Vegas girl, reclining above what was once Frederick Prime's Hardware Store. Perhaps, in her next life, she'll come back as a PlaceMakers, for social change is the true nature of this road.

For much of the last century Karangahape Road was Auckland's premier shopping street. Queen Street was a dowd. The road bulged with department stores, fashion stores, cinemas, churches of every stripe, all good business.

In 1965, the year New Zealand went to war in Vietnam and Ray Columbus and the Invaders won the Loxene Golden Disc Award, other wild roads took

ABOVE Karangahape Road in the late 1930s.

over. Auckland's burgeoning motorway system slashed the district to pieces. The big, prosperous names left one by one, leaving behind not much more than Auckland's most architecturally beautiful streetscape. Much of that was, and is, hidden by signs: the Las Vegas girl is not on lonesome street.

Rents fell, low-rent businesses moved in. K Road became, in the public mind, the nation's premier red-light district. But fashion is always fickle. As the millennium gasped its last, so did Karangahape Road's notoriety. New apartment buildings sprang up, bringing a whole new population to the district. Cafés, art galleries, restaurants, bars and boutiques took over. But we have a much better memory for infamy than propriety. The Vogue Picture Palace had become a gay bar then nightclub; Hellaby's Corner had turned into a pub; the George Wallace building morphed into the Pink Pussycat Club; the Ambury & English building accommodated a lesbian nightclub.

Did we celebrate the grand old Karangahape buildings' return to virtue? Hell no. We remember the street as it was, not for all those solid years of most of the 20th century, but for a few decades at its end.

All of this means you're going to be entertained much more by taking the biggest risk on the whole short length of K Road: finding a parking space.

Leave your car. Walking this wild road is much more fun.

TUATAPERE

OREPUKI

COSY NOOK
PAHIA

RIVERTON

DEEP SOUTH HIGHWAY

RIVERTON TO PORT CRAIG

'IT IS TRULY, WILDLY, SPECTACULARLY DIFFERENT.'

You're driving through a lot of country here on the South Coast. Ngati Mamoe and Ngai Tahu pa and villages lay all along the route. European sealers moved in not long after Captain Cook's third voyage to New Zealand in the late 1770s. John Boultbee, a literate sealer, left the best account of their harsh life, killing seals, scouring the land for food, fighting with Maori, all of which, his diary records, left him 'as rough a piece of goods as ever weathered the wide world'.

So this is as juicy a ride as you'd find anywhere in New Zealand. The weather ranges from riotous to the kind of perfect calm that makes you want to rush out and buy a Lotto ticket.

Winds scream through Foveaux Strait beside you, laying the scrub on its side and tying macrocarpa in knots.

The essence of old New Zealand seems to have been preserved here, and I won't even mention

blast-frozen. It is truly, wildly, different. Its people even have an accent of their own: the Southlanders' rolling *rrrr*, as in arrrrctic, distinguishes them anywhere in the country. A Southlander is a Southlander, recognisable wherever they go.

Riverton, proudly announced in brochures as 'the Riviera of the South', is a proper starting place, an ancient port, a road for both Maori and Pakeha. It's the oldest town in Southland, celebrating its 175th anniversary in 2011, one of the oldest in New Zealand. Now it is a quiet fishing port, with a dwindling number of fishing boats, but you can see where it has been. The cottage owned by the whaler Captain John Howell, the European town's founder, still stands, along with a fine collection of old colonial houses and cottages, for this was once a prosperous town.

Ngati Mamoe called it Aparima, founding whalers called it Jacob's River (Jacob was the name given to a local Maori), and the townspeople's rather uninspired

country, home of such spots as the Pumps, Trees and the famously destructive Porridge.

The route leaves the coast again and passes Round Hill, where miners once dug for gold.

A signpost on a road leading off to the left points to Mullet Bay. There seems no reason why you should detour, but it's worth the trouble. This is Pahia, once the site of a big Maori village, later boasting a railway and a cheese factory, a school until 1997. The biggest Maori settlement in coastal Southland stood here. John Boultbee saw it in 1826, and recorded between 40 and 50 substantial houses. The great Ngai Tahu/ Ngati Mamoe chief Pahi lived on his namesake Pahia until he was drowned in the Strait along with some 40 of his people when his waka broke up. Another European noted 26 years later that the village had disappeared.

Everything else has gone now too, leaving you to wonder why so many narrow roads go off in so many different directions in such a small space: I once managed to get lost in them.

If you persevere you'll finish up at Cosy Nook. It's a tiny, circular, rocky bay, with the cottages of the fishermen who lived in it spaced around its edge. The entrance is guarded by an island called Matariki, so spiky it seems impossible to have accommodated a strong fighting pa. But it did, until sacked by Ngati Mamoe, its Ngai Tahu chief Te Wera dying while urging his sons to die the same way, fighting. Te Wera was buried at Howells Point, Riverton: this is a small tight world.

Cosy Nook has been abandoned by its fishing fleet too: the last time I was there one boat remained, hauled up high and dry, and the village's sole permanent inhabitant puzzled over a crush of tourists, perhaps 20 or 30 cars that day. Like Piccadilly Circus, he said.

If you can stand the crush, this tiny place is one of the most unusual in New Zealand, a gem.

choice of Riverton won. Following the Ngai Tahu claim settlement it is officially Riverton/Aparima. By whatever name, it's an interesting place, best viewed, I thought, from the public bar of the Aparima Tavern, which stood beside the main road overlooking the Jacob's River Estuary and across burnished plains to the flanks of the Longwood Range. Alas, the 135-year-old hotel burned down in 2013.

Down at the bay, surf peaks over the Riverton Bar but the beach is fine. Islands jut from the Strait, Stewart Island smoky in the distance. From further around, on a fine day, you might glimpse Solander Island, a forbidding lump of rock that became home to five sealers marooned in 1808. For five years they lived off seal meat and dressed in their skins until one glorious day, hairy and stinking, they were rescued.

The road bends around the estuary, climbs over the base of Howells Point and drops into Colac Bay, or Oraka, where the settlement is announced by a statue of a surfer riding a wave. For this is serious surf

PREVIOUS SPREAD
Riverton.

LEFT Orepuki, 1955.

ABOVE Cosy Nook.

Real gems can be picked up by anyone who cares to look on the other side of Pahia Point at Orepuki, back on the main road. The tiny town lies in the crook of Te Waewae Bay. Coal, shale and later sawmilling founded and sustained Orepuki. Today it seems barbered to the nub by the Foveaux Strait gales, trees uniformly leaning.

On almost any day here you can join hunched figures searching for gemstones, blue, red, yellow, lumps of milky jade, even gold, if you know where to look, for veins ran down from Round Hill and Orepuki. A Maori village here was swept away by a tidal wave.

The road tracks around Te Waewae Bay and up the Waiau River to Tuatapere, once a sawmilling centre, now self-styled sausage capital of New Zealand. These are the last lit streets you'll find in the south-west corner of New Zealand, and as you stand in its main street, you feel a very long way from Auckland. Locals will tell you part of its appeal is exactly that.

From here roads penetrate deep into Fiordland but the truly adventurous might loop back down to Te Waewae Bay. The road threads along the edge of the bay, that end-of-the-world feeling getting stronger kilometre by empty kilometre, the sea thrashing about and the Fiordland mountains looming.

It stops at the Rarakau car park. This is the famed Hump Ridge Track. Once, a road continued around to Port Craig in the far western corner of Te Waewae Bay, a logging town of some 200 souls who really did want to get away from it all. Not much is left of it now, but the old school building has become a trampers' hut.

The loggers left some valuable artefacts behind, however, notably their timber viaducts carrying the timber trams over deep streams. Now all of this is part of a popular three-day walk, no more appropriate way to end such a drive.

INVERCARGILL

BLUFF

THE BLUFF HIGHWAY

'THE COLD SOUTHERN OCEAN STRETCHES ALL THE WAY TO THE ICE. YOU SHIVER.'

Something about this road is always enticing, for no readily apparent reason. You drive into Invercargill, turn when Dee Street meets Tay Street and becomes Clyde Street, aka State Highway 1. You take the roundabout under the stoic gaze of a soldier high on the Troopers' Memorial. You head south along a road shaped like a backwards letter S.

You could have gone somewhere else. There's plenty of choice from Invercargill. One route takes you along the south coast and into Fiordland; another to Te Anau or Queenstown. You can go north to Dunedin, or east, through Fortrose and into the Catlins.

That's a better choice than you'll get anywhere else in the country.

But chances are you've used State Highway 1, New Zealand's longest highway, for at least part of the journey.

After 2047 kilometres from Cape Reinga, might as well see where it finishes.

All New Zealand's mountains, lakes, rivers, beaches, the plains and the paddocks and the bush are running out here, flattening and fading, with the New River Estuary on one side of the road and the Awarua Plain on the other, the Mataura River and the Oreti meeting in one huge, 35-kilometre marsh.

Swamp simply swallowed the first road in 1861. The provincial council built a railway instead and left the road to meander through marshland and sandhills and fight with the tides.

The plain is one of our biggest remaining wetlands, a complex system of lagoons, swamps and estuaries which from road level seem to roll on forever. Birds love it.

So do electronics engineers. A clutter of masts and receivers rises from the tableland. Latitude, isolation and an empty landscape have served this place well. Awarua Radio was set up in 1913 and served shipping through war and peace for 82 years. Its history is now celebrated in a museum. Meanwhile Awarua has become an international space-tracking station and upper-atmosphere research base.

History was once sieved through this flat place. Charles Kingsford Smith's trans-Tasman flight in 1928, the first, was monitored by Awarua. Admiral Richard

E. Byrd's Antarctic expedition of 1928–30 kept in touch with the world through the station. Awarua notified New Zealand that World War II had been declared.

Much later, in 2008, the resupply spacecraft *Jules Verne* was tracked from here, and in 2011 the *Johannes Kepler*. An exotic electronic cocktail on a bog on the Bluff Highway.

Bluff Hill shares the skyline with the Tiwai Point aluminium smelter's chimney, an unlikely monument to the birth of modern New Zealand's conservation movement. When the government of the day proposed raising Lake Manapouri to supply power to the smelter in the late 1960s the protest culminated in a petition signed by 10 per cent of the population. Conservation won.

Bluff also claims to be New Zealand's oldest town. It lies at the end of the road. The first visiting ship was recorded in 1813 although sealers and whalers are believed to have visited much earlier.

A Ngai Tahu settlement once lay beneath Bluff Hill, although when the English novelist Anthony Trollope visited in 1872 and asked to be shown some Maori he reported, 'I might as well have asked for a moa.' And perhaps he might have been shown one. Who knows? This is a strange place.

Bluff's entrance is guarded by its castle: the blocks and towers of the Ocean Beach Freezing Works, closed in 1991. If you pause you can hear the Strait pounding, for the works are set on an isthmus which all but makes Bluff Hill an island.

On the other side of the road you can buy the delicacy which has made Bluff famous: oysters.

Its third great feature, the reason why it was settled in the first place, lies just ahead: its harbour. God knows they need one here. At least 125 boats have sunk around Bluff and the Strait's archipelago since 1831: 14 people drowned in just two fishing boat tragedies, the *Kotuku* in 2006 and the *Easy Rider* in 2012. Both were capsized by rogue waves.

Cottages huddle on the hill against the gales. Hard lives, tight community. Fred and Myrtle Flutey's famous paua-shell-covered house stood beside the highway until they died and the house was pulled down. It has been recreated, rather incongruously, in Canterbury Museum.

State Highway 1 proceeds majestically along Bluff's main street, edges around the hill and ends at Stirling Point. The narrow harbour entrance is beside you. You're standing on the full stop of New Zealand's most-used geographical expression, 'from North Cape to the Bluff'. A signpost shows distances to other cities around the world. It says, in short, that you're a very long way from anywhere.

But you're close to islands. Over there is Ruapuke, once armed with seven pa, stronghold of the paramount chief of the South, Tuhawaiki, or Bloody Jack. A string of smaller islands fills the gap between. And behind them the cold southern ocean stretches all the way to the Antarctic ice. You shiver a little. It's like reaching the end of a long and gripping book and finding the epilogue has a compelling story to tell.

If all's well that ends well, then it has been a good journey.

ABOUT THE AUTHOR

Bruce Ansley's love of New Zealand roads goes back to a boyhood often spent crammed into a Ford Zephyr as his large family cruised far and wide. Slips, washouts, precipitous grades and roads sometimes hardly more than tracks were just part of the day's drive.

Since then, a lifetime as a writer — much of it for the *New Zealand Listener* — has taken him to every corner of the country. A full-time author since 2007, *Wild Roads* is his eighth book. His previous book *Coast: A New Zealand Journey* won a New Zealand Post Book Award in 2014. He now lives on Waiheke Island with his wife Sally and remains addicted to the sense of freedom that comes from being on the road.

THIS SPREAD
Road through the
Mackenzie District,
near Burkes Pass.

NEXT SPREAD
The Lindis Pass.

IMAGE CREDITS

123RF

168 (ref: 16317087. Steep icy mountain road in winter leading to Haast Pass)

ALAMY

105 (Darroch Donald)

ALEX HEDLEY

15, 31, 40, 44-45, 68, 71, 78, 110, 112, 118, 120, 121, 122, 184, 248-249

ALEXANDER TURNBULL LIBRARY

14 (left, ref: EP/1976/2498/20A. Tractor pulling a car out of snow on the Rimutaka Hill Road, Wellington. John Nicholson. Negatives of the *Evening Post* newspaper), 14 (right, ref: WA-19005-F. Rimutaka road and hill. Whites Aviation Ltd), 20 (ref: WA-51241-F. Arthurs Pass. Whites Aviation Ltd), 24 (ref: 1/2-042683-F. Kuripapango), 27 (ref: WA-33550-F. Lewis Pass, Maruia, near Summit, showing car and two boys on road. Whites Aviation Ltd), 38 (ref: 1/4-100704-F. Unidentified group of people with William and Lydia Williams, standing on summit of Crown Range, Central Otago. Edgar Richard Williams, 1891-1983), 44 (inset, ref: 1/2-055975-F. Road to Duntroon, Otago. Mrs R E Campbell: Photographs of the Reynolds family), 48 (ref: 1/2-026575-G. Newman Bros service car driving through snow on the summit of Takaka Hill. Frederick Nelson Jones, 1881-1962: Negatives of the Nelson district), 50 (ref: 1/2-000550-G. Swing bridge across the Maruia River leading to the springs at Maruia. William Archer Price, 1866-1948: Collection of post card negatives), 55 (ref: WA-32779-F. View from Turangahunui Saddle, Tarawera, Napier-Taupo Road, showing bus along road. Whites Aviation Ltd), 61 (ref: WA-25706-F. Road, Punakaiki, West Coast. Whites Aviation Ltd), 67 (ref: 1/2-034676-G. French Pass, Marlborough. John Dickie, 1869-1942: Collection of postcards, prints and negatives), 74 (ref: 1/2-024836-F. Men at work on the Homer Tunnel, Southland. William Hall Raine, 1892-1955: Negatives of New Zealand towns and scenery, and Fiji), 88 (ref: APG-0602-1/2-G. Part 1 of a 2 part panorama overlooking Whangamomona. Albert Percy Godber, 1875-1949), 96 (ref: 1/2-C-027022-F. Scene overlooking the road to Denniston, West Coast. New Zealand Free Lance), 100 (ref: WA-07309-F. View including Collingwood and Aorere River mouth, Tasman region. Whites Aviation Ltd), 116 (ref: 1/4-097876-F. View across Rangitata River with mountains in the background, Rangitata Valley, Canterbury Region. Edgar Richard Williams, 1891-1983: Negatives, lantern slides, stereographs, colour transparencies, monochrome prints, photographic ephemera), 119 (ref: 1/2-143528-F. Edgar Williams' trip to Mount Aspiring, two unidentified men and car on farmland in the lower Matukituki River Valley with snow covered mountains beyond, Central Otago Region. Edgar Richard Williams, 1891-1983: Negatives, lantern slides, stereographs, colour transparencies, monochrome prints, photographic ephemera), 121 (ref: WA-23333-F. Castlepoint, Masterton. Whites Aviation Ltd), 123 (ref: WA-63205-G. Kuaotunu Beach, Coromandel Peninsula. Whites Aviation Ltd), 127 (ref: WA-30899-F. Weka Pass, Waipara County, showing Seal Rock and a car parked on side of road. Whites Aviation Ltd), 132 (left, ref: 1/2-007735-F. Car ferry landing at Rawene, Hokianga. John Reece Cole:

Photographs of Rawene and the Far North), 132 (right, ref: WA-27153-F. Rawene, Northland. Whites Aviation Ltd), 134 (ref: 10x8-0919-G. Ferry, Motueka River. Tyree Studio: Negatives of Nelson and Marlborough districts), 136 (ref: WA-42219-F. Riwaka and the Motueka River with Road Bridge and surrounding farmland, Motueka, Nelson Region. Whites Aviation Ltd), 140 (left, ref: WA-27846-F. Piopio, Waitomo District. Whites Aviation Ltd), 140 (right, ref: WA-47758-F. Marokopa township and River, Waikato District, including coastline and hills. Whites Aviation Ltd), 145 (ref: PA1-q-003-02-2. Scene with Tavistock Hotel, Waipukurau. George Leslie Adkin, 1888–1964: Photographs of New Zealand geology, geography, and the Maori history of Horowhenua), 154 (left, ref: EP/1980/0192/21A-F. Cook Strait ferry, the *Aratika*, coming into Wellington. Further negatives of the *Evening Post* newspaper), 154 (right, ref: WA-58500-G. Marlborough Sounds, including Aramoana ferry. Whites Aviation Ltd), 156 (ref: PICT-000166. Car travelling up Ngauranga Gorge, Wellington. John Dobree Pascoe, 1908–1972. Making New Zealand: Negatives and prints from the Making New Zealand Centennial collection), 158 (ref: PA1-o-415-10. Brunner bridge and township. Mr J Perkins, 1967: Photograph album and loose prints), 159 (ref: WA-28446-F. Townships of Taylorville and Wallsend, and the Grey River, West Coast. Whites Aviation Ltd), 160 (ref: 1/2-000711-G. View of McDonald's house at Taramakau, West Coast. William Archer Price, 1866–1948: Collection of post card negatives), 161 (ref: Eph-POSTCARD-Ellis-10. Postcard. 4786 P. Revel St., Hokitika, N.Z. New series. Muir & Moodie series, issued by Muir & Moodie, Dunedin N.Z. from their copyright series of views. Made in Germany [1904–1914]), 164 (ref: 1/2-112398-F. Port Awanui township and waterfront, Janet Stewart McGeorge, 1980: Photographs relating to Archibald Hugh Bogle), 170 (left, ref: 1/4-111406-F. Cars on the new Haast Road, Westland, New Zealand. John Dobree Pascoe, 1908–1972: Photographs of family, holidays and tramping trips), 170 (right, ref: 1/4-111460-F. Cars on the new Haast Road, Westland, New Zealand. John Dobree Pascoe, 1908–1972: Photographs of family, holidays and tramping trips), 176 (left, ref: WA-28110-F. Burkes Pass, Mackenzie District, Canterbury Region. Whites Aviation Ltd), 176 (right, ref: WA-41476-F. Hakataramea rural area from Kurow, Otago, includes Waitaki River. Whites Aviation Ltd), 181 (ref: 1/2-080922-F. Rock called 'Old Woman on Leaning Rock' (left) and smaller rocks surrounding it, on the summit of the Dunstan Range, Central Otago District. New Zealand Free Lance), 187 (ref: WA-70233-F. Garston, Southland. Whites Aviation Ltd), 190 (ref: 1/2-140993-G. Unidentified man driving horse drawn cart on Skippers Canyon Road, Skippers Gorge, Queenstown-Lakes District, Otago Region. Edgar Richard Williams, 1891–1983: Negatives, lantern slides, stereographs, colour transparencies, monochrome prints, photographic ephemera), 196 (ref: WA-71669-F. Jollies Pass, North Canterbury. Whites Aviation Ltd), 202 (left, ref: 1/1-021772-G. Frank James Denton, 1869–1963. The Dress Circle on Pipiriki Road, Pipiriki. Tesla Studios: Negatives of Wanganui and district taken by Alfred Martin, Frank Denton and Mark Lampe), 202 (right, ref: PAColl-7171-62. Sheep and drover on the Parapara Road to Wanganui, from Raetihi. New Zealand Free Lance), 203 (ref: WA-37642-F. Whanganui River. Whites Aviation Ltd), 212 (ref: WA-39442-F. Nugget Point, South Otago. Whites Aviation Ltd), 219 (ref: 1/2-001898-G. View of Blacks Point, a gold-mining settlement on the Inangahua River. William Archer Price, 1866–1948: Collection of post card negatives), 222 (ref: WA-40822-F. Oamaru Bay, Coromandel, includes farmland, roads and housing. Whites Aviation Ltd), 228 (ref: WA-24988-G. Buller Gorge, West Coast. Whites Aviation Ltd), 230 (ref: 1/2-070753-G. A view of Buller Gorge showing rock fall.

Frederick Nelson Jones, 1881-1962: Negatives of the Nelson district), 231 (ref: 1/2-050061-F. Covered wagon on the Buller Gorge Road. *Greymouth Evening Star*: Photographs of the West Coast), 235 (ref: WA-20100-G. Manawatu Gorge. Whites Aviation Ltd), 237 (ref: 1/1-039570-G. Hughson's coach on New Plymouth-Opunake road. Daroux, Louis John, 1870-1948: Photographs of New Zealand and the Pacific), 238 (ref: 1/2-071823-F. Karangahape Road, Auckland city), 242 (ref: WA-38210-F. Orepuki, Southland District. Whites Aviation Ltd), 246 (ref: WA-39062a-F. Unidentified boys watching the Stewart Island ferry from the side of the road, Bluff, Southland. Whites Aviation Ltd)

DAVID WALL
22, 56, 80, 148, 180, 183, 229

DREAMSTIME
63 (Lukesergent - West Coast Road Photo), 174 (Kiwichris - Waitaki River Bridge Photo)

GETTY IMAGES
26 (Joseph Johnson), 82 and 85 (CGIbackgrounds.com), 211 (Paul Kennedy), 217 (picturegarden)

ISTOCK
2-3, 10, 101 (LazingBee), 197 (dchadwick), 213 (Hpuschmann)

JOHN MILES
25

MARIE ARMSTRONG
66

MEGHAN MALONEY
146

MYCHILLYBIN
42 (Michi Krauss), 58 (Haupiri Net Images), 98 (Myles Andrews), 130 (Rebekah Emerson), 133 (Mark Ewington), 141 (Alistair Lang), 144 (Barry Doig), 155 (Myles Andrews), 166 (Karen Doidge), 177 (Lynn Clayton), 186 (William Connell), 226 (Haupiri Net Images), 232 (Mark Roberts), 239 (Mike Mackinven)

NEW ZEALAND STOCK LIBRARY (NEW ZEALAND STOCK LIBRARY / STEVE BICKNELL)
46, 52, 126, 138, 142

PHOTO NEW ZEALAND
21 (Kim Christensen), 32 (Rob Brown), 49 (Kim Christensen), 77 (Derek Morrison), 89, 90-91, 92 (Arno Gasteiger), 94, 97, 102, 108 (Mike Langford), 115 (Geoff Marshall), 117 (Jason Hosking), 124, 157 (Terry Hann), 171 (Ben Smith), 173 (Ann Worthy), 198 (Paul Kennedy), 214 (Mark Watson), 223 (Alex Wallace), 234 (Paul Stieller), 240 (Miz Watanabe), 244 (Arno Gasteiger)

ROB SUISTED / NATURE'S PIC
15, 19, 76, 106, 150, 162, 165, 204, 207, 208, 209, 218, 220, 224, 243

SHUTTERSTOCK
4-5, 16, 28, 34, 35, 36, 39, 43, 60, 64, 72, 75, 86, 128, 152, 179, 187 (left), 188, 191, 192, 193, 194, 200, 236, 252, 247, 250-251, 252

THINKSTOCK
4-5, 250-251 (Andrew Conway), 256